Bernard Burke

Vicissitudes of families and other essays;

First series

Bernard Burke

Vicissitudes of families and other essays;
First series

ISBN/EAN: 9783337809805

Printed in Europe, USA, Canada, Australia, Japan

Cover: Foto ©ninafisch / pixelio.de

More available books at **www.hansebooks.com**

Vicissitudes of Families,

AND

OTHER ESSAYS.

FIRST SERIES.

BY

SIR BERNARD BURKE,

ULSTER KING OF ARMS,
AUTHOR OF THE "PEERAGE AND BARONETAGE."

FIFTH EDITION.

LONDON:
LONGMAN, GREEN, LONGMAN, AND ROBERTS,
PATERNOSTER ROW.
1861.

TO

THE COUNTESS OF EGLINTON AND WINTON,

This little Volume,

THE PRODUCTION OF WHICH ORIGINATED IN A
SUGGESTION OF HER EXCELLENCY'S,

is inscribed,

WITH THE AUTHOR'S HIGHEST RESPECT
AND SINCEREST ESTEEM.

RECORD TOWER, DUBLIN CASTLE.

CONTENTS.

	PAGE
VICISSITUDES OF FAMILIES	1
The Percys	13
The Nevilles	18
Rise and Fall of the Cromwells	26
The Bairds of Gartsherrie	40
Kirkpatrick of Closeburne	46
Anstruther of Anstruther	50
Macdonell of Glengarry	54
The Princess of Connemara	65
The Doom of Buckingham	74
The Royal Stuarts	83
The House of Albany	86
Earls of Stratherne and Menteith	101
Lindsay of Edzell	113
St. Clair of Roslyn	117
Stewart of Craigiehall	135
Gargrave and Reresby	142

VICISSITUDES OF FAMILIES—*continued.* PAGE

   A Dethroned Monarch 144

   The O'Neills 149

   MacCarthy More 162

   The Maguires of Tempo 171

   The Fall of Desmond 186

   Umfraville 192

   Hungerford, the Spendthrift 195

   Sir Edward Castleton, Bt. 197

   Lady Roche 197

   Theodore Palæologus 199

LANDMARKS OF GENEALOGY 203

THE DOUBLE SOJOURN OF GENIUS AT BEACONSFIELD 238

RECOLLECTIONS OF ENGLISH COUNTIES . . 257

HERALDRY 340

THE GERALDINES 406

INTRODUCTION.

VICISSITUDES OF FAMILIES:—THE PLANTAGENETS—DECAY OF HISTORIC HOUSES IN ENGLAND—FULLER'S REMARKS THEREON—FAMILY DECADENCE IN SCOTLAND AND IN IRELAND—MILESIAN NAMES INCLUDED IN THE PEERAGE—IRISH OFFICERS IN FOREIGN SERVICE—ENCUMBERED ESTATES' COURT—D'ARCY OF KILTULLAGH—HYDE OF CASTLE HYDE—MARTIN OF CONNEMARA.

VICISSITUDES OF FAMILIES.

The "vicissitudes of great families" form a curious chapter in the general history of mankind; in fact, the interest attaching to individual fortunes is of a more human character, and excites more of human sympathy, than that which belongs to the fate of kingdoms. But such details are seldom to be found close at hand. They lie for the most part scattered about in unread chronicles and private papers, overwhelmed, buried, as it were, under the dryness or the weight of the superincumbent materials, from which they must be disinterred, and the dust swept off, before they can be fitly presented to the public at large. The absence of such epitomizing aids may be considered as one reason for these domestic stories having excited so little general notice. Another cause must, no doubt, be sought in the multitude of subjects that press upon the reader's time and attention, from every side, leaving but a narrow space for the development of any particular study. The history even of kingdoms has, in the course of ages, grown to a size so monstrous, that a lifetime is scarcely sufficient to grapple with it. Every day we are more and more compelled to take refuge in abridgment, omitting all minor details, and recording only the salient portions of events, though even then, it may be said, that nearly as much of every reader's time is employed in forgetting as in learning. As, however, in spite of all this, books go on flooding the world with the rapidity of a winter torrent, there appears to be no valid reason why a few drops from the source from which I am about to draw should not be thrown into the general rush of waters. They will hardly cause the stream to overflow. Besides, dropping all metaphor, the decline and fall of illustrious houses is a subject that cannot fail to amuse those who delight in "moving accidents by flood and field," while to minds of another cast it may supply something more solid than mere amusement. That spirit of emulation and perseverance, which so mainly contributes to success, may be awakened by the example of greatness built up from the lowest grounds by well-directed energy, while pride may derive a no less useful lesson from seeing how little stability there is in the highest gifts of fortune, and that family trees, like all other trees, must eventually perish, the question being only one of time. Truly does Dr. Borlase remark, that "the most lasting houses have their seasons, more or less, of a certain constitutional strength: they have their spring, and summer sunshine glare, their wane, decline, and death." What race in Europe surpassed in royal position, personal achievement, and romantic adventure, our own Plantagenets—equally wise as valiant, and no less renowned in the Cabinet than in the Field? But let us look back only so far as the year 1637, and we shall find the great-great-grandson of Margaret Plantagenet, herself the daughter and heiress of George, Duke of Clarence, following the cobbler's craft at Newport, a little town in Shropshire! Nor is this the only branch from the tree of royalty that has dwarfed and withered. If we were to closely investigate the fortunes of the many inheritors of the royal arms, it would soon be shown that, in sober truth,

> "The aspiring blood of Lancaster
> Had sunk in the ground,"

aye, and deeply too. The princely stream flows through very humble veins. Among the lineal descendants of Edmund of Woodstock, Earl of Kent, sixth son of Edward I., King of England, entitled to quarter the royal arms, occur a butcher, and a toll gatherer; the first, a Mr. Joseph Smart, of Hales Owen; the latter, a Mr. George Wilmot, keeper of the turnpike gate at Cooper's Bank, near Dudley. Then, again, among the descendants of Thomas Plantagenet, Duke of Gloucester, fifth son of Edward III., we discover Mr. Stephen James Penny, the late sexton at St. George's, Hanover Square—a strange descent, from sword and sceptre to the spade and the pickaxe!

In the ranks of the unennobled aristocracy time has effected wondrous changes. The most stately and gorgeous houses have crumbled under its withering touch. Let us cast our eye on what county we please in England, and the same view will present itself. Few, very few, of those old historic names that once held paramount sway and adorned by their brilliancy a particular locality, still exist in a *male* descendant. It has been asserted, I know

not exactly with what truth, that in Herefordshire, a
county peculiarly rich in ancient families, there are but
two or three county gentlemen who can show a male descent from the proprietors recorded in the Visitations. In
the North, these genealogical vicissitudes have been hastened by the influence of commercial success, which has
done so much to uproot the old proprietary of the soil,
that one marvels how, in Lancashire and the West Riding
of Yorkshire, such families as Towneley, Hulton, Gerard,
Blackburne, Blundell, Trafford, Ramsden, Tempest, and
Wentworth, " have stood against the waves and weathers
of time." Others, of no less fame and fortune, have
passed altogether away, and others have dwindled from
their proud estate to beggary and want:

"Eversæ domûs tristes reliquiæ."

It has often been remarked, that the more distant a
county is from London, the more lasting are its old families. The merchant's or manufacturer's gold tends to
displace the ancient aristocracy; but its action is most
generally felt within a limited circle round the metropolis,
or the great city wherein its accumulation has been made.
The aim of the prosperous trader is to fix himself on some
estate in his own immediate neighbourhood. Thus it is
that few old resident families are to be found in Middlesex, Surrey, or Essex; while in Northumberland, Cheshire,
Shropshire, Devon, and Cornwall—all remote from London
—many a stem is still flourishing, planted in the Plantagenet times. Quaint old Fuller is not altogether of my
way of thinking. Here are his own words:

"It is the observation of Vitruvius, alleged and approved by Master Camden, that northern men advancing southward cannot endure the heat, but their strength melteth away, and is dissolved, whilst southern people removing northward, are not only not subject to sickness through the change of place, but are the more confirmed in their strength and health. Sure I am that northern gentry transplanted into the south by marriage, perchance, or otherwise, do languish and fade away within few generations; whereas southern men, on the like occasions, removing northward, acquire a settlement in their estates with long continuance. Some peevish natures (delighting to comment all things in the worst sense) impute this to the position of their country, as secured from sale by their distance from London (the staple place of pleasure), whilst I would willingly behold it as the effect and reward of their discreet thrift and moderate expense."

This is a curious subject, and I may be pardoned for giving another extract from the same agreeable author:—

"The fable is sufficiently known of the contest betwixt the wind and the sun, which first should force the traveller to put off his clothes. The wind made him wrap them the closer about him; whilst the heat of the sun soon made him to part with them. This is moralized in our English gentry. Such who live southward near London (which, for the lustre thereof, I may fitly call the sun of our nation), in the warmth of wealth, and plenty of pleasures, quickly strip and disrobe themselves of their estates and inheritance; whilst the gentry living in this north country on the confines of Scotland, in the wind of war (daily alarmed with their blustering enemies), buckled their estates (as their armour) the closer unto them: and since have no less thriftily defended their patrimony in peace than formerly valiantly maintained it in war."

It must not be imagined for a moment that such alternations of fortune are confined to England. North of the Tweed, the same results occur. Scotland has had her full share of family vicissitudes. Her national and civil wars, her religious strifes, and her chivalric devotion to the feeling of loyalty, produced in many instances disastrous consequences. The royal house of Stuart affords in itself so many striking examples, that I shall have to devote a whole chapter to it. During the Usurpation, Anne, Duchess of Hamilton, the proudest, and richest, and best born heiress in Scotland, was at one time so reduced in circumstances, as to be dependent for her daily subsistence on the industry of a young companion and friend, Miss Maxwell, of Calderwood, who was an expert sempstress, and maintained herself and her ruined mistress by the produce of her needle. Better times, however, came, and the Duchess, restored to her lost estate, rewarded her preserver with the gift of Craignethan Castle, in Lanarkshire, which, after Miss Maxwell's marriage to a Mr. Hay, gave designation to the respectable Scottish family of Hay of Craignethan. But we need not travel so far back. Not very long ago, indeed within the memory of many still alive, Urquhart, laird of Burdsyard, a scion of the famous family of Urquhart of Cromarty, after passing many years as an officer in a distinguished regiment, and mixing in the first society of London and Edinburgh, was necessitated, by his extravagance, to sell his estate, sank, step by step, to the lowest depth of misery, and came at last a wandering beggar to his own door—or rather to that door which had once been his own.

A somewhat similar story is told of a Scottish peer. Frazer of Kirkhill relates that he saw John, Earl of Traquair, the cousin and courtier of King James VI., "begging in the streets of Edinburgh, in the year 1661. He was"—(these are Frazer's own words)—"in an antique garb, and wore a broad old hat, short cloak, and pannier's breeches, and I contributed, in my quarters in the Canongate, towards his relief. We gave him a noble. He was standing with his hat off. The master of Lovatt, Culbrockie, Glenmoriston, and myself, were there, and he received the piece of money from my hand as humbly and thankfully as the poorest supplicant."

Across the Irish channel, the story is even more significant. There is, perhaps, no part of the world where such violent and almost incessant internal convulsions have disorganised society, and overturned all social happiness and prosperity, as in Ireland. The attentive reader of Irish history rises from his studies wearied with the record of perpetual wars. From the earliest period of its history until within our own memory, that fine country was the scene of civil discord, and for more than ten centuries it can scarcely be said to have enjoyed fifty consecutive years of calm. As a necessary consequence, the Irish annals present a series of the most striking vicissitudes; and there is scarcely a family or a seat that has not shared deeply in those feverish changes and calamities.

An Irish "Peerage" gives a very inadequate account of the royal and noble blood of Ireland. But few of the Milesian races have found their way into the peerage,* though some still inherit a portion of their ancient possessions; and it is in the Austrian, French, or Spanish service,†

* The only Milesian families granted peerages by the sovereigns of England, have been the O'Neills, earls of Tyrone, and barons of Dungannon, and, in modern times, viscounts and earl O'Neill, in Antrim; the O'Donnells, earls of Tyrconnel; the MacDonells, earls of Antrim, who were Scots of Irish descent; the Maguires, barons of Enniskillen: the Magenisses, viscounts of Iveagh, in the county of Down; the O'Haras, barons of Tyrawly, in Mayo; the O'Dalys, barons of Dunsandle, in Galway; the O'Malones, barons of Sunderlin, in Westmeath; the O'Carrols, barons of Ely, in the King's County, and co. Tipperary; Kavanagh of Carlow, baron of Ballyane for life; the MacGilpatricks, or Fitzpatricks, barons of Gowran in Kilkenny, and Earls of Upper Ossory in the Queen's County; the O'Dempseys, viscounts of Clanmalier and barons of Philipstown, in the King's and Queen's Counties; the O'Briens of Clare and Limerick, earls and marquesses of Thomond, earls of Inchiquin, viscounts of Clare, &c.; the MacCarthys of Cork and Kerry, earls of Clancare and Clancarty, and viscounts of Muskerry and Mountcashell: the O'Callaghans of Cork and Tipperary, viscounts Lismore, in Waterford; the O'Quins of Clare, barons of Adare, and earls of Dunraven, in Limerick, and the O'Gradys of Clare and Limerick, viscounts Guillamore.

† The army list of Austria exhibits a long roll of officers of Irish ancestry;—The First Aide-de-camp to the Emperor is Maximilian, Count O'Donnell, and the senior Field Marshal, Laval, Count, and Prince Nugent, K.C.B., on whom the Emperor of Austria conferred the Order of the Golden Fleece, transmitting the very ribbon worn by Radetsky. The catalogue includes, besides, Count Albert Nugent (eldest son of the Field Marshal), Col. Daniel O'Connor (Kerry), Commandant of Mantua, Count Charles Taaffe (Viscount Taaffe, in the peerage of Ireland),

among the middle classes, or, perchance, in the mud-walled cabins of the Irish peasant, that search should be made for the real representatives of the ancient reguli. The territories of most of the old princes, and the lordships of very many of the old chieftains, are now enjoyed by the descendants of Henry the Second's barons, of the knights and gentlemen of Elizabeth and James, of the shrewd countrymen of the latter monarch, of the staid soldiers of Cromwell, and of the troopers of William III. A Psalter of Tara and an Irish "Peerage" have little in common; still the descendants of some of the aboriginal royal races hold their own* even to

Baron Herbert of Rathkeale, Baron Piers, Count McCaffrey Maguire, Count Walsh of Carigmain, &c. &c.

France has also a formidable array of officers of Irish descent. First and foremost are the gallant Marshall Mac Mahon, Duc de Magenta, and his equally distinguished companion in arms, Marshal Niel, both sprung from Milesian ancestry, the one a descendant of the Mac Mahons, Lords of Corca Baiscinn, co. Clare, sprung from the famous Bryan Boru, King of Munster; the other, a scion of the royal and illustrious O'Neills. I have seen a very interesting letter of Marshall Niel's addressed to a kinsman in Ireland, Mr. Charles H. O'Neill, Barrister, of Dublin, in which the gallant officer refers with no inconsiderable pride to his Irish origin. Among the officers of the Cuirassiers of the French Imperial Guard, lately serving in Italy, is Louis O'Brien, the lineal descendant of the O'Briens of Munfin, co. of Wexford, a branch of the once royal O'Briens.

In Russian history, De Lacy and O'Rorke are as famous as they were in the Irish annals; and in Spain, O'Donnell, Magennis (Conde de Iveagh), Sarsfield, O'Neill, and O'Reilly, have not forfeited their old renown.

* A valuable and probably unique collection of THE RENTALS of the various estates sold in the Encumbered Estates' Court has been made by Joseph Burke, Esq., of Fitzwilliam Place, this day. Kavanagh of Borris in the county of Carlow, male representative of MacMurrough, King of Leinster, retains a splendid estate in the very heart of MacMurrough's kingdom; Mr. O'Neill of Shane's Castle, the heir general of the Kings of Ulster, has succeeded to full 30,000 acres of the old Clanaboy principality, stretching for miles along the banks of Loughneagh; and it was only within the last two years that the vast Thomond property passed from the regally derived O'Briens. Many of the descendants of the minor dynasts could probably be discovered under the frieze coats of the peasants; and a genealogical enquirer might trace in the sunburnt mendicant the representative of the O'Rorkes, the O'Reillys, the O'Ryans, or the O'Sullivans, who were of fame

"Ere the emerald gem of the western world
Was set in the crown of a stranger."

Ireland is, indeed, the Tadmor in the desert of family vicissitude; time out of mind it has been the prey of the

Dublin, Barrister-at-Law, so long associated with the administration of the Poor Law in Ireland. These Rentals may be considered the fullest history of Irish landed property ever brought together. They contain a description of the lands under sale, the tenants' names, descriptions of the demesnes, and frequently views of the mansion houses, with maps and local statistics, much more important than the particulars of sales at Chichester House under the direction of the Court of Claims.

Mr. Burke has also collected reports of the sales, the names of the purchasers, and the amount of purchase-money :—in fine, this collection is, I believe, the sole perfect series of papers connected with the Encumbered Estates' Court. The Court itself does not possess so complete a set, and I doubt if the British Museum possess any.

spoiler. Strongbow, Cromwell, and William III. spared few of the aboriginal lords of the soil, and the recent alienation of property, under the Encumbered Estates' Court, has effected a fearful revolution amongst the landed gentlemen of English descent. Confiscation, civil war, and legal transfer have torn asunder those associations between "the local habitation and the name," which have for centuries wound round each other. The gentry of Ireland are now, in many cases, dispossessed: new manners and new men are filling the land, and the old time-honoured houses are passing rapidly away. Whoever collects instances of fallen families, some thirty years hence, will have a fruitful field to gather in. No one will gainsay the beneficial influence the Encumbered Estates' Court has exercised in a national point of view, or fail to trace to its introduction into Ireland the dawn of the prosperity which is now shining on that most improving of countries. That it has worked infinite public good is undeniable; but it is equally certain, that the general benefit has been effected at the cost of much individual misery. The condition of the country is increased by it, as the state of a boat's crew, tempest-tossed, with only a slender basket of provisions, is improved by some of the unhappy sufferers being thrown overboard and drowned. But the relatives of the doomed cannot but lament, and even the unconnected spectators of such stern and sharp justice cannot remain unconcerned. No cases of vicissitudes would be so pathetic, no episodes of decadence so lamentable as those that could be told in connection with the transfer of land in Ireland; but the wounds are too fresh, and the ruin too recent, for me to enter on so painful a theme. Many a well-born gentleman—torn from his patrimony — has sought and found on the hospitable shores of Australia and America the shelter and happiness denied to him in the land of his birth; while some I might mention, who stayed at home in the vain hope of retrieving the past, or were too old to enter on a new career, ended their days in the Poor-House. What story of fiction is more striking than that of Mr. D'Arcy, of Kiltullagh and Clifden Castle, in the county of Galway, who, after the ruinous sale of his estates, took orders and became a working clergyman in the very district which used to be his own; or, what more marvellous instance of the depreciation of property, than in the sale of Castle Hyde, in the county of Cork, the inheritance of Mr. Hyde, a scion of the Clarendon Hydes, and cousin of the Duke of Devonshire, who was deprived of his fine old place in the worst times of the famine?

Ιμεροεν παν τ' εστ' ερατεινον
Αμφ' αλσεα γαρ Πυργ' Ψδεον.

One tale only of those tragic times I will in a future page venture to relate, and that will be the story of the heiress of Connemara. I can do so, as no one remains alive to whom the narrative will bring a pang.

The Percys.

"Now the Percy's crescent is set in blood."
OLD BALLAD.

THE Percys and the Nevilles held almost regal sway in Northumberland and Durham. "The two great Princes of the North were Northumberland at Alnwick, and Westmoreland at Raby Castle." Yet, how strikingly unfortunate were the Percys during the reign of the Tudors, and, indeed, long before! Sprung from the marriage of Josceline of Lovaine (son of Godfrey Barbatus, Duke of Lower Brabant, and brother of Adeliza, second Queen of Henry I.) with Agnes de Percy, daughter and eventual heiress of William, third Lord Percy, this illustrious and eminently historical family is conspicuous alike for its achievements and its sufferings. Henry, first Earl of Northumberland, was slain at Bramham Moor; and his brother, Sir Thomas Percy, K.G., the early companion in arms of the Black Prince, and subsequently the renowned Earl of Worcester, was beheaded in 1402. The first Earl's son, the gallant "Hotspur," the best captain of a martial epoch, had already fallen at Shrewsbury. Henry, second Earl of Northumberland (Hotspur's son), passed his youth, attainted and despoiled of estate, an exile in Scotland; subsequently restored by Henry V., he returned to England, and, true to the tradition of his race, achieved martial fame, and found a soldier's death at the battle of St. Albans. In the same wars, his two sons, Sir Thomas Percy Lord Egremont, and Sir Ralph Percy, were also both killed; Egremont at Northampton, and his brother at Hedgeley Moor. None were more chivalrously true to the Lancastrian cause than the Percys. " I have saved the bird in my bosom !" that is, " my faith to my king," were the last words of the dying Sir Ralph.

The next and third possessor of the title, Henry, Earl of Northumberland, the husband of the great heiress of Poynings, was slain at Towton in 1461, still on the side of the Red Rose; and his son, Henry, the fourth Earl, endeavouring to enforce one of King Henry VII.'s taxes, was murdered by a mob, at Thirsk, in 1480.* Henry, the fifth Earl, died a natural death; but his second son, Sir Thomas Percy, was executed at Tyburn, in 1537, for his concern in Aske's rebellion. Henry, the sixth Earl, the first lover of Anna Boleyn, compelled by his father to marry against his own wish the Lady Mary Talbot, lived a most unhappy life, childless and separate; at last, sinking under a broken constitution, he could not bear up against the sorrow brought on by his brother's execution and his house's attainder, but died in the very same month in which Sir

* The funeral of this Earl is a memorable instance of the lavish expenditure of the time; at the present valuation of money, the cost was £12,080! Of his magnificent monument in Beverley Minster, a few vestiges only remain, although that erected to his Countess is still in the highest preservation, and is one of the most beautiful sepulchral specimens in this kingdom. Dugdale has a memorandum that the grave of this lady, in the church at Beverley, was opened on the 15th Sept. 1678,—nearly two hundred years after her death,—and that "her body was found in a fair coffin of stone, embalmed and covered with cloth of gold; and on her feet slippers embroidered with silke; and therewith a wax lampe, a candle and plate candlestick."

Thomas had been consigned to the block. This Earl, known as "Henry the Unthrifty," disposed of some of the fairest lands of his inheritance. After his decease, the peerage honours of the Percys were obscured by Sir Thomas's attainder, and during the period of their forfeiture the rightful heirs had the mortification to see the Dukedom of Northumberland conferred on John Dudley, Earl of Warwick. This nobleman, however, being himself attainted in 1553, the Earldom was restored, in 1557, to Thomas Percy, in consideration that his ancestors, "ab antiquo de tempore in tempus," had been Earls of Northumberland, but the sunshine of his prosperity was soon eclipsed. He joined the Rising of the North against Queen Elizabeth, and ended his life on the scaffold, August 1572. His brother Henry, eighth Earl of Northumberland, still blind to the hereditary sufferings of his race, intrigued in favour of Mary, Queen of Scots, and, being imprisoned in the Tower, was shot, or shot himself, there. His son Henry, ninth Earl, was convicted on a groundless suspicion of being concerned in the Gunpowder Plot, stripped of all his offices, adjudged by the Star Chamber to pay a fine of £30,000, and sentenced to imprisonment for life in the Tower. His grandson, Joscelyn, eleventh Earl of Northumberland, outlived his only son, and with him ended the male line of the most historic, perhaps, of all our English families. The last Earl's daughter, the Lady Elizabeth Percy—twice a wife and twice a widow before she was sixteen—was the greatest heiress of her time. Her first husband, Henry, Earl of Ogle, died the year after his marriage, and her second,

Thomas Thynne, of Longleate, "Tom of ten thousand," was assassinated by Count Koningsmark.

Eventually the Lady Elizabeth became the wife of Charles Seymour, the proud Duke of Somerset, and thus her splendid inheritance passed to the Seymours. A singular claimant had, however, arisen to the hereditary renown, broad lands, and nobility of the illustrious House of Percy in the person of a humble trunk-maker of the city of Dublin, one James Percy, who went over in 1670, the very year the Earl died, especially to prefer his claim, which he subsequently pursued with all the enduring boldness of a Percy against the might and wealth of the most powerful nobleman in the kingdom. The trunk-maker contended against the Duke of Somerset for full fifteen years, and obtained during the contest some temporary triumphs, although I firmly believe that he had no right whatsoever to the title he sought; but he was hardly dealt by, and of consequence excited no little sympathy pending the affair; nor did his defeat and total annihilation finally set his pretensions at rest, for it is even still believed by many, that the trunk-maker was the true Percy. Certain it is, that the poor claimant was absolutely treated as criminal for presuming to "trouble the House of Lords," and daring to enter the lists with the potent and haughty Duke of Somerset.

During the struggle, between the years 1674 and 1681, no less than five suits connected with the matter were tried in the Courts of Law. The first action brought by Percy was against one James Clark for scandal in having declared that he, Percy, was an impostor; but in this he suffered a nonsuit — a result he attributed to the venality of his attorney, in a printed pamphlet, in which he further states that Lord Hale, the Chief Justice, had declared that James Percy had as much right to the Earldom of Northumberland as he, Lord Hale, had to his coach and horses, which he had bought and paid for. The claimant next brought an action against one John Wright, another of his adversaries, also for slander, for having declared that he was illegitimate, and the case was tried before Chief Justice Rainsford, when, having proved his legitimacy and pedigree, he had a verdict for £300. Subsequently Percy had protracted litigation with the sheriff of Northumberland for the twenty pounds granted out of the revenues of the county to the earldom, by the patent of creation. During these lawsuits, several proceedings were instituted in the House of Lords; and at length, in 1689, the Lords' Committee for Privileges declared Percy's conduct to be insolent in persisting to call himself Earl of Northumberland, after the former decisions of the House, and finally adjudged that " the pretensions of the said James Percy to the Earldom of Northumberland are groundless, false, and scandalous," and ordered that the said claimant be brought before the four courts of Westminster Hall, wearing a paper upon his breast, on which these words were written, " The false and impudent pretender to the Earldom of Northumberland." Thus ended the attempt of the trunk-maker, and nothing further was ever heard of the unfortunate man or his family, beyond the fact that his son, or supposed son, Sir Anthony Percy, filled the office of Lord Mayor of Dublin, in 1699.

The Nevilles.

"The sun shone bright, and the birds sung sweet,
The day we left the North countrie,
But cold is the wind, and sharp is the sleet,
That beat on the exile over the sea."
                                        OLD BALLAD.

BRIGHT as is the halo which romance and song have shed round the name of Percy, I question much whether any one of that illustrious race ever reached the pinnacle of power attained by Ralph Nevill, the first Earl of Westmoreland, or by Richard Neville, Earl of Warwick, "the greatest and last of the old Norman chivalry—kinglier in pride, in state, in possessions, and in renown than the king himself." A recent writer remarks with much truth, that "the Neville was to mediæval England what the Douglas was to Scotland. No family surpassed it in the brilliancy of its alliances and honours, or the vastness of its estates. Of the house of Neville, there have been six Earls of Westmoreland, two Earls of Salisbury—one of whom, and the more renowned, was also Earl of Warwick—eighteen Barons, and four Earls of Abergavenny, one Earl of Kent, two Marquesses of Montacute—one of whom was also Duke of Bedford—five Barons Latimer, one Lord Furnival, and one Lord Fauconberg. The illustrious names that adorn the family tree of the Neville are numerous beyond all precedent. A Neville was Queen of England,

and a Neville, mother of two of our English monarchs. Twice was a Neville consecrated Archbishop of York, and twice did a Neville fill the dignified office of Lord High Chancellor: seven Nevilles were Duchesses, nine Nevilles were Knights of the Garter, a Neville presided over the Commons as Speaker, and Nevilles without end pervade our national records as warriors and statesmen. The annual income in land of Richard Neville, Earl of Warwick, independently of his own patrimony, would be calculated in our present money at full £300,000. Sir Edward Bulwer Lytton has vividly pourtrayed "the Last of the Barons." "His wealth," says the novelist, "was enormous, but it was equalled by his magnificence, and rendered popular by his lavish hospitality. No less than thirty thousand persons are stated to have feasted daily at the open tables with which he allured to his countless castles the strong hands and grateful hearts of a martial and unsettled population."

The genealogist will recollect that, when Josceline de Louvaine received in marriage the heiress of the Percys, the proud condition was imposed on the Flemish Prince, on his accepting the Norman alliance, that he should relinquish either his own name or coat of arms in favour of that of his bride, and that he decided the option by assuming the name of Percy. Whether in performance of some similar agreement, or out of gratitude for their large maternal inheritance, or from the mere fashion of that day to Normanize, the descendants of Robert Fitz Maldred, the Saxon Lord of Raby, by Isabel Neville, his wife, the Norman Lady of Brancepeth, assumed the surname of Neville. The vast estates thus united devolved in due course of time on Robert Neville of Raby, who married Mary, daughter and sole heiress of Ralph Fitz Randolph, Lord of Middleham, and thus added the famous castle and estates of Middleham to his already overgrown possessions. The issue of this—if the narrative of contemporary historians be correct — unfortunate marriage was Ralph de Neville, a noble baron, careless in the management of his affairs, and fonder of residing with the monks of Coverham and Marton than in his own castles. He married twice, and by his first wife, Euphemia Clavering, had two sons, on the elder of whom, Robert, called, from his love and show of finery, "the Peacock of the North," his grandmother settled the castle and lordship of Middleham, with all its appendages in fee; but dying before his father, who survived until the year 1331, and was buried on the south side of the altar at Coverham, he was succeeded by his only brother, Ralph, Lord Neville of Raby, who in the fifth year of Edward III. obtained a fresh charter of free warren in all his lands and lordships in the county of York. At one time he was Ambassador to treat with Philip of Valois, in the presence of the Pope, and on various occasions he was engaged in the Scottish and French wars. At length, having spent a long and active life, he died in 1367, and was buried in Durham Cathedral, where his monument still remains, he having been the first layman who had sepulture there. His son and heir, John, third Lord Neville, of Raby, who fought in Scotland, France, and Turkey, was such a gallant soldier that John of Gaunt, in consideration of fifty marks a year, charged on his estates in Danby and Forcett, Yorkshire, retained him in his service for life. By his first marriage with Maud, daughter of Lord Percy, he had Ralph, his heir; by his second union with Elizabeth, heiress of William, Lord Latimer, he had John, subsequently Lord Latimer. John, third Lord Neville of Raby, died on St. Luke's day, anno 12 Rich. II., and was interred near his father at Durham. His eldest son and successor, RALPH DE NEVILLE, having first won the golden spurs of knighthood, was, in the 21st year Rich. II., created Earl of Westmoreland, and subsequently received from Henry IV. a grant of the Earldom of Richmond (which title, however, he never assumed). During the time of this—the great Earl of Westmoreland—the power and grandeur of his race seem to have attained a very high degree of eminence. He was a Knight of the Garter, Warden of the West Marches, and Earl Marshal of England, and died possessed of the honours and castles of Richmond, Middleham, and Sheriff Hutton, with many a dependent manor, and many a fair southern lordship. His eldest son (by the Lady Margaret Stafford, his first wife, daughter of Hugh, Earl of Stafford, K.G.) John, Lord Neville, who died before him, was the direct ancestor of Charles, sixth Earl of Westmoreland, whose miserable end I will by and by narrate. The eldest son of the second princely alliance of the first Earl of Westmoreland with Joan Beaufort, daughter of John of Gaunt, Duke of Lancaster, was Richard Neville, Lord of Middleham, who, by his marriage with Alice, daughter and heiress of Thomas Montagu, Earl of Salisbury, acquired that title, and having joined the standard of Richard Plantagenet, Duke of York, who had married his sister, the

Lady Cecilia Neville, was beheaded after the disastrous battle of Wakefield, A.D. 1460, when his estates became forfeited to the crown. But in the following year Edward IV. regained the throne of his ancestors, and Middleham Castle, with all its vast domains and wide-spread manors, reverted to their rightful owner, the renowned "King Maker," Richard Neville, Earl of Salisbury, K.G., and (by his union with Anne, sole heiress of her brother Henry, Duke of Warwick) Earl also of Warwick:

"For who liv'd king, but he could dig his grave,
And who durst smile when Warwick bent his brow?"

Under him the ancient fortress of Middleham seems to have reached the height of its magnificence, and within its walls he kept all but royal state. To quote the words of the gifted author of "the Last of the Barons," "the most renowned statesman, the mightiest Lords flocked to his Hall: Middleham—not Windsor, nor Shene, nor Westminster, nor the Tower—seemed the Court of England." Here it was that the Duke of Gloucester, his future son-in-law, learned the art of war from the princely Earl: here it was that the fourth Edward, conducted as a prisoner-guest, by his gallant bearing and soul-stirring address, bowed the barons, knights, and retainers of his overgrown subject to his will. Hence, (being left, as tradition states, under the surveillance of Warwick's brother, the Archbishop of York, and indulged with the privilege of hunting in the park,) Edward escaped on a fleet horse, and resumed the reins of government. But I must not dilate too much. That mighty Earl, who had made and unmade kings, found a bloody grave at Barnet; and Middleham, with its dependencies, was allotted to Richard, Duke of Gloucester, in right of his wife, the Lady Anne Neville, Warwick's youngest daughter.

In 1469, the House of Neville attained the acme of its glory. Within exactly one hundred years, its ruin was accomplished. In 1569, Charles Neville, sixth Earl of Westmoreland, received at his castle of Brancepeth his neighbour the Earl of Northumberland, and there was concocted "the Rising of the North:"

> "And now the inly-working North
> Was ripe to send its thousands forth,
> A potent vassalage to fight
> In Percy's and in Neville's right."

But the insurrection was ill-planned and rashly determined on. It resulted in total defeat and in the utter destruction of the Nevilles of Raby. Lord Westmoreland fled to Scotland, and found protection and concealment for a long time at Fernyhurst Castle, Lord Kerr's house, in Roxburghshire. Meanwhile, the Earl's cousin, Robert Constable, was hired by Sir Ralph Sadler to endeavour to track the unfortunate nobleman, and, under the guise of friendship, to betray him. Constable's correspondence appears among the Sadleir State Papers — an infamous memorial of treachery and baseness. Despite, however, the efforts of Government, the Earl succeeded in effecting his escape to Flanders; but his vast inheritance was confiscated, and he suffered the extremity of poverty. Brancepeth, the stronghold of the Nevilles in war, and Raby, their festive Hall in peace, had passed into strangers' hands, and nothing remained for the exiled lord. He was living in the Low

Countries in 1572, on a miserable pittance allowed him by the bounty of the King of Spain, and so deplorable had been his previous condition, that Lord Seton, writing two years before to Mary Queen of Scots, states that "the Earl of Westmoreland had neither penny nor half-penny." The petition to the Spanish Monarch which obtained the trifling pension, gives a pathetic description of the poor nobleman's wretchedness, and sets forth that the estates of which he had been deprived were worth 400,000 doubloons per annum (that is £150,000 of our money). His lordship survived his flight from Scotland more than thirty years, eking out a wretched existence, and dying penniless and almost forgotten in Flanders in 1601. By his high-spirited and devoted wife, the Lady Jane Howard, the worthy daughter of Henry Howard, Earl of Surrey, he left four children, viz., Catherine, married to Sir Thomas Grey of Chillingham; Elizabeth, who died unmarried; Margaret, married to Sir Nicolas Pudsey; and Anne, married to David Ingelby of Ripley. Pecuniary pressure and severe suffering were the lot of these ladies; the third, Margaret, endured persecution and oppression. There is a letter from Hutton, Bishop of Durham, to Lord Burghley, dated 1594, suing for the Lady Margaret's pardon, wherein he says:—"I sent up in the beginning of the term to sue for the pardon of the Lady Margaret Neville, taken in company with Boast, the seminary priest. She lamented with tears that she hath offended God and her soverçign. She is wholly reclaymed from Popery. Dr. Aubrey hath had her pardon drawn since the beginning of term. If it come not quickly I fear she will die with sorrow. It were very honourable for your good lordship to take the case of a most distressed mayden, descended as your lordship knoweth of great nobilitie, the House of Norfolk, the House of Westmoreland, and the House of Rutland, in memory of man, and was but a child of five years old when her unfortunate father did enter into the rebellion; and now she is a condemned person, having not one penny by year to live upon since the death of her mother, who gave her £33 6s. 8d. a-year, part of that £300 which her Majesty did allow her. It were well that her Majesty were informed of her miserable state: she is virtuously given, humble, modest, and of very good behaviours."

Thus tragically closed the last act of the eventful drama of the Nevilles of Raby. The Bishop of Durham's supplicatory letter in behalf of "the distressed maiden," is indeed a sad end to the history of the mightiest and noblest race in our English annals. What a different scene does the Bishop's petition disclose from the gorgeous display of power and wealth of the preceding century. The crowd of retainers has dispersed, the castles are dismantled, and the broad lands parcelled out among strangers. In their stead is the poor desolate lady, dwelling in a lowly residence in a foreign land, and suing for some small pittance to stave off actual want:

"As highest hilles with tempests be most touched,
And tops of trees most subject unto winde,
And as great towers with stones strongly couched,
Have heavy falls when they be under mynde,
E'en so by proofe in worldly things we finde,
That such as clime the top of high degree,
From perill of falling never can be free."

Rise and Fall of the Cromwells.

"Why, what is pomp, rule, reign, but earth and dust?"
SHAKESPEARE.

LONG before the time of the great OLIVER, the Cromwells were of consideration and high county standing in Huntingdonshire, seated at their fine old mansion of Hinchinbrooke.

They came originally from Wales, and bore the surname of Williams: the first who took that of Cromwell was Sir Richard Williams, and he did so as nephew of Thomas Cromwell, Earl of Essex, the "maleus monachorum," or, as old Fuller renders it, "the mauler of monasteries." The alteration was made at the express desire of Henry VIII., and, through the favourite's influence, great wealth and station were conferred on Sir Richard.

"As Vicar-general of all things spiritual," (I quote from Thomas Cromwell's "Memoirs"), "the Earl of Essex had an opportunity of obliging his kinsman, then Richard Williams, alias Cromwell, Esq., and others, with the sale of the lately dissolved religious houses, at sums infinitely below their very great value, some of the most advantageous purchases were made by this ancestor of the Huntingdonshire Cromwells; and amongst others, those of the nunnery of Hinchinbrooke, and the monastery of Saltry-Judith in that county, together with the site of the rich abbey of Ramsey. Additions were made to his possessions by the king, even after the fall of the favourite Cromwell; so that at the period of his death, Sir Richard's estates probably equalled (allowing for the alteration in the value of money) those of the wealthiest peers of the present day. At a tournament held by his royal master in 1540, and described by Stowe, Richard Cromwell, Esq., is named as one of the challengers; all of whom were rewarded on the occasion by the king, with an annual income of an hundred marks granted out of the dissolved Franciscan monastery of Stamford, and with houses each to reside in. His Majesty was more particularly delighted with the gallantry of Sir Richard Cromwell (whom he had knighted on the second day of the tournament), and exclaiming, 'formerly thou wast my *Dick*, but hereafter thou shalt be my *Diamond*,' presented him with a diamond ring, bidding him for the future to wear such an one in the fore-gamb of the demi-lion in his crest, instead of a javelin, as heretofore. The arms of Sir Richard, with this alteration, were ever afterwards borne by the elder branch of the family, and by Oliver himself on his assuming the Protectorate, although previously he had borne the javelin."

In 1541, Sir Richard Cromwell served as High Sheriff of Cambridgeshire and Hunts; in 1542, was returned knight of the latter shire to Parliament, and in 1543, became one of the gentlemen of the privy chamber to the king. In this year, a war breaking out with France,

Sir Richard proceeded to that kingdom as General of the English infantry, and joined the army of the Emperor, then engaged in the siege of Landrecy; but after a few months' service, the auxiliary force returned to England, and Sir Richard Cromwell received, as a mark of royal favour, the office of Constable of Berkeley Castle. The date of the death of this renowned soldier has not been ascertained, but certain it is that he left a prodigiously large estate, derived chiefly from ecclesiastical confiscation. He had married early in life, A.D. 1518, Frances, daughter and coheir of Sir Thomas Myrffin, the then Lord Mayor of London, by Elizabeth, his wife, daughter and heir of Alderman Sir Angel Don, whose wife was a descendant of the ancient Cheshire house of Hawardine. This alliance brought several quarterings into the Cromwell family. Sir Richard's son and heir, Sir Henry Cromwell, called from his liberality and opulence "The Golden Knight," rebuilt, or, at all events, remodelled and as good as built the mansion of Hinchinbrook. Here he resided in princely state, and here he received a visit from Queen Elizabeth, on her progress from the university of Cambridge. In 1563 he was elected M.P. for his native county, and served as High Sheriff no less than four times. At length, 7th January, 1603, at a good old age, he died, leaving the character of "a worthy gentleman, both in court and country." By Joan, his first wife, daughter of Sir Robert Warren, Knt., he had several sons and daughters; the latter were, I. Joan, married to Sir Francis Barrington, Bart.; II. Elizabeth, who married William Hampden, Esq. of Great Hampden, and was mother of JOHN

Hampden, the patriot; III. Frances, who married Richard Whalley, Esq., of Kirkton, Notts, and had three sons; 1. Thomas Whalley, father of an only son, Peniston, of Screveton, (who, after dissipating a considerable fortune, passed the latter years of his life a prisoner for debt in London); 2. Edward Whalley, the regicide, who died an exile, after the Restoration; and 3. Henry Whalley, Judge Advocate, whose ultimate fate is unknown; IV. Mary, who married Sir William Dunch, of Little Whittenham, Berks, and had a son, Edmund, whose representatives are the present Sir H. C. Oxenden, Bart., and the Duke of Manchester; and V., Dorothy, who married Sir Thomas Fleming, son of the Lord Chief Justice Fleming, ancestor of the Flemings of Stoneham, in Hampshire. The sons of Sir Henry Cromwell, the Golden Knight, were Oliver, his heir; Robert, father of the Lord Protector; Henry of Upwood;* Richard, M.P., who died unmarried, and Philip.

The eldest, Sir Oliver Cromwell, who succeeded to the family estates, magnificently entertained King James I. at Hinchinbrooke, on his Majesty's journey from Scotland to London, and was made a Knight of the Bath, previously to the coronation. At the outbreak of the civil war, Sir Oliver remained not an idle spectator, but enrolling him-

* Henry Cromwell, of Upwood, third son of Sir Henry, of Hinchinbrooke, left one son, Richard (whose only surviving child, Anne, a poetess, married her kinsman, Henry Williams, alias Cromwell, of Ramsey), and two daughters; Elizabeth, married to the Lord Chief Justice Oliver St. John, and Anna, married to John Neale, Esq., of Dean, co. Bedford, ancestor, by her, of the Rev. Edward Vansittart, who inherited the estate of Allesley, and assumed the surname of Neale.

self under the royal banner, raised men, and gave large sums of money to support the king's cause. This devotion to an unfortunate party obliged him to sell Hinchinbrooke to the Montagues, since Earls of Sandwich, whose stately pleasant house it still is, on the left bank of the Ouse, and a short half mile west of Huntingdon. Sir Oliver retired to Ramsey Abbey, and there ended his days, on the 28th August, 1655, in his 93rd year, impoverished and broken-hearted, but still unshaken in his allegiance. He married, first, Elizabeth, daughter of the Lord Chancellor Bromley; and secondly, Anne, widow of Sir Horatio Palavicini; by the former, he had issue, four sons, HENRY, Thomas, John, and William, and four daughters. The sons were all cavalier officers, and suffered much in consequence. The eldest, Colonel HENRY CROMWELL, who inherited the wreck of his ancestors' vast estates, took a very active part for the king, and had his property sequestered, but on a petition to parliament, 9th July, 1649, the sequestration was discharged, and the fines for delinquency remitted, "at the request of the Lord Lieutenant of Ireland, Oliver Cromwell." From this time Henry Cromwell appears to have led a private life, harassed, however, by debt and difficulties, the consequence of his family's devotion to the royal cause, and the hereditary misfortune—extravagance and ostentation. He died 18th September, 1657, and was interred in the chancel of Ramsey church the day following, to prevent, it was reported, the seizure of the corpse by his creditors. By his second wife, Battina, daughter of Sir Horatio Palavicini, Colonel Henry Cromwell left a son, HENRY CROMwell, Esq., of Ramsey, baptized there 22nd June, 1625. This gentleman, either swayed by interested motives, or won by the favour of the Protector (who in the worst of times, was a kind and considerate kinsman), gave in his adhesion to the new order of things, and took his seat in parliament. The moment, however, the proposal for the restoration of the monarchy was mooted, it had his hearty support, and fearing that the name of Cromwell would prove distasteful at the court of King Charles, he resumed the original patronymic of his ancestors, and styled himself Henry Williams. Under this designation, we find him set down as one of the intended knights of the Royal Oak. He died 3rd August, 1673, leaving no issue; and thus expired the great Huntingdonshire line of Cromwell, for a long series of years the most opulent family in that part of England. Their estate of Ramsey alone, with the lands and manors annexed, would now be valued at £80,000 per annum; and besides that, they had extensive possessions in other parts of the county, and in Essex. From the last Henry Cromwell, alias Williams, the abbey of Ramsey passed by sale to the famous Colonel Titus, and became afterwards, by purchase also, the property of Coulson Fellowes, Esq., whose descendant still enjoys it.

The second son of Sir Henry Cromwell, "the Golden Knight," of Hinchinbrooke, was Robert Cromwell, Esq., at one time M.P. for Huntingdon, who by the will of his father, had as his portion an estate in and near that town, which, at our present valuation, would be worth about £1000 per annum. On this he resided as a country gentleman, managing his own lands and acting as a justice of the peace for the county. His wife was Elizabeth, daughter of William Steward, of Ely, an opulent man, a kind of hereditary farmer of the cathedral tithes and church lands round that city, in which capacity his son, Sir Thomas Steward, Knt., in due time succeeded him, resident also in Ely. Elizabeth was a young widow when Robert Cromwell married her: the first marriage, to "one William Lynne, Esq., of Bassingbourne, in Cambridgeshire," had lasted but a year; her husband and an only child are buried in Ely Cathedral, where their monuments still stand. By this lady, (whose descent Noble and Brooke both derive, with little or no proof, from the royal house of Stuart) Mr. Robert Cromwell left at his decease, in 1617, (his widow survived until 1654, when she died at her apartments in the Palace, Whitehall), one son, the renowned OLIVER, and five daughters: Catherine, married first to Captain Roger Whetstone, and secondly, to Colonel John Jones, one of King Charles' judges; Margaret, married to Colonel Valentine Waughton, another of the regicides; Anne, married to John Sewster, Esq., of Wistow; Jane, married to Major-General John Desborough, and Robina, married first to Dr. Peter French, Canon of Christ Church, Oxford (by whom she was mother of Elizabeth French, wife of Archbishop Tillotson), and secondly, to Dr. John Wilkins, Bishop of Chester.

OLIVER CROMWELL was born in St. John's parish, Huntingdon, 25th April, 1599, and christened there, on the 29th of the same month, receiving his baptismal name from his uncle and godfather, Sir Oliver Cromwell, of Ramsey.* At the age of twenty-one, he married a lady of fortune, Elizabeth, daughter of Sir James Bourchier, of Felsted, in Essex, a civic gentleman of some wealth, and had with four daughters† as many sons, viz.: ROBERT, born in 1621, who died unmarried; OLIVER, born in 1622, killed in 1648, fighting under the parliamentary banner; RICHARD, who succeeded to the Protectorate, and HENRY, Lord Deputy of Ireland.

Oliver Cromwell, who was declared Lord Protector, 12th December, 1653, died in 1658, at Whitehall, at four o'clock in the afternoon, on "his beloved and victorious third of September," and was buried with more than regal pomp, in Henry VII.'s chapel, on the 23rd of November following. His remains, with those of Ireton and Bradshaw, were dug up after the Restoration, and, being pulled out of their coffins, were hanged at Tyburn, 30th January,

* The fiction of Oliver Cromwell having been a brewer rests upon no better authority than this:—the little brook of Hinchin, flowing through the court-yard of the house towards the Ouse, offered every convenience for malting or brewing; and there is a vague tradition that, at some remote time before the place came into possessions of the Cromwells, it had been used as a brewery.

† The Lord Protector's daughters were, 1. BRIDGET, married first to Lieutenant-General Henry Ireton, and secondly to General Charles Fleetwood; 2. ELIZABETH, married to John Claypole, Esq.; 3. MARY, married to Thomas Belasyse, Viscount Fauconberg; and 4. FRANCES, married first to Robert Rich, grandson of Robert, Earl of Warwick, and secondly, to Sir John Russell, Bart. Since the first edition of this Work appeared, an esteemed correspondent informs me that a lineal descendant of General Ireton's eldest son is at this present time a basket-man in the Cork market.

1661, until sunset; when they were taken down, beheaded, and flung into a deep hole under the gallows. On Cromwell's coffin being broken open, a leaden canister was found lying on his breast, and within it a copper plate gilt, with the arms of England impaling those of Cromwell on one side, and on the other, the following inscription:—
" Oliverius, Protector Reipublicæ, Angliæ, Scotiæ, et Hiberniæ, natus 25 Aprilis, anno, 1599; inauguratus 16 Decembris, 1653: mortuus 3 Septembris, anno 1658: hic situs est." Oliver's widow survived her husband fourteen years, living in great obscurity, and died 8th of October, 1672, aged 74, at Norborough, her son-in-law, Claypole's house.

At the decease of his father, Oliver, RICHARD CROMWELL, succeeded to the sovereign power, as tranquilly and as unopposedly, it has been remarked, as though he had been the descendant of a long line of princes; yet his reign lasted but seven months and twenty-eight days. He subsequently resided abroad until about 1680; but where his various peregrinations led him is not known with any degree of certainty. On his return to England, he appears to have assumed the name of Clark, and to have resided at Sergeant Pengelly's house at Cheshunt to the end of his life, courting privacy and retirement, and cautiously avoiding so much as the mention of his former elevation even to his most intimate acquaintance. He died at Cheshunt, 13th July, 1712, in the 88th year of his age. Pennant mentions, that his father had told him that he used often to see, at the Don Saltero Coffee House at Chelsea, poor Richard Cromwell, " a little and very neat old man, with a most placid countenance, the effect of his innocent and unambitious life." By Dorothy, his wife, daughter of Richard Major, Esq., of Hursley, Hampshire, he had three daughters, the youngest of whom, the wife of John Mortimer, Esq., F.R.S., died at the age of twenty, without issue; of the other two, Miss Elizabeth Cromwell and Mrs. Gibson, Mr. Luson says, " I have several times been in company with these ladies; they were well-bred, well-dressed, stately women; exactly punctilious; but they seemed, especially Mistress Cromwell, to carry about them a consciousness of high rank, accompanied with a secret dread that those with whom they conversed should not observe and ackowledge it. They had neither the great sense nor the great enthusiasm of Mrs. Bendysh; but, as the daughter of Ireton had dignity without pride, so they had pride without dignity." Their unfilial conduct to their father remains a sad blot on their memory; and the meekness of poor Richard Cromwell makes their want of feeling more especially painful.

The male representative of the Lord Protector Oliver's family, vested, at the decease of this his eldest son, in the descendant of his second, HENRY CROMWELL, of Spinney Abbey, at one time Lord Deputy of Ireland, who, on the death of his father, quietly resigned his government, and returned to England, where he continued afterwards to reside as a country gentleman, at Spinney Abbey, in Cambridgeshire, unconcerned in the various changes of the State, and unembittered by the ills of ambition. By Elizabeth, his wife, eldest daughter of Sir Francis Russell, Bart., of Chippenham, he left, at his decease, in 1673, five sons and one daughter. To the latter, Elizabeth, wife of William Russell, Esq., of Fordham Abbey, I shall refer in the sequel. Of the sons, all died without issue except the second, HENRY CROMWELL, Esq., who was born in Dublin Castle, during his father's government of Ireland, 3rd March, 1658. He inherited eventually the estate of Spinney Abbey, but was compelled, by the pressure of circumstances, to sell that property, and experienced great vicissitudes and pecuniary distress. A letter of his is still preserved, in which he deplores his condition. " Our family," he writes to Lady Fauconberg, his aunt, "is low, and some are willing it should be kept so; yet I know we are a far ancienter family than many others; Sir Oliver Cromwell, my grandfather's uncle, and godfather's estate that was, is now let for above £50,000 a-year." Shortly after, so deep was his distress, that he petitioned the Lord Lieutenant of Ireland to give him some employment, but prayed to be excused from going over with his Excellency, as he was in want of the necessaries of a gentleman to appear in the Viceroy's suite. At length, the Duke of Ormonde procured for him the commission of Major of Foot, and he joined Lord Galway's army in the Peninsula, where he died of a fever in 1711. By Hannah, his wife, daughter of Benjamin Hewling, a Turkey merchant, he had a large family, of which the only son, whose descendants still exist, was THOMAS CROMWELL, who, " sic transit gloria mundi," carried on the business of a grocer, on Snow Hill, and died in Bridgewater Square, London, Oct. 2, 1748. He married, first, Francis Tidman, the daughter of a London tradesman, and by her was father of a daughter

Anne, the wife of John Field, of London.* He married, secondly, Mary, daughter of Nicholas Skinner, a merchant of London, and had, to leave issue, an only son, OLIVER CROMWELL, a solicitor, and clerk to St. Thomas's Hospital, who succeeded, under the will of his cousins, the Miss Cromwells, to an estate at Theobalds, Herts, which had been granted by Charles II. to General Monk, for his services in restoring the monarchy. Mr. Oliver Cromwell married, in 1771, Mary, daughter and co-heir of Morgan Morse, and left an only daughter and heir, ELIZABETH OLIVERIA CROMWELL, of Cheshunt Park, born in 1777, who married, in 1801, Thomas Artemidorus Russell, Esq., and had several children. With this OLIVER CROMWELL, who died in 1821, the attorney, and the son of the grocer, the male line of the Lord Protector's family expired. Thus, the house of Cromwell, which, even before the great Oliver's time, possessed estates in Huntingdonshire and other counties of immense value, dwindled from its high and princely station, and, within four generations, sank into absolute security, and became altogether extinct. No better destiny awaited many of the female descendants of the Lord Protector.

Elizabeth Cromwell (daughter of Henry Cromwell, Lord Deputy of Ireland) left, by her husband, William Russell, Esq., of Fordham Abbey, seven sons and six daughters. Of the former, Francis Russell, Esq., baptized at Fordham

* The issue of Anne Cromwell and John Field were, 1. Henry, of Woodford, Essex; 2. Oliver; 3. John, an officer in the Mint; 4. William; 5. Anne, married to Thomas Gwinnell; 6. Elizabeth; 7. Sophia; 8. Mary; and 9. Letitia, married to the Rev. John Wilkins.

Abbey, 1691, was father of Thomas Russell, Esq., a military officer, whose daughter, Rebecca, married, first, James Harley, Esq., by whom she had no issue, and secondly, William Dyer, Esq., of Ilford, a magistrate and deputy-lieutenant for Essex, by whom she had William Andrew Dyer, Esq., two other sons and two daughters. Of the daughters of Elizabeth Cromwell and William Russell, the eldest, Elizabeth, married Robert D'Aye, Esq., of Soham, a gentleman of ancient family, who dissipated his fortune, and became so reduced that HE DIED IN A WORKHOUSE, leaving his widow (the great granddaughter of the Lord Protector) dependent on an annual present from the daughters of Richard Cromwell; this ceasing towards the latter years of her life, she endured the severest hardships and the bitterest penury. She survived until 1765: her only surviving daughters were both married, one to Thomas Addeson, a shoemaker at Soham, and the other to one Saunders, a butcher's son, who was a fellow-servant in the family in which she lived.

Mary (the fourth daughter of Elizabeth Cromwell and William Russell) was left a poor, destitute, and forsaken child, in the village of Fordham, until Sir Charles Wager, who purchased her ancestral estate of Fordham Abbey, heard of her miserable condition, and had her educated. Eventually she married a Mr. Martin Wilkins, a respectable resident of Soham, and died without children. The fifth daughter, Margaret, formed a very humble connection; and the youngest married Mr. Nelson, of Mildenhall, by whom she had a son, a jeweller, and a daughter, who, after the death of her husband, Mr. Redderock, an attorney, kept a school at Mildenhall. How pointedly does this story of the downfall of Oliver Cromwell's family tell of the instability of all human greatness! Within the scope of a single century, and after the lapse of a few generations, we find the descendants of one, who in power equalled the mightiest princes of the earth, reduced to the depths of poverty, and almost begging their daily bread. To sum up:—Thomas Cromwell, the Lord Protector's great grandson, was a grocer on Snow Hill, and his son, Oliver Cromwell, the last male heir of the family, an attorney of London. But it was in the female line that the fall was most striking. Several of the Lord Protector's granddaughters' children sank to the lowest class of society. One, after seeing her husband die in the workhouse of a little Suffolk town, died herself a pauper, leaving two daughters; the elder, the wife of a shoemaker, and the younger, of a butcher's son, who had been her fellow-servant. Another of Oliver Cromwell's great granddaughters had two children, who earned their scanty bread by the humblest industry; the son as a small working jeweller, and the daughter as the mistress of a little school at Mildenhall.

The Bairds of Gartsherrie Ironworks and their Predecessors.

"He hath put down the mighty from their seats, and exalted them of low degree."

About the end of the last century, there lived in the parish of Monkland, near Glasgow, a small farmer, in humble circumstances, of the name of Baird. By his wife, who had been employed in a neighbouring farm house, he had a numerous family of sons, who, between the year 1820 and the present year, 1860, have, by dint of ability, judgment, honesty, and frugality, raised themselves to the position of the first mercantile men in Scotland. To this must be added the advantage of rare good fortune and propitious circumstances, which does not diminish their merit, for there is no use in a ball being placed at a man's feet if he has not strength and dexterity to kick it, and to keep it up. The coal and iron trade in the Monklands had not yet been developed. The sagacity and enterprise of the Bairds were devoted to that object, and in the course of a few years they rose from the position of farmers to that of thriving ironmasters, and then gradually advanced until they distanced all others in the same line in Scotland, and placed themselves on a footing with the Guests and Baileys of South Wales.

Merchants are proverbially princes to-day and beggars to-morrow; and as long as enormous capital is invested in speculation, however prosperous and apparently secure, permanency can never be certain. Those who are alive in the year 1900 will be in a condition to know whether or not the heirs of the Bairds belong to the richest landed aristocracy of Great Britain; and whether or not the immense estates already acquired by them have been preserved so as to found great territorial families.

In the meantime, these numerous and enterprising brothers have acted with praiseworthy ambition in acquiring landed possessions, which give them an influence in the country far beyond the mere accumulation of pounds, shillings, and pence. Within the last twelve or fifteen years they have secured by purchase magnificent estates, which, if preserved, will, before two generations are over, raise their descendants to a place among the magnates of the land.

The present generation of Bairds, regarded as they are by the public among the richest commoners of Scotland, have reason to be proud of the lowly origin from which prudence and industry have raised them. Possibly their grandchildren may desire to cover that origin with the blazon of pedigree; but the fabricators of a colossal fortune have good cause to glory, with thankfulness, in a rise which has been mainly owing to their own merit.

The brothers Baird have been too busy in transmuting iron into gold, to have time, or probably inclination, to think of pedigree, or to care for ancient blood. Possibly, however, in one or two descents, a family already founded, and by that time allied among the aristocracy, may think it worth while to seek out a generous stem for their golden branches; and it is a matter of fact, that Lanarkshire, which has witnessed the gradual rise of these brothers to wealth, numbered, many centuries ago, among its most considerable barons, an ancient race of their name.

In the reign of Alexander III., Richard Baird had a charter of lands from Robert, son of Waldeve de Biggar, and King Robert Bruce gave a grant of the barony of Camnethan to Robert Baird. In the ancient mansion of Camnethan, as it existed in the days of the lordly Somervilles, the most ancient portion was called the Bairds' Tower. The prosperity of this race was, however, speedily blighted by treason. Baird of Carnwath, and three or four other barons of that name, being convicted of a conspiracy against King Robert Bruce, in the Parliament held at Perth, were forfeited and put to death.

Baird of Auchmedden in Banffshire has long been considered the principal family of the name;* and it is a curious circumstance, that among the many estates which the brothers Baird have acquired, Auchmedden is one. The main line of Auchmedden is extinct, but there are two baronets' families descended from it, viz., **Baird of Saughton Hall**, and **Baird of Newbyth**.

I must leave to some genealogist of a future generation the task of connecting the many-millioned brothers

* A still older line of Bairds in Banffshire, viz. of Ordinhuiff, died out in the 16th century.

of Gartsherrie Ironworks with the races of their name which have been distinguished in olden time, or which now claim a place among our well-descended gentry. My intention is to record the rise of this most remarkable and meritorious family, and, while I congratulate them on their present posterity, to cast a look of regret on one or two of the ancient races which have passed away and given place to them. Nothing can more strikingly depict the vicissitudes of fortune in considerable families than the transfer of hereditary property; and therefore I will attempt to trace the fortunes of one or two of the Bairds' predecessors.

I trust that I shall not wound aristocratic feelings—I will not call them prejudices (for such feelings are good in their proper place and within due bounds)—when I say that such transfer of great estates from the old to the new races is an immense benefit to the country. Not that the new man is a better landlord, neighbour, magistrate, or member of Parliament, than the man of ancient lineage; generally quite the reverse. Not that the individual instances of a noble and time-honoured race being forced to give way to one fresh from the ranks of the people, are otherwise than repugnant to our tastes and habits of thought. But such changes serve as the props and bulwarks of the existing social and political institutions of Great Britain. In this country there is happily no conventional barrier raised against the admission of a man of the people into the ranks of the aristocracy. Industry and good conduct, favoured by providence, in the acquisition of wealth, may raise a poor man to a place among the rich landed gentry of the country, and another generation may see him not only in the House of Lords, but allied by blood to the highest families of the land.

Therefore it is the true interest of the people to maintain those social and political institutions which are thus liberal towards them.

If the insurmountable barrier of a proud nobility of sixteen quarters existed in England, as it is, and as it still does, in some continental countries, our government and constitution would not be worth six months' purchase. It is the safeguard of English institutions that admission to the aristocracy is not exclusively barred against the ambition of a man of humble birth, and that a place there, when once obtained, is jealously guarded by the right of primogeniture. Each generation witnesses the ascent of numbers of men of the people among the upper ten thousand of English aristocracy, and when there, they generally become the most exclusive preservers of the footing which they have gained. It is well for England that men like the Bairds hasten to invest their hundred thousand or their million in great landed estates; and moreover, that they centre their wealth on their eldest sons. What a contrast does this rich, flourishing, popular aristocracy exhibit to the poverty-stricken nobility of most continental countries, which, on the one hand, rarely admits of accessions from the people, and on the other, fritters away its possessions by eternal subdivisions of titles and estates among every branch of its race, however remote.

This forms one of the most striking and beneficial

discrepancies between our social institutions and those of most of the great continental states. With us, a merchant no sooner realizes a fortune than his ambition is to be a country gentleman, and to push upwards among the old families of a county. He sends his son to Eton and Oxford, where he associates on equal terms with young men of birth. He seeks matrimonial alliances for his children among those of a superior class: and, unless there is something ridiculous or forbidding about him and his family, his efforts are generally successful, and the next generation sees the Liverpool merchant or the Manchester cotton-spinner's son or grandson associated and allied with houses which were founded at the Conquest or during the Barons' wars. There is scarcely a peer, however exalted his rank may be, who has not some degree of cousinhood with families of very ordinary pretensions; and not a few of our Cabinet ministers in modern times are but one remove from the counting-house, through the intermediate step of a merchant or cotton-spinner turned squire.

Having thus paid tribute to the beneficial influence of new blood on our political institutions, let us indemnify ourselves by dwelling for a few moments on one or two of the great landed families who have been supplanted for the present by the Gartsherrie Iron Kings.

The estates which these brothers have purchased are numerous, valuable, and wide-spread in every direction throughout Scotland. In the north, Strichen has been acquired from Lord Lovat, Urie from Mr. Barclay-Allardice, and Auchmedden, the patrimony of the ancient family of Baird. In the south, Stitchill has been bought from Sir John Pringle, and Closeburne from Sir James Stuart Menteath. In the east, Elie and the ancient barony of Anstruther have been purchased from Sir Windham Anstruther; and in the west, Knoydart, the last remnant of the territories of the chieftain of Glengarry, has added to the victories of the prosperous Iron Kings over the old lords of the soil.

I believe that I have only enumerated a portion of their purchases; for proprietors, small as well as great, have been swallowed up.

With a view to mark the vicissitudes of fortune, I will give a sketch of the history of the principal families whose estates have been transferred to these prosperous men:—Kirkpatrick of Closeburne, Anstruther of Anstruther, and Macdonell of Glengarry chieftain of Clanronald.

I. Kirkpatrick of Closeburne, Baronet.

The Kirkpatricks were proprietors of Closeburne from a very early period. John de Kirkpatrick obtained a royal charter for those lands which had formerly belonged to his ancestors from King Alexander II. His descendant, Roger Kirkpatrick, was one of the first who stoutly maintained the cause of King Robert Bruce; and he proved his zeal by murder and sacrilege.

Bruce met his powerful rival, "the red Comyn," in the town of Dumfries, and burning with ill-dissembled indignation at the treachery of which he had discovered him to be guilty, he requested a private interview with him in the church of the Minorite Friars. Comyn agreed, and they had not reached the high altar before Bruce arraigned him of treachery. "You lie," said Comyn; on which Bruce stabbed him with his dagger; and, hurrying from the sanctuary, he met Kirkpatrick in the street. "I doubt," said Bruce, as he hastily mounted his horse, "that I have slain Comyn." "Do you doubt?" said Kirkpatrick, fiercely; "I'll make sure!"—and, immediately entering the convent, he found the victim weltering in his blood, and writhing in agony in front of the high altar. Having despatched him as he lay helpless on the steps of the altar, he speedily joined Bruce. This achievement has ever since been the proud boast of the family; and in memory of the murderous sacrilege, they adopted for their crest a hand grasping a sword, dropping blood, with "I make sicker" (or sure) for their motto.

The Barons of Closeburne continued to flourish among the principal gentry of the South of Scotland for many centuries. In the year 1685 Thomas Kirkpatrick was created a Baronet of Nova Scotia by Charles II., to reward him for his fidelity to his royal father. The present is the sixth baronet of the family; but they have been, for three generations, deprived of their family estates; for in the latter part of last century, Closeburne was sold to the Rev. James Stuart Menteath, rector of Barrowby, in Lincolnshire. His son, Charles, was created a baronet in 1838; and his son, Sir James, sold the ancient inheritance of the Kirkpatricks to one of the brothers Baird for upwards of two hundred thousand pounds.

The family of Kirkpatrick of Closeburne has been recently brought from the profound obscurity into which it had fallen, and presented to the public under very peculiar circumstances. The complaisance of genealogists has attributed to Eugenie, Empress of the French, the Spanish Countess of Theba, a maternal descent from this ancient race. The mother of her Imperial majesty was certainly a Kirkpatrick, and of Dumfrieshire origin; but if the Kirkpatricks from whom the Empress is descended, are of the family of Closeburne, it remains yet to be ascertained and proved when and how they diverged from the ancient tree. They held the rank of mere provincial gentry, and all their alliances that can be traced are with families of name and station far inferior to those with whom the house of Closeburne intermarried.

Robert Kirkpatrick, of Glenkiln, married Henrietta Gillespie, and was father of William Kirkpatrick, of Conheath in Dumfrieshire, who married Mary Wilson, by whom he had several children. One of his sons, William, settled as a merchant in Malaga, and married the daughter of a foreign consul there, by whom he had three daughters. The eldest, who was very beautiful, attracted the notice and became the wife of the youngest son of the great family of Montijo, grandees of Spain of the first class. The daughter of the Scottish merchant was considered a mesalliance for a young man of so distinguished a family, and her inferior birth was stated as a reason for consent being refused. An application was made hereupon by the friends of the family to the late ingenious Mr. Charles Fitzpatrick Sharpe, a gentleman who, from his wit and fondness for virtu, was called by Sir Walter Scott the Horace Walpole of Edinburgh. Mr. Sharpe, it is said, undertook, with considerable zest, the task of supplying his fair countrywoman with a long and flourishing genealogical tree, in which the dagger dripping the heart's blood of "the red Comyn" made a conspicuous figure. The pedigree was, it is asserted, beautifully drawn up, and sent to Spain. When it was submitted to King Ferdinand VII., he indulged in a joke on the occasion. Looking at the document, where the origin of the Kirkpatricks seemed lost in the mists of ancient Caledonia, his Majesty said, "O, by all means let the young Montijo marry the daughter of Fingal."

The husband of Miss Kirkpatrick eventually succeeded to the titles and estates of his family, and left two daughters: of these the elder espoused the Duke of Berwick and Alva, (representative of the Marechal Duc de Berwick, natural son of King James II.,) and died deeply deplored in the autumn of this present year, (1860), while the younger, long celebrated for her beauty and grace as Countess de Theba, is now Eugenie, Empress of the French. Until within the last few years, a Miss Kirkpatrick, grand aunt of the Empress, resided in the county town of Dumfries; and her Imperial Majesty has several first cousins of the name of Kirkpatrick, sons of her mother's sister, who married a cousin of her own name. One of them was not long ago settled as a merchant at Havre.

II. Anstruther of Anstruther.

In the year 1100, William de Candela was Lord of Anstruther. At that early period it was customary for nobles to adopt their surnames from their lands, and it was rare to find a Scottish baron who possessed a family name besides his territorial designation. One of the few ancient Scottish nobles of the time of King David I., who enjoyed this distinction, was William, Lord of Anstruther. He had already a noble name. He was not the founder of his family. He was a son of the noble race of De Candela, and in the year 1100 he was one of the most considerable of the barons of Fife. It is not known how long his ancestors had possessed the barony of Anstruther before that period. It is more probable that he was a foreign nobleman, who obtained grants of land from King David I., as was the case with so many distinguished strangers at that period. Few, however, brought with them a family name. The greater number of the ancient races in Scotland spring from ancestors who had no name except that of their lands, and it is an honour to the house of Anstruther to be descended from an ancestor already noble so early as 1100: a fact which determines the ascertained nobility of the family for eight hundred years.

William de Candela is known to have been Lord of Anstruther about the year 1100, but there is no original grant of the barony to shew the exact year in which it was first conferred on him or on his ancestor. He lived through the reign of David I., and did not die until the commencement of that of Malcolm IV., who ascended the Scottish throne in the year 1153. His son William, Lord of Anstruther, was a pious benefactor to the Abbey of Balmerino, and died in the reign of William the Lion, which commenced in 1165. His son Henry, in compliance with the usage of Scotland, assumed the name of his lands as his surname, and disused that of De Candela. He is styled Henricus de Anstruther Dominus de Anstruther in a charter wherein he confirms his father's pious donations to the Abbey of Balmerino, in 1221, in the reign of Alexander II. His son Henry, Lord of Anstruther, was also a pious benefactor to religious houses in charters granted during the reign of Alexander III. He was a crusader, and accompanied St. Louis to the East. He assumed for his arms the three nails of the cross, now represented by three piles sable on a silver shield. In his old age he was compelled to swear fealty for his barony of Anstruther to Edward I., in 1292 and 1296.

For many generations the chiefs of this family were munificent benefactors to religious houses. In the reign of Louis XII. of France two sons of the family held high commands in the Scottish guards, attending the person of that monarch and his successor. In 1513 Andrew, Baron of Anstruther, was killed, along with James IV., at Flodden. His grandson of the same name was killed at Pinkie in 1547. Sir James, the thirteenth in descent from William de Candela, was high in favour with King James VI., by whom he was knighted, and in 1585 appointed hereditary Grand Carver to His Majesty, an office still held by his descendant. In 1592 he was the Master of the royal household. Sir William, his son, was gentleman of the bedchamber to James VI., and was made a Knight of the Bath at his coronation in London in 1603. His brother, Sir Robert, was a diplomatist of great eminence. He was employed by James I. and Charles I. on many important embassies. In 1628 he was sent as Ambassador Extraordinary to his master's near connection, the King of Denmark, with whom he was in especial favour as a boon companion no less than as a diplomatist. In a protracted revel the Danish King was so much delighted with his company that he actually resigned the Danish crown to him, with which Sir Robert was invested during the remaining days of the feast. In 1629 he was Ambassador to the Emperor of Germany; and he was sent by Charles I. and the Elector Palatine as their Plenipotentiary to the Germanic Diet at Ratisbonne, and in 1630 he was Ambassador to the princes of Germany at Heilbronn.

The Ambassador's son, Sir Philip, was a most zealous and devoted royalist. He had a high command in the King's army, and was taken prisoner at the battle of Worcester. He was severely fined by Cromwell, and his estates were sequestered until the Restoration. He lived until 1702, and saw two of his sons created, in the same year, 1694, baronets of Nova Scotia. He had five sons, two of whom were baronets, and three knights. 1. Sir Philip carried on the line of the family. 2. Sir James, whose line is extinct. 3. Sir Robert, ancestor to the baronets of Balcaskie. 4. Sir Philip, who had a daughter married to the Earl of Traquair. 5. Sir Alexander, who married the Baroness of Newark, and was father of the third and fourth Lords Newark. Sir Robert, the third son, was created a baronet in 1694. His son, Sir Philip, second Baronet of Balcaskie, married a granddaughter of the Marquis of Tweeddale, by a daughter of the Earl of Buccleugh, and had issue, I. Sir Robert, who carried on the line of his family, and was grandfather to Sir Ralph, the present Baronet; II. Colonel John Anstruther, whose son, John Anstruther, took the name of Thomson for the estate of Charleton, and was father of the present Mr. Anstruther Thomson of Charleton, who is twenty-first in direct male descent from the founder of the house of Anstruther.

Sir William Anstruther, the old royalist's eldest son, was created a baronet in 1694. By a daughter of the Earl of Haddington he had a son, Sir John, who married Lady Margaret Carmichael, eldest daughter of the second Earl of Hyndford; a most fortunate alliance, as it has saved the eldest branch of the house of Anstruther from beggary. On the extinction of the house of Hyndford by the death of Andrew, last Earl, in 1817, the great Carmichael estates devolved upon the Baronet of Anstruther as heir general of the family, and these estates are now all that remain to the present Baronet, who is the twenty-first in direct male descent from the founder of the family, and who succeeded his youthful nephew in 1831. He was not long in possession before he became inextricably involved, and at length, after many years, he succeeded in breaking the entail of his Anstruther estates, and sold them in 1856, together with the mansion of Elie House, to one of the brothers Baird, who has thus come into possession of one of the most ancient family properties in Scotland. Sir Windham Anstruther is still possessed of the great Carmichael estates in Lanarkshire, which are in value equal to those he has alienated. But had he not inherited them, he would have been as much the landless representative of a fallen house, as the other great proprietors who have yielded to the colossal wealth of the Bairds.

III. Macdonell of Glengarry, Chief of Glengarry.

THE possessions of the house of Somerled, King of Inisgael, have, in the course of centuries, been strangely scattered. Without attempting to enumerate other alienations, I may state that the great island of Isla, which formed one of the important territories of the old Hebridian Kings, passed in later times to Mr. Morrison, the rich London merchant; and the estates of Somerled's direct descendant, the chief of Clanronald, have become the spoil of two iron kings; the one patrician, and the other plebeian. Glengarry was purchased some years ago by the prince of Staffordshire ironmasters, Lord Ward; and Knoydart, still more recently, by the iron potentate of Gartsherrie.

In the middle of the twelfth century, the "Orkneyinga Saga" calls Somerled and his sons (who were the chiefs of the Gallgael) the Dalverian family; a term derived from Dala, the Norse name for the district of Argyle, and which implies that they had been for some time indigenous in the district. In fact, Somerled was the descendant of a long line of chiefs, of whom the names are on record; but it is unnecessary to trace them, for a direct male descent from a renowned warrior-king, who died in the year 1164, is honour enough, without a further search into the mists of antiquity.

Somerled was already Lord of Argyle. He married Efrica, daughter of the King of Man and the Southern islands. In 1156, he attacked his brother-in-law, King Godred, who was obliged to detach the Southern Hebrides from Man, and to cede them to the conqueror. Somerled hereupon styled himself King of the Isles, or King of Inisgael. Next year, he invaded Scotland, and made terms, as an equal, with King Malcolm IV. He then expelled his brother-in-law from Man, and took possession of the whole of the Isles. In 1164, he again invaded Scotland with one hundred and fifty-three galleys; but he was slain, and his fleet was repulsed.

On his death there was a division of his territories. A portion of the mainland devolved on his son Dougal, who was ancestor of the great house of De Ergadia, Lord of Lorn, which was ruined by its adherence to the English interest against King Robert Bruce, and which is now represented by Macdougald, of Dunolly Castle.

The principal portion of Somerled's insular dominions was inherited by his son, Reginald, who, like his father, was styled King of the Isles, and King of Man, under which title he was acknowledged by John, King of England, to whom he swore fealty as a vassal king, in 1212. He was succeeded by a line of island princes, who generally styled themselves King, and never acknowledged the supremacy of the monarchs of Scotland, excepting when compelled to do so by force of arms. They always courted the English alliance, and were considered by the successive Plantagenet monarchs in the light of valuable confederates to undermine the integrity of the Scottish kingdom.

A different line of policy, however, was pursued by Angus More, or the great Lord of the Isles, the fourth in descent from Reginald, who succeeded his father in 1303, for he sheltered King Robert Bruce, when a fugitive, in his castle of Dunaverty, when no other would incur the risk. He afterwards helped to maintain him on the Scottish throne, by fighting for him at Bannockburn, with two thousand men under his banner. And for these good deeds he was rewarded by the grateful monarch with large grants of lands. He died before 1337.

John, his son, followed a wavering policy. He was at first tempted by the offers of King Edward Balliol to forsake the party of the Bruces, and he went to England very soon after his father's death, and made terms with King Edward III. in 1337. But when King David Bruce regained the crown, he made his peace with him, was admitted to favour in 1344, and continued in undisturbed possession of his vast territories.

There has been a great controversy concerning the family of John, Lord of the Isles. And it will be necessary to pay some attention to it, in order to understand the claims of the different branches, who trace themselves to him as their common ancestor, and several of whom claim to be his representative. In 1337, John, Lord of the Isles (for that was now the title of the family, the style of King having been long disused), had a papal dispensation for marrying one of his cousins, Annie Mac Rory, a daughter of Roderick of the Isles, the head of an important branch of his family. By her he had three sons: 1. JOHN; 2. GODFREY; 3. RONALD. John, Lòrd of the Isles, afterwards married the Princess Margaret, daughter of Robert II., the first Scottish king of the house of Stuart, and by her, also, he had three sons: 1. DONALD; 2. JOHN; 3. ALEXANDER.

From that day to the present, there has been a fierce controversy as to which of these two sets of sons was the legitimate inheritor of the blood and the honours of the Hebridian princes. The partisans of the sons of the first marriage maintained, that they were not only elder, but lawfully born; that their mother was divorced in order to make way for the second and royal marriage of their father, and that their rights were sacrificed to those of the eldest son of the Scottish princess. On the other side it is admitted, indeed, that they were the elder sons; but it is contended, that they were not born in lawful wedlock, and that none of them succeeded to the dignity of Lord of the Isles, while Donald, the eldest son of the princess, from whom they themselves held their lands, was their father's acknowledged heir.

Without presuming to decide on so difficult a question, which has served for five centuries as a subject of fierce dispute, I will observe that the contest has been carried on between the descendants of Donald, the eldest son of the Princess, and those of Ronald, the youngest son of Annie MacRory. Now, this Ronald had two elder brothers, John and Godfrey, both of whom are known to have had issue, and there is no positive proof that the descendants of either are extinct; so that even if Ronald, the third son of the first marriage, was legitimate, it would be impossible to prove that his descendants are the true representatives of John, Lord of the Isles. Be this, however, as it may, the fact is, that Donald, the eldest son of John, Lord of the Isles, by the Princess Margaret, was acknowledged to be his heir, and he accordingly succeeded as "Dominus Insularum," on the death of John, in 1380.

Of these six sons, JOHN, the eldest, died before his father, leaving a son, Angus, of whom little is known; GODFREY, the second, was Lord of Uist and Garmoran, whose descendants are traced in history for several generations, when they seem to have sunk into obscurity. RONALD is the ancestor of the great house of Clanronald. DONALD, the fourth son, but eldest son of the royal marriage, was his father's heir. JOHN MORE was ancestor of Macdonald of Isla, Kintyre, and the Glens, and the Earls and Marquises of Antrim in Ireland. ALEXANDER was Lord of Lochaber, and ancestor of Macdonald of Keppoch.

Donald, Lord of the Isles, who succeeded in 1380, carried on the old line of his family policy, intriguing with the English king, and endeavouring to shake off the allegiance which he owed to the King of Scotland. He invaded Scotland with ten thousand men, and fought the famous battle of Harlaw, in 1411, against Robert, Duke of Albany, the Regent, who was his uncle. In right of his wife, Donald became Earl of Ross. He died in 1420, and was succeeded by Alexander, Lord of the Isles, and Earl of Ross, whose early years of rule were spent in intrigues and treaties with the English, and in wars against his Scottish sovereign, to whom he was at last forced to submit. In 1429, he threw himself on the king's mercy, and in his shirt and drawers, and on his knees, before the altar of Holyrood, in the presence of the queen and nobles, he presented his sword to the king. His life was spared, and he was shut up in the Castle of Tantallon. In 1431, he was pardoned, and restored to his dominions. He died in 1449. He had three sons: JOHN, his successor; HUGH, ancestor of Macdonald of Sleat, now Lord Macdonald; CELESTINE, Lord of Lochalsh, whose granddaughter and coheir, Margaret, carried great possessions to her husband, Alexander of Glengarry, which raised the fortunes of that family.

John, Lord of the Isles, and Earl of Ross, succeeded his father in 1449. His life and reign are similar to those of his predecessors:—an invasion of Scotland with one hundred galleys and five thousand men: a treasonable treaty with Edward IV. of England, in 1462, on the footing of an independent prince; a submission, and a pardon from the Scottish king; a deprivation of his earldom of Ross, and the conversion of this great insular lordship into a Scottish peerage. He again entered into a treasonable treaty with Edward IV. in 1481; but he was permitted to resume possession of his estates after the violent death of his son, who was a sacrilegious plunderer and rebel to the Scottish king. The old lord's nephew, Alexander of Lochalsh, made an insurrection in 1491, but was wounded and defeated. He himself was forfeited in

1493, but he submitted, surrendered, and finally died in the abbey of Paisley, in 1498.

The power of the Isles was now broken. The old lord's grandson, Donald-Dhu, was the last of the direct line, and was set up by the Islesmen as their lord, in 1503. But he was, ere long, taken and imprisoned for forty years in the Castle of Edinburgh. In the meantime, various pretenders, of the race of the Isles, claimed the insular sovereignty, but without permanent success. Donald-Dhu at length escaped from his long captivity, and raised an insurrection in 1544, when he made a treaty with England, as Earl of Ross, and sovereign Lord of the Isles. He crossed over with one hundred and eighty galleys to Ireland, in order to raise more men, but died of a fever at Drogheda, in 1544. With him ended the direct male line, and he may be considered as the last "Dominus Insularum."

The descent of Clanronald is derived from Ronald, the third son of John, Lord of the Isles, by Annie Macrory; and those who contend for the right of Glengarry to be chief of all the Macdonalds, maintain that the issue of John and Godfrey, Ronald's two elder brothers, became extinct. From Donald, the son of Ronald, descended the family of Knoydart and its cadet, Glengarry, while from Allan, another son, descended the family of Moydart. There appears to have existed an inveterate animosity between the Lords of the Isles, Earls of Ross, and the family of Knoydart, who for several generations became depressed, and were deprived of many of their territorial possessions. They were in the course of a few generations completely reduced, and, on their extinction, Glengarry, the next branch, succeeded to their rights, and he was the better able to maintain his pretensions, from having, about the beginning of the sixteenth century, acquired great possessions by marriage with the granddaughter and co-heiress of Celestine, Lord of Lochalsh.

But the descendant of Allan of Moydart resisted the pretensions of Glengarry, and, in vindication of what he deemed his right, placed himself at the head of Clanronald, by adopting the title of Captain of Clanronald, a designation retained until the latter part of the last century, when the Highland title of Captain of Clanronald was abandoned for that of Macdonald of Clanronald.

At the time of the extinction of the Lords of the Isles, the family of Knoydart consisted of two branches, Knoydart and Glengarry: and while the former never recovered from the depressed state to which it had been reduced and soon became extinct, the latter continued to flourish, with an accession of wealth and influence, and always vehemently opposed the claim of Moydart to be chief. The successive chieftains of Glengarry have ever loudly asserted their right to be the chiefs of Clanronald, and have maintained their claims to the present day. "Non nostrum est tantas componere lites." But it is, alas! an empty claim, both on the part of Knoydart and Moydart. For the representatives of both families have not an acre of Macdonald land between them; and the vast possessions over which their ancestors bore sway, are subdivided among strangers and aliens.

It is a circumstance, perhaps, not generally known, that the adoption of Macdonald as a family name is comparatively recent. The clan was, doubtless, anciently called Clandonald, from a remote ancestor. The old family name, however, was "de Insulis," or "of the Isles," or "de Yla," and the distinctive denomination of the chief was "Dominus Insularum." But, above four hundred years ago, when the great chiefs were extinguished, the custom of designation by patronymics superseded the old name of "de Insulis," or "de Yla," and continued down to the time of King James VI. The inconvenience of this custom was manifest, and caused it to be disused in the beginning of the seventeenth century. And it so happened, that in the three chief families of the Clandonald existing at that time in the Highlands, the Christian name Donald having occurred in all of them, they all adopted the surname of Macdonald. Thus, Sir Donald of Sleat became Sir Donald Macdonald, in 1625, when he was created a baronet; Donald MacAngus Mac Alister of Glengarry, and Donald Mac Allan Mac Ian, Captain of Clanronald, were the contemporary heads of the other two most potent families of the race in Scotland, and Roland Mac Sorlie, afterwards Earl of Antrim, was first called Macdonnell in 1618, when he was created Viscount Dunluce.

The undoubted representative of the later Lords of the Isles was the Lord of Sleat; as he was descended from Hugh, son of Alexander, Lord of the Isles, and grandson of Donald, the eldest son of John and Princess Margaret; and his descendant, the present Lord Macdonald, is generally regarded as the head of the Clan. However, this is most vehemently disputed by the chieftain of Clanronald, whether he be Moydart or the unfortunate Glengarry, whose last territorial possessions have passed into the hands of the many-millioned Bairds.

I have stated, that the third son of John, Lord of the Isles, and his first wife, Annie MacRory, was Ronald or Ranald, the successor of a great and powerful race, which was called, from his name, Clanronald, and which has branched into several families. It is probable that if the power of the Lords of the Isles had been handed down to successors in a direct line, the pretension of the chieftains of Clanronald to be chiefs of the great Clan of Macdonald might never have been advanced. But the extinction of the direct line of the reigning family of the Isles produced a confusion in the succession, and excited the ambition of a powerful branch to dispute the claims of the more immediate representative of the later island lords.

The power of Macdonald, or as it is called Macdonell, of Glengarry, seems to have attained to its culminating point in the reign of King Charles II., at which period a Scottish peerage was conferred on its representative, Angus, in 1660, with the style and title of Lord Macdonell and Aross. But he died without issue in 1682, when his peerage became extinct, and when arose the *vexata quæstio* of chieftainship, and the conflicting claims of Glengarry and Moydart, each asserting his right to be chieftain of Clanronald.

In the beginning of the present century, Alexander Ranaldson Macdonell, of Glengarry, claimed to be chief of Clanronald, and as he was ambitious of being recognized as head of the Clan Macdonald, he revived, with considerable ardour, the ancient controversy; and he accordingly put forth his pretensions in a letter addressed to Alexander Wentworth, second Lord Macdonald. To this the peer very tersely replied —" Till you prove that you are my chief, I am yours, MACDONALD."

Glengarry died in 1828; and since then all his estates have been sold, and are now held partly by Lord Ward, and partly by one of the Bairds of the Gartsherrie ironworks.

The Princess of Connemara.

"Good Heaven! what sorrows gloom'd that parting day
That called her from her native walks away;
When the poor exile, every pleasure pass'd,
Hung round the bowers, and fondly looked her last,
And took a long farewell, and wish'd in vain
For seat like this beyond the western main."
  GOLDSMITH.

WHO has not heard of the eccentric but benevolent Richard Martin, the Lord of Connemara, the renowned for hospitality in a land of hospitality, and for many years the representative of the county of Galway in the British house of Commons? Weighed accurately in the scales of merit, he may have fallen short of his ancestors. Most certainly he was not the man to have accumulated the family estates, but somehow his name stands out to the eclipse of those who went before him, and I am thus tempted to give him a momentary precedence.

Even those who have forgotten the eccentricities of this singular character, will yet recollect him in connection with a certain act for "preventing or punishing cruelty to "animals," an act which is popularly known under his name, "Dick Martin's Act." Nor did he content himself with having obtained this parliamentary defence for his four-footed clients, and then leaving the carrying of it out to others; he was equally strenuous in seeing that they had the full benefit of the law enacted for their protection, and when he was in London never failed to bring up before the police-magistrates such delinquents as had the ill-luck to come under his eye, when he would press the law against them to the utmost. There was something of the το γελαιον—of the ridiculous—which for a long time accompanied his best efforts, but eventually the cause of humanity was triumphant.

In Connemara, where, like Selkirk upon the island of Juan Fernandez, he was "monarch of all he surveyed," and could do pretty well as he pleased, without the intervention of a magistrate, his benevolence took a shorter cut to its object, and the memory of his doings in behalf of his dumb friends is perpetuated in the ruins of an ancient fortalice upon the shores of Ballynahinch Lake. The peasants of the neighbourhood still know these mouldering fragments by the name of *Dick Martin's Prison,* and will tell how the Lord of Connemara used, in the somewhat doubtful exercise of his feudal rights, to confine therein such of his tenants as sinned against the laws of humanity towards the brute creation. But I must now leave this redresser of animal grievances, and trace my steps back to the commencement of my story.

The founder of the Martin family in Ireland was Oliver Martyn, who accompanied the first English army, under

Strongbow, and settling in Galway, originated one of the thirteen tribes in that ancient town. But the prosperity of the race would seem to have been greatly increased in the time of Captain Richard Martin of Donegan, who received large grants from the confiscated possessions of the O'Flaherties of Ire Connaught. He was a warm partizan of James the Second, and after the abdication, or more properly the flight, of that monarch, joined for a time the so-called Irish army. It seems, however, that he knew how to trim his sails to the wind, for upon the Jacobite cause becoming manifestly hopeless, he submitted to King William, and had the good fortune to retain his lands. He then petitioned the reigning sovereign that he might be allowed to erect his estates into a manor, urging as a ground for this request his desire to improve the property by encouraging dealers and handicraftsmen of every kind to become settlers upon it. His prayer was accordingly granted by a patent, July 5th, 1698, which, moreover, ratified the title of all his previous acquisitions. Nor was it probably any drawback to his satisfaction that he had constantly to fight with some one or other for the maintenance of these new rights, which, in proportion as they enlarged his bounds, had curtailed those of his neighbours. Amongst the most troublesome of the enemies so raised up against him was Edmund O'Flaherty, surnamed *Laider*, or the Stoney, who was far from tamely acquiescing in the alienation of his paternal territories. Many and desperate were the conflicts between the feudal chieftains, for the most part sword in hand, on horseback. But the praise of chivalry must, we think, in fairness, be awarded to the

Laider, who seems to have trusted in a great measure to his own good right arm. Martin, being always surrounded by a troop of followers, ran comparatively little risk, while the more adventurous O'Flaherty had often to cut his way to safety through opposing numbers by dint of superior strength.

The estate of the Martins might well be called a principality. Situated in the county of the town of Galway and the baronies of Moycullen, Ballynahinch, and the half-barony of Ross, in the county of Galway, it contained upwards of one hundred and ninety-two thousand statute acres, and extended almost uninterruptedly from the town of Oughterard to Clifden and Claggan Bays, a distance of at least thirty miles, having the navigable Lough Corrib on the north of the Bay of Galway, and the Atlantic ocean as the south and south-western boundaries. Yet their dwelling of Ballynahinch, although styled a castle, was unworthy of the surrounding land. The prodigious extent of the demesne may be imagined from the fact that the grandfather of the last possessor could boast to George the Fourth, " he had an approach from his gate-house to his hall of thirty miles length." Were the greater part of these enormous domains either waste, rock, or moorland, there would be less matter for surprise ; but such is not altogether the fact ; the whole is infinitely diversified with glens, lakes, rivers, and some portion of cultivated land, though far below what the soil would naturally admit of. Many of these waters exhibit scenes of surpassing beauty, their wide surface being broken by beautifully wooded islets. There are about sixty-four of the larger of such watery oases, not to mention a multitude of islets that occur singly or in clusters, and are not the less lovely from oftentimes presenting themselves in the midst of desolation. Moreover the whole coast, washed by the Atlantic, is indented with numerous bays, offering the same panorama of islands that seem to float upon the reflecting element. And then, as might be expected from the natural history of Ireland, the waters abound in salmon and trout, while the land is not less amply provided with grouse, woodcocks, and divers sorts of waterfowl, which make a country life so delectable to sportsmen. At the same time, amidst all these agreeable attractions, there is no want of the useful. The sea affords an abundant supply of manure for agricultural purposes, various parts are rich in blue limestone, and in the *Twelve Pin Mountains* are inexhaustible quarries of marble. Nothing is wanted but the hand of industry, aided by modern science, to render Connemara equal to some of the favoured regions of the earth, unless I must add thereto a healthier social system, and a better education of the people.

Within this prodigious extent of territory the Martins exercised something very nearly akin to feudal rule, the arms of the law being much too short on most occasions, to stretch into the wilds of Connaught. They were lords paramount. Every head was bared in submission to the owners of so many thousands upon thousands of acres, which, if not generally remarkable for cultivation, at least impressed the imagination by extent. Yet, immense and almost unbounded as the estate was, the seeds of decay had been sown in it by the profuse hospitality of its improvident owners; and with such marvellous rapidity did they spread, that when Richard Martin ceased to be returned to parliament, he was fain to seek refuge from his creditors by flying to the continent, where, at Boulogne, he died, January 6th, 1834.

Affairs do not seem to have much improved under his immediate successor. Perhaps the evil was already too deeply rooted to admit of cure. At all events, when, upon the death of Thomas Barnewall Martin, Esq., M.P., of Ballynahinch Castle, the property descended to his daughter, popularly styled "the Princess of Connemara," she found it so encumbered by the prodigality of her ancestors that it became a serious question in what way she was to keep her inheritance together. Still she struggled on bravely, and for some time maintained a decent appearance upon the balance that remained after paying off the interest of the various mortgages. A continuation in the same line of prudence might perhaps eventually have restored the family estates to something of their former splendour; but, though sought in marriage by many of wealth and name, she gave her hand in preference to a near relation— Mr. Gonne Bell—who, whatever else might be his gifts, had not the gift of fortune. In this case, as in so many others it was "all for love, or the world well lost," a poetical creed which is seldom very strongly believed in when the heyday of life is over.

On the day of marriage Mr. Gonne Bell assumed by royal licence, dated 15th Sept. 1847, the name of his bride, and shortly afterwards both parties united in borrowing a large sum of money from the *Law Life Assurance*

Company, in order to consolidate the incumbrances upon the estate at a lower rate of interest. But this attempt to save themselves was defeated by events over which they had no control. The year of famine came on, government works were commenced, and the tenants soon ceased to pay any rents whatever, and as a natural consequence the owners of so many thousand acres were no longer able to pay up the instalments due upon their mortgage. Men acting in large bodies are seldom so merciful as when they are individually responsible for their deeds, and the Law Life Assurance Society formed no exception to this rule of general experience. They insisted upon the due performance of their bond, and that being under the circumstances impossible, this vast Connemara property came into the Encumbered Estates' Court, and the famous old race of Martin of Ballynahinch was sold out: the times were the worst possible for an advantageous sale; and the Assurance Company bought in almost the entire of the estate, at a sum immeasurably below its real value, and quite inadequate, even with the produce of the remnant of the lands bought by other parties, to the liquidation of its heavy liabilities. Not a single acre remained for the poor heiress of what was once a princely estate, and while others were thus fattening upon her ancient inheritance, the "Princess of Connemara," without any fault of her own, became an absolute pauper. The home of her fathers had passed away to strangers, leaving nothing behind but debts and the bitter recollection of what she had lately been. A more painful example of family decadence will not easily be found, though the roll of such events, as I

have already shown, is sufficiently extensive. In most
cases the fall is more or less gradual, the downward course
speeding on with each descendant. But here, although
the worm of decay had for some time been at work, eating
and undermining what seemed from its size to be indestructible, yet its progress was almost too rapid for notice,
and when the building fell it seemed to fall at once, sweeping everything before it.

In this total wreck of all her fortunes the ill-starred.
" Princess of Connemara" retired to Fontaine l'Eveque in
Belgium, where for a short while she supported herself by
her pen; but so scanty were the means thus obtained that
she at length resolved to abandon the continent for America,
hoping to find in the New World an ampler field for her
exertions. Some friends of the family now came forward
with a small subscription to enable her to carry out this
object. Much it could not have been, for we find her
embarking on the voyage in a sailing vessel, although she
was far advanced in pregnancy. A premature confinement
was the result in this den of misery, without medical
attendant, without a nurse, without any one of the aids so
indispensable at such a moment of danger and suffering.
Can it be a matter of surprise to any one that she died
soon after she touched the shore; or, as some will have it,
before she left the boat?

Though the home and the broad lands of the Martins are
now in strangers' hands, the echo of their name has not
passed away among the peasants. The people of Connemara yet speak of the Martins as being the legitimate

lords of the soil, and never mention them but with affectionate regret.

> "Pride, bend thine eye from heav'n to thine estate;
> See how the mighty sink into a song!
> Can volume, pile, preserve the great?
> Or must thou trust Tradition's tongue,
> When flattery sleeps with thee, and history does thee wrong?"

The Doom of Buckingham.

"So much for Buckingham."

THE DUKES OF BUCKINGHAM afford one of the most singular pages in the misfortunes of great families: the title, by whatever race it was borne, uniformly ending in the same disastrous result. To begin with the Staffords, the earliest bearers of this ill-omened but honourable distinction:—

Humphrey de Stafford, the sixth Earl of that name, and first Duke of Buckingham, closely allied to the royal house of Lancaster, may be said to have opened that tragedy, which deepened as it progressed towards a catastrophe with his successors. His eldest son was killed at the fatal battle of St. Albans, in which the Yorkists so signally defeated their opponents, and he himself fell gallantly fighting for the Lancastrians at the battle of Northampton in 1459. Such a death, however, was much too common in those times of civil warfare, to have deserved of itself any particular notice; but it acquires a deep significance from after circumstances, as if being an omen of misfortune.

The second Duke of Buckingham, Henry de Stafford, thus becoming according to the custom of the times, a ward to the reigning monarch, was naturally brought up so far as education could influence him, in attachment to the House of York. He was even a main instrument in elevating to the throne King Richard III., who made him a Knight of the Garter and Lord High Constable of England. But, as every reader of Shakespeare knows,—

" High-reaching Buckingham grew circumspect.
The deep, revolving, witty Buckingham
No more shall be the neighbour to my counsels;
Hath he so long held out with me untired,
And stops he now for breath?"

Whatever might be the cause—whether the old family attachment, or the neglect of King Richard—the Duke collected a force to join Richmond; but his army being defeated, he himself fled, and was finally taken, when, all other services forgotten, it was—

" Off with his head! so much for Buckingham."

The Duke was decapitated in the market-place of Salisbury in 1483, and so recently as 1838, his headless skeleton was exhumed in the yard of the Blue Boar Inn, in that city.

The success of the Lancastrians restored the next heir of this house, Edward de Stafford, to the family honours, and he became the third Duke of Buckingham. The favour this nobleman found with Henry VII. was rather increased than diminished with that monarch's despotic successor. But he had the misfortune to offend the all-powerful Wolsey—who, if Buckingham was proud, was yet prouder. The first occasion of dispute between them, according to the gossip of the day, was this:—It chanced on one occasion, that Buckingham held a bason for the king to wash his hands, when, Henry having completed his ablutions, the prelate dipped his fingers into the water. Buckingham was so offended at this, which he considered derogatory to his rank, that he flung the contents of the basin into the cardinal's shoes; and the latter being no less incensed in his turn, declared aloud, that he "would stick upon the Duke's skirts." To show his contempt for such a menace, the Duke came to court soon afterwards richly dressed, but without any skirts; and the king demanded the reason of so strange a costume; he replied it was "to prevent the cardinal from sticking, as he had threatened, in his skirts." How the bluff monarch received this jest we are not told, but, from subsequent events, we may only too well infer how little palatable it was to the haughty cardinal, who had long before resolved that—

" Buckingham
Should lessen his big looks."

It seems that the Duke had dismissed from his employ a steward named Knevet,—not, as Shakespeare has it, a surveyor,—the man having oppressed the tenants. Wolsey made use of this renegade's agency to accuse Buckingham of a design against King Henry's life; and, being tried at Westminster, before Thomas, Duke of Norfolk, who sat as Lord High Steward of England for the occasion, the duke was found guilty, and beheaded upon Tower Hill. When the Emperor Charles V. heard of this atrocious murder, he is said to have exclaimed, " A butcher's dog has killed the finest *Buck* in England!"—the allusion being to the occupation of Wolsey's father.

The title of Duke of Buckingham fell at the same time

under attainder; but in the reign of Edward VI. an act passed, by which the then heir of the house was "taken and reputed as Lord Stafford, with a seat and voice in parliament as a baron." The original curse, however, of the ducal family slept only for a few generations. In Roger Stafford, born at Malpas, in 1572, the old disasters of this house broke out, and with him the male line of the Staffords became extinct. "This unfortunate man," says Banks, "in his youth went by the name of Fludd, or Floyde, for what reason has not yet been expressed—perhaps, with the indignant pride that the very name of Stafford should not be associated with the obscurity of such a lot. However, one Floyde, a servant of Mr. George Corbet, of Cowlesmore, near Lee, in Shropshire, his mother's brother, is recorded in a manuscript, which was once part of the collections of the Stafford family; and it is not improbable that this was some faithful servant, under whose roof he might have been reared, or found a shelter from misfortunes, when all his great alliances, with a cowardly and detestable selfishness, might have forsaken him, and that he might have preferred the generous, though humble name of Floyde, to one that had brought him nothing but a keener memorial of his misfortunes."

At the age of sixty-five, the sun of fortune seemed for a moment to shine upon him; but it was only for a moment. By the early death of Henry, Lord Stafford, the great grandson of his father's eldest brother, in 1637, he became the male heir of the family, and petitioned parliament accordingly. With his usual ill-luck, he was persuaded to refer his claim to King Charles, who decided, "that the said Roger Stafford, having no part of the inheritance of the said Lord Stafford, nor any other lands nor means whatever, should make a resignation of all claims and title to the said barony of Stafford, for his majesty to dispose of as he should see fit." With this mandate the unfortunate Roger complied, and the king, by patent, dated 7th December, 1640, created Sir William Howard, and Mary Stafford, his wife, Baron and Baroness Stafford.

Jane Stafford, the sister of the luckless Roger, married a joiner, and had a son, a cobbler, living at Newport, in Shropshire, in 1637!

The title of the Duke of Buckingham, which we have thus seen sleeping for so many years, was once again revived in the person of George Villiers, the son of Sir George Villiers, Knight, of Brokesby. Although the favourite of two monarchs, he was heartily detested by the nation, and seems to have been under the usual malignant star of all who had hitherto borne the same title. His expedition to the island of Rhee, for the relief of the Rochellers, proved a most inglorious failure, from the consequences of which he was only saved by the ill judged favour of the sovereign. He then endeavoured to regain his lost credit with the nation by a second and more fortunate attempt. With this view he repaired to Portsmouth, to hasten the necessary preparations by his presence. Here, while passing through a lobby after breakfast, with Sir Thomas Fryer, and other persons of distinction, he was stabbed to the heart with a penknife, by one John Felton, a lieutenant in Sir John Ramsey's regiment. He died almost instantly of the wound, being then only in his thirty-sixth year.

The son of this unfortunate man, George Villiers, second Duke of Buckingham, was no less remarkable for the absolute perfection of his form, than for the extent and variety of his talents. , He had a command in the royal army at the battle of Worcester, and, upon the king's defeat, made his escape to Holland. When, through the agency of Monk, royalty was restored, he returned to England, and by his admirable versatility, mingled, no doubt, with some degree of falsehood, he managed, at one and the same time, to ingratiate himself with Charles and the Presbyterians. But his vices would seem to have been more than equal to his abilities. He formed one of the unpopular administration called the *Cabal*, from the initials of the names of those composing it; and, having first seduced the wife of Francis Talbot, Earl of Shrewsbury, he killed that nobleman in a duel. It is said that the no less profligate countess was a looker-on at this bloody scene, and held the Duke's horse by the bridle while he killed her husband.

This singular compound of vice and talent has thus been characterised by Walpole, in his " Catalogue of Noble Authors :"—" When this extraordinary man, with the figure and genius of Alcibiades, could equally charm the Presbyterian Fairfax and the dissolute Charles; when he alike ridiculed the witty king and his solemn chancellor; when he plotted the ruin of his country by a cabal of bad ministers, or, equally unprincipled, supported its cause with bad patriots; one laments that a man of such parts should be devoid of every virtue. But when Alcibiades turns chemist, when he is a real bubble and a visionary miser, when ambition is but a frolic, when the worst designs are for the foolishest ends, contempt extinguishes all reflections on his character."

Such a career could hardly terminate otherwise than it did. He forfeited his friends, wasted his estate, and completely lost his reputation. Pope thus describes his death, which he affirms to have taken place at a remote inn in Yorkshire:—

" Behold what blessings wealth to life can lend,
And see what comfort it affords our end!
In the worst inn's worst room, with mat half hung,
The floors of plaster, and the walls of dung.
On once a flock-bed, but repaired with straw,
With tape-tied curtains never meant to draw,
The George and Garter dangling from that bed
Where tawdry yellow strove with dirty red,
Great Villiers lies: alas! how changed from him
That life of pleasure, and that soul of whim!
Gallant and gay in Cliveden's proud alcove,
The bower of wanton Shrewsbury and love;
Or just as gay, at council, in a ring
Of mimic statesmen, and their merry king.
No wit to flatter left of all his store!
No fool to laugh at, which he valued more!
There, victor of his health, of fortune, friends,
And fame, this lord of useless thousand sends."

In the Parish Register of Kirby Moorside, the entry of the Duke's death occurs in these words—I give the exact spelling—" George Vilaus, Lord dooke of bookingham."

John Villiers, who assumed, on questionable right, the dignities of Viscount Purbeck and Earl of Buckingham, had his share of the evil destinies that seem for ever attached to the name of Buckingham. He became the associate of gamesters, and having lived a life of debauchery and squandered his fortune, he married Frances, the daughter of the Rev. Mr. Moyser, and widow of George Heneage, Esq., of Lincolnshire, a woman of dissolute character, whose only recommendation was her large jointure. By her he had two daughters, who, pursuing the course of their mother, sank to the lowest state of degradation. The last survivor, "Lady Elizabeth Villiers," died in a disreputable purlieu, Tavistock Court, near Covent Garden, 4th July, 1768.

The next possessor of the Dukedom of Buckingham was John Sheffield, third Earl of Mulgrave, and 1st Marquess of Normanby, who attained the ducal dignity in 1703. He was both a soldier and a statesman, and affected the character of a poet.

His race did not escape the doom of Buckingham; his grace's successor, Edmund, second Duke, died at Rome, of a rapid consumption, before he reached his majority. With him the honours and male line of the ducal house of Sheffield expired.

The last family, that of Grenville, on whom the Ducal coronet of Buckingham has been conferred, adds the final link to the chain of this Dukedom's disasters.

How strange, that he who bore the noble name of Chandos should so soon forget the fate of Canons, where the Duke of Chandos expended a fortune in raising an immense structure, which his heirs dared not inhabit, and which vanished from earth almost as soon as the extravagant builder! Much more than Canons did Stowe deserve to be preserved. The whole British nation had a species of property in that seat of a family pre-eminently distinguished among our statesmen. The names of Pitt, Buckingham, and Grenville would of themselves call forth many a sigh from us, at the fall of that Stowe, with which they were connected; but when, in addition, we remember the superb library, and the *chefs-d'œuvre* of art, with which successive generations had enriched the mansion, and when we think of the change in the future position of the generous and noble-hearted Marquess of Chandos, who should be heir to these riches as truly as he is to the blood of Plantagenet, our national regret is absorbed in our personal sorrow.

May I not be allowed to express a fervent prayer, that the long stream of misfortune has now run its course, and that a bright future may even yet attend the fortunes of this illustrious title?

The Royal Stuarts.

"All a true Stuart's heritage of woe."
AGNES STRICKLAND.

THE ROYAL STUARTS had no precedent in misfortune, and their vicissitudes form the most touching and romantic episode in the story of Sovereign Houses. Sprung originally from a Norman ancestor, Alan, Lord of Oswestry in Shropshire, they became, almost immediately after their settlement in North Britain, completely identified with the nationality of their new country, and were associated with all the bright achievements and all the deep calamities of Scotland. James I., sent to France by his father to save him from the animosity of Albany, was unjustifiably seized by Henry IV. on his passage; suffered eighteen years' captivity in the Tower of London; and was at last murdered by his uncle, Walter, Earl of Athol, at Perth. James II., his son, fell at the early age of twenty-nine, at the siege of Roxburgh Castle, being killed by the accidental discharge of his own artillery, which, in the exuberance of his joy, he ordered to be fired in honour of the arrival of one of his own Scottish earls with a reinforcement. James III., thrown into prison by his rebellious subjects, was assassinated by the confederated nobility, involuntarily headed by his son, the Duke of Rothsay, who became in consequence King James IV. The hereditary mischance of his race attended the fourth James to Flodden, where he perished, despite of all warning, with the flower of the Scottish chivalry. His son, James V., broken-hearted at the rout of Solway Moss, where his army surrendered in disgust, without striking a blow, to a vastly inferior force, took to his bed, and never rose from it again. Just before he breathed his last, news came that the Queen had given birth to a daughter: " Farewell !" exclaimed pathetically the dying monarch, " farewell to Scotland's crown ! it came with a lass and it will pass with a lass. Alas! alas!" The child— thus born at the moment almost of her father's death— was the beautiful and ill-fated Mary Stuart, who, after nineteen years of unwarranted and unmitigated captivity, was beheaded at Fotheringhay Castle; and her grandson, the royal martyr, Charles I., perished in like manner on the scaffold. Charles's son, James II., forfeited the proudest crown in Christendom, and his son's attempt to regain it brought only death and destruction to the gallant and loyal men that ventured life and fortune in the cause, and involved his heir, " Bonny Prince Charlie," in perils almost incredible. A few lines more are all that are required to close the record of this unfortunate race. The right line of the royal Stuarts terminated with the late Cardinal York, in 1807. He was the second son of the old "Pretender," and was born at Rome, 26th March, 1725, where he was baptized by the name of Henry Benedict Maria Clemens. In 1745, he went to France to head an army of 15,000 men assembled at Dunkirk for the invasion of England, but the news of Culloden's fatal contest counteracted the proposed plan. Henry Benedict returned to Rome, and exchanging the sword for the priest's stole, was made a cardinal by Pope Benedict XIV.

Eventually, after the expulsion of Pius VI. by the French, Cardinal York fled from his splendid residences at Rome and Frascati to Venice, infirm in health, distressed in circumstances, and borne down by the weight of seventy-five years. For a while he subsisted on the produce of some silver plate which he had rescued from the ruin of his property, but soon privation and poverty pressed upon him, and his situation became so deplorable, that Sir John Cox Hippisley deemed it right to have it made known to the King of England. George III. immediately gave orders that a present of £2,000 should be remitted to the last of the Stuarts, with an intimation that he might draw for a similar amount in the following July, and that an annuity of £4,000 would be at his service so long as his circumstances might require it. This liberality was accepted, and acknowledged by the Cardinal in terms of gratitude, and made a deep impression on the Papal Court. The pension Cardinal York continued to receive till his decease in June, 1807, at the age of eighty-two. From the time he entered into holy orders, his Eminence took no part in politics, and seems to have laid aside all worldly views. The only exception to this line of conduct was his having medals struck at his brother's death, in 1788, bearing on the face a representation of his head, with this inscription —" Henricus Nonus Magnæ Britanniæ Rex; non voluntate hominum, sed Dei Gratiâ."

With Cardinal York expired all the descendants of King James II., and the representation of the Royal Houses of

Plantagenet, Tudor, and Stuart thereupon vested by inheritance in Charles Emmanuel IV., King of Sardinia, who was eldest son of Victor-Amadeus III., the grandson of Victor-Amadeus, King of Sardinia, by Anne, his wife, daughter of Henrietta, Duchess of Orleans, daughter of King CHARLES I. of England. Charles Emmanuel IV. died s. p. in 1819, and was succeeded by his brother Victor-Emanuel I., King of Sardinia, whose eldest daughter and co-heiress, Beatrice, Duchess of Modena, was mother of FRANCIS V., EX-DUKE OF MODENA, SENIOR CO-REPRESENTATIVE by descent OF THE ROYAL HOUSE OF STUART. Mr. Townend, who has written a very curious and interesting work on " The Descendants of the Stuarts," remarks on the curious coincidence, that in the ducal family of the little State of Modena are combined the representations of three of the greatest dynasties in Europè: the Duke is himself the eldest descendant of the Royal Stuarts of England; his eldest sister, Theresa, is married to Henri, Comte de Chambord, *de jure* King of France; and his younger sister, Mary, wife of John of Spain, is mother of the infant Charles, who stands in the position of heir-presumptive, in the male line, to the monarchy of Spain.

Having thus summed up the vicissitudes of the royal line of Stuart, I will give more at length—as the details are less generally known—the history of the HOUSES OF ALBANY AND STRATHERNE.

The House of Albany.

ROBERT BRUCE is justly revered by the grateful enthusiasm of Scotland as the founder of its national independence, but his grandson, Robert II., has scarcely met with due appreciation from posterity. If the former placed the liberties of his country on a more solid foundation than in past ages, the latter had the merit of preserving and confirming them. During the wretched reign of the degenerate David, Robert the High Steward was the unflinching asserter of national independence, and when at length, in mature years, he ascended the throne of the country which he had so long ably governed as Regent, his reign was alike creditable to himself and beneficial to the people.

During the most stirring epoch of the dread struggle which the heroic Bruce carried on for his crown and his country, his only child, the Princess Marjory, was united to the bravest and worthiest of the Scottish magnates, Walter, the youthful hereditary Lord High Steward. This marriage, which gave birth to the long and hapless line of Stuart kings, took place in 1315; and the death of the bride and the birth of her son occurred within the year, on the 2nd of March, 1316. Tradition records a tale of an accident to the Princess while hunting, which resulted in a premature confinement, the lady's death, and the preservation of the child by the Cæsarean operation. The bloodshot eyes of King Robert the Second have been accounted for by a mishap in this violent birth. In his infancy he was declared heir to the Scottish crown, and it was not until some years after that his royal prospects were blighted by the birth of his uncle David, the child of the Bruce's second marriage. The historian Fordun describes him while a youth as "comely, tall, robust, modest, liberal, gay, and courteous." In 1338 he was appointed Regent and he held that high office until King David's return from his French asylum in 1341. He was again placed at the head of the realm when David was taken prisoner by the English at the battle of Durham in 1346; and so he continued until the unworthy King's liberation from captivity in 1357. During the remainder of his uncle's reign he had a continual struggle to maintain his own rights and the independence of his country against the King's treasonable intrigues to place an English prince as his successor on the throne of Scotland, and against the cowardly promptitude with which both David and a large party of the Scottish nobles desired to answer the call of Edward III., by paying him homage.

At length, fortunately for Scotland, David II. died in February 1371, and the succession to the crown opened to the Lord High Steward, then a grey-headed and experienced veteran, in his fifty-fifth year. His title was acknowledged in the most solemn manner at his coronation at Scone, on the 26th of the following month. Thus commenced the reign of the Stewarts, and it would have been well for them if they had inherited the wisdom and vigour of the founder of their dynasty. King Robert's first wife was Elizabeth, daughter of Sir Adam Mure, Lord of Rowallan in the shire of Ayr; for which marriage, as the parties were distantly related, a dispensation was obtained from Pope Clement VI., dated at Avignon, 22d Nov., 1347, by which it appears that they had then several children of both sexes, who were thereby legitimated. This does not imply that Elizabeth had been the mistress of the Lord High Steward; but that they were married irregularly, so that without this dispensation and legitimation their issue would have forfeited their right to the crown. This came afterwards to be a subject of much serious anxiety, and for many generations the royal posterity of King Robert II.'s first marriage were branded with the suspicion of illegitimacy. No one was bold enough actually to dispute the succession of the Stewart Kings; but the succeeding generations of a great family descended from the eldest son of King Robert II.'s second marriage were in the habit of boasting of their preferable claim to the crown. Indeed, it is a curious circumstance that the absolute right of the Stuarts to reign was only clearly proved exactly one hundred years after their reign had ceased, and when the direct line was on the verge of extinction. In 1789 the learned and talented Andrew Stewart of Castlemilk and Torrance discovered, after a long search in the Vatican at Rome the dispensation of Pope Clement VI. which legalized the marriage between the Lord High Steward and Elizabeth Mure. King Robert was father of a very numerous family by both his marriages, as well as of several illegitimate sons, who were the founders of distinguished families. But it is concerning the fortunes of his second surviving son and his descendants that it is my purpose here to treat.

Robert, the third but second surviving son of the Lord High Steward and Elizabeth Mure, was born in 1339, and while yet a very young man, obtained the great Earldom of Menteith by his marriage with its heiress, the Countess Margaret. He subsequently became Earl of Fife, and in 1383 he was appointed Great Chamberlain of Scotland. His father, Robert II., died at a good old age in 1390, and for several years previously, the Earl of Fife and Menteith exercised the office of Regent of the kingdom, which his father from age, and his elder brother John, Earl of Carrick, from bodily infirmity, were incapable of governing with vigour.

The Earl of Carrick, on ascending the throne, relinquished his baptismal name of John, which the remembrance of Balliol had made unpopular with the country, and ill omened in the royal family, and assumed that of Robert, as being connected with more glorious associations. But the change of name could not render Robert III. fitted for governing a turbulent and disturbed country. The King was amiable, prudent, and sensible. His Queen, Anabella, daughter of the Lord of Stobhall, of the house of Drummond, was virtuous, wise, and affectionate. But their domestic virtues were buried beneath a load of adverse circumstances. The King was incurably lame, and unable to lead his barons to war, or to join with them in the tournament or the chase. As the second King of a new race, he had the same difficulty to contend against which beset the first Capetian monarchs,—a proud and haughty nobility, many of whom reckoned themselves great as the King, and some a little greater. He was not allied either by mother or wife to any of the puissant native magnates, nor to a foreign prince; and in a position which would have required great vigour both of body and mind, he had nothing to depend upon but piety, sound sense, and kindness of heart. His marriage had been long unfruitful, as his eldest son that lived, the miserable Duke of Rothsay, was born, after twenty years, in 1378, and his son James, who afterwards reigned, not until sixteen years after, in 1394. He must have been fifty two or three years old when he mounted the throne, in 1390. Unsupported by powerful alliances, infirm of body and mild in spirit, with a son in boyhood, he was quite incapable of wielding the strong sceptre of the Bruce. It is not, therefore, to be wondered at, that he gladly left the supreme power of the state in the vigorous hands in which his father had already placed it, and was thankful to devolve his authority on his brother, Robert, Earl of Fife and Menteith, whom, in 1398, he still further dignified with the high-sounding and imposing title of Duke of Albany, *i.e.* of all Scotland north of the Frith of Forth and Clyde. It was a fortunate circumstance for Robert III. and his descendants, that the Duke of Albany was his full brother, and was thus involved in the same suspicion of spurious birth with himself, as son of Elizabeth Mure, born before her marriage was legalized. There can be little doubt that if Albany had been the eldest son of Robert II.'s second marriage, his elder brother would never have reigned, or his reign would have been brief. But Albany had a common interest with the King in repressing the ambitious aspirations of the sons of their father's second marriage, the Earls of Stratherne and Athol.

In his irresolution, timidity, and anxious desire to conciliate the goodwill of all parties, the King commanded the respect and allegiance of none; and, accordingly, from the moment of his accession to the crown, he surrendered himself entirely to the guidance of his strong-minded and able brother, who was in every way, but one, fitted to be a good master to the bold and lawless barons. He was entirely wanting in justice, honour, and generosity.

The year 1402 was marked by the tragical death of David, Duke of Rothsay, the King's eldest son, at the age of twenty-four; a tale of which the romantic interest can scarcely be said to have been heightened by the faithful colouring of the first of Scottish writers. It is sufficient here to say, that this young Prince, who had been for the moment deprived of his liberty by the King, in order to punish him for some youthful excesses, was, at the instigation of Albany, delivered into his keeping, and was most barbarously starved to death in the Regent's castle of Falkland, in March, 1402. No one should visit the county of Fife without reading Walter's Scott's masterly description of the last days of this unhappy Prince, and afterwards visiting Falkland palace, where he will see a locality, which, whether or not it is *the vrai*, is, at all events, the *vraisemblable* Two months after, a parliament held at Edinburgh went through the form of investigating the facts of the case. Albany, and his ally the Earl of Douglas, admitted the imprisonment, but denied the murder. The Prince, they said, had died a natural death. However, their crime is proved by the words of the act of remission which was granted them, and which was given them in terms quite as ample as if they had actually murdered the heir of the crown.

Three years after Rothsay's murder, in 1405, the poor king, anxious to save his remaining son James, Earl of Carrick, then a boy in his twelfth year, from the plots of his cruel uncle, confided him to the care of Henry Sinclair, second Earl of Orkney, Fleming of Cumbernauld, Halyburton of Dirleton, and Sinclair of Hermandston, who conducted him to North Berwick, where he embarked for France. But they had been only a few days at sea, when their vessel was captured by an armed English ship, and the Scottish Prince and his suite were conveyed to London and shut up in the Tower. The old King, worn out by infirmity, and broken by sorrow, did not long survive his child's captivity, and died in April, 1406.

On the King's death, the estates of the realm assembled at Perth, and declared the Earl of Carrick to be King, as James I. The Duke of Albany was chosen Regent. The young King, in the meantime, continued a prisoner at the English court, where he was treated with great distinction, where he received a most finished education, and where, above all, he was in security. During his absence, the chief power of the state remained in the hands of Albany, who continued to be Regent or governor of Scotland until his death, which happened at Stirling, at the age of eighty, in 1419. He had ruled supreme over Scotland during thirty-four years, commencing with the latter years of his father's reign. And so effectually had he secured the favour of the nobility, or subdued them by terror, that his son, a quiet, unambitious man, succeeded without challenge to the power which he had so artfully and wickedly wielded. By his first marriage with the Countess of Menteith he had his son and successor, Duke Murdoch, and several daughters married to the greatest of the Scottish nobility. By his second marriage, with Muriella Keith, daughter of the Great Marischal, he had, with two younger sons who died without issue, a son John, Earl of Buchan, born 1380, appointed Constable of France after the battle of Beaugè in 1421. He afterwards died in the bed of honour at the bloody battle of Verneuil, in August, 1424; and he was thus spared the pain of witnessing the utter ruin of his family, which took place in the following year. Buchan married Elizabeth, daughter of Archibald, fourth Earl of Douglas, Duke of Touraine, by whom he had an only child, Margaret, who married George, second Lord Seton, and her lineal descendant and representative, Archibald William, present EARL OF EGLINTON AND WINTON, K.T., is one of the very few entitled to quarter the ROYAL STUART ARMS. Buchan's widow married William Sinclair, third Earl of Orkney, and was ancestress* of a long line of Lords Sinclair, from whom the existing holder of that title is not even remotely descended.

In 1423, King James I. was restored to his kingdom, through the intervention of the new regent, Duke Murdoch, whose gentleness seems to have deserved a better fate than to expiate with his blood the offences of his father. The country fell into great disorder as soon as the vigorous arm of Duke Robert was unnerved by death. Murdoch was unable to control the turbulence of his own family, much less that of the haughty Scottish barons and chiefs.

In illustration of the insubordination of his family, a tale is told of a falcon, which was coveted by his son, Walter, but which the Regent loved too well to part with.

* Elizabeth, Countess of Buchan and Orkney, was ancestress to Mr. Anstruther-Thomson and the Earl of Rosslyn.

One day the unruly youth tore the bird from his father's wrist, and twisted off its head in a fit of spite. The Regent's remark was fraught with the fate of Scotland, and with that of his race: "Since I cannot govern *you*, I will send for one who can." This is supposed to allude to the negociation which restored the captive King to his country.

In the year 1391, Murdoch, son and heir of Robert, Duke of Albany, the Regent, was married to Isabella, the eldest daughter and heir of Duncan, Earl of Lennox, one of the most noble and powerful of the native magnates of Scotland, and this union was for many years eminently happy and prosperous, as well as fruitful. They had four sons, who, as is said by a contemporary writer (Cupar MSS. of the Scotichronicon), were men of "princely stature and lovely person, eloquent, wise, agreeable, and beloved." Robert, the eldest, died without issue before him, in 1421. Walter and Alexander were beheaded along with their father, and James survived to transmit the blood of his race, through many lines, to our own day.

The restored King was not slow in commencing the work of vengeance on the race by whom he had been so long supplanted. The first victim was Walter, the Regent's eldest surviving son, who was called Walter of the Lennox, as heir to the earldom of his maternal grandfather. He was carried off before the King's coronation, and confined in the Rock of the Bass. Soon after, the aged grandfather, Duncan, Earl of Lennox, was seized with Sir Robert Graham, and confined in the castle of Edinburgh. In March, 1425, James felt himself sufficiently secure on his throne to order the arrest of the late Regent himself, along with twenty-six of the most illustrious men in Scotland, many of whom, however, were immediately released, and were, in fact, compelled to sit in judgment on the distinguished and fore-doomed victims. When the Regent was arrested, the Duchess Isabella was also seized, at their castle of Doune, and dragged to the fortress of Tantallon. James, the youngest son, alone escaped, and being a daring youth, he made one desperate effort to succour or avenge his family. With a body of armed followers he sacked Dumbarton, and put to death its commander, John Stewart of Dundonald, natural son of King Robert II.; but his struggle was unavailing, and he fled to Ireland, where he became father of many families which have been great in the history of their country.

In a parliament, where the King presided, in May, 1425, Walter Stewart of the Lennox was tried by his peers, convicted, and instantly beheaded. On the next day, his brother, Alexander, had his head struck off; and he was followed to the scaffold, a few hours later, by Duke Murdoch, his father; and the Earl of Lennox also perished, at the age of eighty. They were all put to death on the castle hill of Stirling, from which high position the unhappy ex-regent was enabled to cast a last look on his rich and romantic territory of Menteith, and the hills of Lennox, to which his Duchess was heir; and he could even descry the stately castle of Doune, which had been his own vice-regal palace. The companion of those most unhappy princes, Sir Robert Graham, was released, and he lived to consummate his long-planned vengeance on the King, in 1437. He it was who, when James cried for mercy, in his extremity, replied, "Thou cruel tyrant, thou never hadst any mercy on lords born of thy blood, therefore no mercy shalt thou have here!"

This ruin seems to have smitten the house of Albany most unexpectedly. On May, 1424, Duke Murdoch, as Earl of Fife, seated his royal cousin on the throne, to receive the unction and the crown. His son, Alexander, then was made a belted knight by the king's hands, and the duchess appeared as the greatest lady at the court; but in the commencement of the following year she had to mourn the violent deaths of her husband, her father, and two sons.

It is said that when the relentless monarch had wreaked his vengeance on Albany and Lennox, and the young men, he sent all their bloody heads to the duchess! to try whether, in the distraction of her grief, she might not reveal political secrets. But she endured the horrid spectacle with unshaken calmness, allowing no other words to pass her lips than these: "If they were guilty, the king has acted wisely, and done justice."

The widowhood of the Duchess of Albany was long and dreary, though rich and great. She inherited the vast estates of her father, which were not confiscated, and his earldom, which was not forfeited. She retired within her princely domains to her feudal castle of Inchmurran, in an island of Loch Lomond, where she bore, with punctilious ceremony, the lofty names of Albany and Lennox, and possessed all the broad and fair domains around that beautiful lake. Yet, widowed and childless, she was haunted by the recollection that her race was extinguished

H

by the hand of the executioner, and that her fair and handsome sons would never return at her call

"To renew the wild pomp of the chase and the hall."

The widowed Duchess outlived the destroyer of her family for twenty-three years; and if she harboured feelings of revenge against him, they were amply gratified by his murder, in 1437, which was attended by every circumstance of horror.

There are many charters of the Duchess of Albany, which prove her to have lived at her castle in Loch Lomond, and in possession of the power and wealth of her family until the year 1460. A very interesting one, conveying lands for the pious purpose of offering prayers for the souls of her murdered husband, father, and sons, and dated 18 May, 1451, is attested by Murdoch, Arthur, and Robert Stewart of Albany, who all seem at that time to have been domesticated with her at Inchmuryne Castle.

Who were these three Stewarts of Albany? They were three of the seven illegitimate children of James Stewart, the duke's youngest son, who fled to Ireland, and who there formed a connection with a lady of the house of the Lord of the Isles, which produced a flourishing progeny. These youths seem to have been adopted, after their father's death, by their grandmother, to bear her company in the melancholy, deserted halls of her feudal castle. These seven sons are all well-known to history. Many of them were legitimated, which, however, did not entitle them to succeed to the great possessions of their family, though some of them and their descendants reached the highest rank and offices in the state, and founded great families. When the Duchess Isabella died, in 1460, her title of Lennox seems to have become dormant. She had no legitimate descendants, and those of her two sisters had each some claim to the succession. Her second sister, Margaret, was wife of Sir Robert Menteith of Ruskey, and her daughters carried her claims into the families of Napier and Haldane. Her third sister, Elizabeth, was wife of Sir John Stewart of Darnley, and her grandson, John, created a Lord of Parliament, as Lord Darnley, assumed the title of Earl of Lennox, in 1478, and was the direct paternal ancestor of James I., King of Great Britain.

I will conclude with a rapid review of the varied fortunes of the seven sons of James Stewart of Albany, the youngest of the fair and noble princes of the House of Albany, and heir of the line of Lennox.

- I. Andrew, invited from Ireland by King James II., raised to high honours, and created Lord Avandale in 1459, was appointed in 1460 Lord High Chancellor of Scotland, (which office he held for twenty-five years), and had a grant for life of the landed estates belonging to the Earldom of Lennox. He died childless in 1488.
- VI. Walter was father of Andrew Stewart, who was Lord Avandale in 1501; and he was the father of three distinguished sons;
    - A. Andrew, third Lord Avandale, exchanged his title for that of Ochiltree. His direct representative, Andrew, third Lord Ochiltree, resigned

his Scottish title, settled in Ireland, and was created a peer as Lord Castlestewart in 1619. His descendant is the present Earl of Castlestewart, who is the representative of the House of Albany. A younger son of the second Lord Ochiltree, Captain James Stewart, achieved a bad notoriety under King James VI., when for a few years he was all-powerful as Earl of Arran and Lord High Chancellor; but his fall was as sudden as his rise had been.

B. Henry Stewart was created Lord Methven in 1528, and married in 1526, Princess Margaret of England, widow of King James IV. He had no issue by the Queen, and his issue by a second wife failed.

C. James Stewart of Beath. His son, James, was created Lord Doun in 1581. His grandson, James Lord Doun, married the daughter and heir of the Regent Earl of Moray, natural son of King James V., and the descendant of this marriage is the present Earl of Moray.

The four intermediate sons between Andrew and Walter were less distinguished, and do not appear to have left issue. They were MURDOCH, ARTHUR, ROBERT, and ALEXANDER; and three of them seem to have been the companions of their widowed grandmother.

VII. JAMES STEWART, the youngest, was ancestor to the still existing families of Stewart of Ardvohrlich, and Stewart of Glenbuckey.

Earls of Stratherne and Menteith.

ROBERT II., King of Scotland, married for the second time, in 1355, the Lady Euphemia Ross, daughter of Hugh, sixth Earl of Ross, by Lady Matilda Bruce, daughter of Robert Bruce, Earl of Carrick, sister of King Robert I., and widow of John Randolph, Earl of Murray. This lady was Robert's near relation, being the first cousin of his mother; and a dispensation was obtained for the marriage from Pope Innocent VI., dated at Avignon, 2 May, 1355. The issue consisted of several daughters and two sons. I. David, Earl Palatine of Stratherne, of whose posterity I am about to treat, and II. Walter, Earl of Athol. The fate of the latter was singular and tragical. Hatred against King James I. rankled deeply in the hearts of some of the principal nobility, who resented his severity, and especially the relentless rigour with which he had destroyed the illustrious princes of the House of Albany. The King's uncles, sons of the second marriage of his grandfather, had escaped at that time, and the Earl of Athol had been distinguished by his nephew's favour. He had even been benefitted at the expense of his grandnephew, Malise, Earl of Stratherne, son of the daughter of his elder brother, David : for under pretence that Stratherne was a male fief, the King deprived Malise of that earldom in 1427, and conferred it on Walter, Earl of Athol, for life.

Notwithstanding the high favour in which Athol and his grandson and heir, Sir Robert Stewart, were held by the King, they were deeply concerned in the conspiracy which terminated in his murder, in the monastery of the Dominicans at Perth, on the night of the 20th of February, 1436. Sir Robert Stewart, who was chamberlain, availed himself of the privileges of his office, in preparing for the admission of the conspirators; and he and his grandfather were in the King's company up to the very moment when the murder took place. Sir Robert Stewart was taken, and, after cruel tortures, was beheaded. The aged Earl was also taken, tried, and condemned; and although he protested his own innocence, he admitted that he had knowledge of his grandson's complicity in the conspiracy, from which he had vainly attempted to dissuade him. The cross on which his grandson had been tortured previous to his death, was taken down, and a pillar was set up in its stead, to which the earl was bound, with a paper crown fastened on his head, inscribed with the title " Traitor !" His head was then struck off, and having been adorned with an iron crown, was stuck on the point of a spear. His extensive estates were forfeited, and among them the spoils of his elder brother. The earldom of Stratherne reverted to the crown, and it was annexed thereto by Act of Parliament in 1455.

David, Earl Palatine of Stratherne, seems to have had

the good fortune to escape the horrors in which so many of the members of his family were involved. The earldom of Stratherne was conferred on him by his father immediately after he ascended the throne, in 1371. He does not appear to have filled a prominent place in the world, and the time of his death is uncertain. He left a daughter, Euphemia, who succeeded to his titles and possessions, and became Countess of Stratherne. She married Sir Patrick Graham, second son of Sir Patrick Graham of Kincardine, ancestor to the Duke of Montrose, and immediate elder brother of Sir Robert Graham, who, with his own hands, murdered King James I. Patrick became, in right of his wife, Earl of Stratherne, and he was assassinated by his own brother-in-law, Sir John Drummond, in 1413. They had issue two daughters: I. Euphemia, wife, first of Archibald, fifth Earl of Douglas, Duke of Touraine, and secondly, of James, first Lord Hamilton; II. Elizabeth, wife of Sir John Lyon of Glamis; and a son, Malise, who succeeded his mother as Earl of Stratherne.

As already mentioned, King James I., considering this earldom to be a desirable acquisition for the crown, deprived Earl Malise of it in 1427, under pretence that it was a male fief, and he transferred it for life to his aged uncle, the Earl of Athol, with a view that it should ultimately revert to himself. By way of compensation, he gave Malise sundry lands, which he erected into an earldom with the title of Menteith, in 1427, and with this honour he and his heirs were forced to be contented; and it continued to be their portion for two centuries, until a singular revolution took place in their family history, in consequence of the talent and ambition of a very remarkable man who held the earldom in the reign of King Charles I.

Although no actual attempt was ever made to set aside the royal family of Stewart on the ground of illegitimacy, there was a very general impression in the country, that the whole issue of the first marriage of King Robert II. were not born in lawful wedlock, owing to a relationship with Elizabeth Mure within the prohibited degrees, and the want of a papal dispensation. Indeed, King Robert III. and the Duke of Albany were said to have been born previous to the marriage of their parents. In the dispensation granted by Pope Clement VI., found by Andrew Stewart in the Vatican in 1789, it is stated, that at that time several children had been born; but it may be doubted whether Robert and Elizabeth had ever lived in a state of concubinage without marriage. It may be, that they were married and had children; but that the papal court would not recognize the marriage as existing previous to the dispensation being granted. At all events, even in the unlikely case that those two princes had been born out of wedlock, the subsequent marriage of their parents would have rendered them legitimate.

The subject was an obscure one. It was very well known that an irregularity existed; and those who were hostile to the royal family kept up, from generation to generation, the assertion that they had no well-founded right to the throne. The question then came to be considered, who was the rightful heir to the crown, setting aside the so-called spurious offspring of King Robert II. and Elizabeth Mure? He, of course, had the best right who was eldest son of the king by his second marriage, viz. Prince David, Earl of Stratherne. He, as already stated, had a daughter and sole heir, Euphemia, wife of Sir Patrick Graham; and her son, Malise, Earl of Menteith, and his descendants, were, according to this view, the rightful sovereigns of Scotland. One might have supposed such a claim to have been formidable to the reigning monarch in the days of King Robert III. or James I.; and if David of Stratherne, had been an able or popular man, or if so talented and powerful a regent as Robert, Duke of Albany, had not existed, the royalty of the earlier kings of the Stuart dynasty might have been endangered. And it would even seem probable that the conspiracy against James I. had some such object in view; for it was said to be the intention of the conspirators to raise Sir Robert Stewart, the chamberlain, Athol's grandson, to the throne, and he was then the male representative of Robert II.'s second marriage, David of Stratherne's heir being in the female line.

But the progress of time and the uninterrupted succession of many Stuart kings had turned this question of the right of succession into a curious matter of genealogical speculation, like the rival claims of Balliol and Bruce. At least, I should have imagined such to have been the case; for it seems almost incredible, that at the end of two hundred years, an Earl of Menteith should have considered himself to be the rightful heir of the crown of Scotland, or that such fantastic and visionary claims should have given real uneasiness to the monarch of Great Britain. Yet so it was.

From Malise, the deprived Earl of Stratherne and Earl of Menteith, there was a regular succession of earls from father to son during seven generations. They had sent forth several younger branches, such as Graham of Gartmore, Graham Viscount Preston, Graham of Netherby, Graham of Gartur, &c. In the year 1589, an heir was born who was destined to raise the family to considerable importance, and to sink it again into greater obscurity.

This was William, son of John Graham, sixth Earl of Menteith, by Mary, daughter of Sir Colin Campbell, of Glenurchy. He succeeded to his family honours when he was only nine years of age, in 1598. The superiority of his talents attracted the notice and gained the esteem of King Charles I., who, in 1628, made him Lord Justice General of Scotland, and in the following year President of the Privy Council. Lord Menteith very naturally wished to avail himself of the royal favour in order to regain for his family the high honours which his ancestor had forfeited by what he regarded as an act of tyranny. As he was heir male of Malise, Earl of Stratherne, he desired to have that distinguished title restored to him; and his ambition was stimulated by the consciousness of royal blood, for he knew that he was heir general of Prince David, Earl Palatine of Stratherne, and representative of a branch of the reigning family. He, therefore, in 1630, went through the legal form, which in Scotland is common to all on succeeding to a father or other ancestor; he had himself *served heir* to Malise, Earl of Menteith, Patrick, Earl of Stratherne, and Prince David, Earl of Stratherne. This was done by the advice and with the concurrence of one of the most distinguished lawyers of the day, Sir Thomas Hope, the Lord Advocate of Scotland.

King Charles, not foreseeing the consequences, and misled by his favour for the earl, was induced to ratify this service, and to admit his claim to the higher honour of Stratherne, in virtue of the charter granted by King Robert II. to the eldest son of his second marriage, David, the ancestor of the earl, who thereupon, in 1621, became Earl of Stratherne and Menteith.

At that time, the fable that Elizabeth Mure was not the wife, but the concubine of King Robert II., was very generally credited as an article of unenquiring popular belief, though it has for the last eighty years been proved on the clearest evidence, from the actual dispensation found in the Vatican, that she was his wife. But, if the marriage with Elizabeth Mure had been set aside, the whole royal race became at once illegitimate, and consequently the children of the second marriage with Euphemia Ross became entitled to the crown: and thus to William Graham, the direct heir of the only child of the eldest son of that marriage, would, of course, have devolved the right of the Scottish crown.

The earl was perfectly aware of all those circumstances, and his ambition or vanity so far got the better of his prudence, that it is said that in his service for the Earldom of Stratherne, he solemnly renounced his right to the crown, reserving the right of his blood, which he rashly and vain-gloriously asserted to be "the reddest in Scotland."

It is difficult for us now to conceive the importance which at the commencement of the seventeenth century was attached to such a question. Every person, however, who is versed in Scottish history knows what discordant opinions were entertained on the subject of King Robert's marriages, and with what acrimony the contest was carried on by disputants in private, from generation to generation. And now this unlucky service of Lord Menteith, and his imprudent expressions, and the restoration of the princely earldom by the king to so ambitious a claimant, brought these controversies to a point. A search in the Vatican would have set everything right. But this was not thought of at the time; and there were very few who did not give credit to the false tale. Even in the genealogical table of the Scottish kings, published along with the acts of parliament, Euphemia Ross is expressly stated to have been the *first* wife of Robert II. This was confusion worse confounded; for if Elizabeth Mure was wife at all, she must have been the first.

King Charles now began to view the earl's claims with considerable uneasiness. Strong remonstrances were made to him by his Scottish ministers; and the learned and ingenious Sir William Drummond of Hawthornden addressed a special memorial to him on this subject in 1632, in which he said "that the restoring of the Earl of Menteith in blood, and allowing his descent and title to the Earldom of Stratherne, is thought to be disadvantageous to the king's majesty," &c. &c. He then goes on to shew the danger of a disputed succession; he regards Graham's ostentatious resignation of his claim to the crown to be highly dishonouring to his majesty, and he adds, that he might, notwithstanding, dispose of his right to some great foreign prince, or that seditious subjects might avail themselves of it; and he urges, that as the posterity of Euphemia Ross had been depressed for two centuries, they ought to continue under depression.

Charles, alarmed at a danger of which he had never thought, and which I am apt to regard as visionary, but which in those times seemed real, immediately ordered a law form to be gone through, to reduce the earl's service and patent; and the court did accordingly set them aside, and deprived him of his patent, not only of Earl of Stratherne, but also of Earl of Menteith; and he was thus stripped of all his honours in 1633. In this proceeding they acted not only unjustly but ignorantly, for they assigned as the reason a manifest falsehood, viz., that David, Earl of Stratherne, had died without issue. At the same time, the king deprived him of his high office of Lord Justice General. However, in order not entirely to crush him, a new title was, in 1633, conferred on him; but a title mean and hitherto unknown, that of Earl of Airth. He was thereafter styled Earl of Airth and Menteith. According to Scott of Scotstarvet, a contemporary, he was confined in the isle of Menteith, where he was when he wrote, in 1654. This, however, is probably an exaggeration of the fact, that the earl, after this unhappy shipwreck of his grandeur, spent the remainder of his days in seclusion.

His son, John, Lord Kinpont, so far from seeking to avenge his father's injuries, was a noble cavalier, and an attached adherent of the great Montrose; and he was stabbed with a highland dirk in 1644, in Montrose's camp, by James Stewart of Ardvohrlich. This incident has been introduced by Sir Walter Scott, in his Legend of Montrose.

Lord Kinpont left a son, William, second Earl of Airth, who succeeded his grandfather, and died without issue, in 1694, and two daughters :—

I. Mary, wife of Sir John Allardice of Allardice.
II. Elizabeth, wife of Sir William Graham, Bart., of Gartmore.

These ladies were the coheirs of Prince David, Earl of Stratherne; and, in conclusion, I may briefly state the circumstances of their direct representatives, which add two more examples of the extraordinary vicisssitudes to which even royal races are so liable.

Mary, or, as she was styled, Lady Mary Graham, the eldest daughter of Lord Kinpont, married, in 1662, Sir John Allardice of Allardice, a gentleman of very ancient family. She died in 1720. Her great grandson, James Allardice of Allardice, died in 1765, leaving an only child, Sarah-Anne, his sole heir, who married Robert Barclay of Ury, the representative of a family which is traced back to the reign of King David I. The son of this marriage, Robert Barclay-Allardice of Ury and Allardice, was a man celebrated in the sporting world, distinguished for his athletic powers, and highly esteemed in general society. He claimed the earldoms of Stratherne, Menteith, and

Airth, as heir of line of William, Earl of Airth, and of his ancestor Prince David, Earl of Stratherne. His death is very recent, and his ancient paternal inheritance of Ury has passed into the hands of one of the members of the firm of Baird, the successful iron-masters at Gartsherrie.

It is painful to allude to a *mésalliance* of one nobly and even royally descended, and that too in our own day. But it is a fact two well known to render it indelicate to make mention of it, that the only daughter and heir of Mr. Barclay Allardice united herself in marriage with a man of low degree of the name of Ritchie. However lamentable this degradation of ancient blood may be, the heir of this marriage has the singular advantage of possessing what is believed to be a well-founded claim to one of the oldest and greatest of the earldoms of Scotland, and to the honour of being representative of one of the Princes of the blood royal of that country.

Elizabeth, or Lady Elizabeth Graham, the second daughter and co-heir of John, Lord Kinpont, married, in 1663, Sir William Graham, Baronet, of Gartmore, a cadet of the house of Menteith. She had a son, Sir John Graham, Baronet, of Gartmore, who died in 1708 without issue, and a daughter, Mary, who married James Hodge, of Gladsmuir. Her only child, Mary Hodge, married, in 1701, William Graham, younger brother of Robert Graham, who in 1708 succeeded to Gartmore as heir male. The issue of this marriage was: 1st. A son, William Graham, who was junior coheir of the Earls of Airth and Menteith; and who, although he had no right to do so (while the line of Allardice existed), assumed the title of

Earl of Menteith, and, as such, voted at various elections of Scottish peers, from 1744 to 1761, when the committee of privileges ordered him to discontinue the title. He died unmarried in 1783. 2nd. A daughter, Mary Graham, wife of John Bogle, employed in the excise, at Glasgow, by whom she had issue, a son, who lived in great poverty, and is said to have died somewhere about the close of last century, a houseless and homeless wanderer, subsisting on charity. Such have been the strange vicissitudes of the two coheirs and representatives of Prince David of Scotland, Earl Palatine of Stratherne, in whose line a right to the crown was, according to the popular belief of many centuries, supposed to be vested.

Lindsay of Edzell.

"Bright star of the morning, that beamed on the brow
Of our chief of ten thousand, O where art thou now?
The sword of our fathers is cankered with rust,
And the race of Clan Lindsay is bowed to the dust."
EARL CRAWFORD'S CORONACH.

SECOND only to the Royal Stuarts were the LINDSAYS, Earls of Crawford. Their Earldom, like those of Orkney, Douglas, March, &c., formed a petty principality, an "imperium in imperio." The Earls affected a royal state, held their courts, had their heralds, and assumed the style of Princes. The magnificence kept up in the castle of Finhaven befitted a great potentate. The Earl was waited on by pages of noble birth, trained up under his eye as aspirants for the honours of chivalry. He had his domestic officers, all of them gentlemen of quality; his chamberlain, chaplains, secretary, chief marischal, and armour-bearer. The property that supported this expense was very considerable. The Earls of Crawford possessed more than twenty great baronies and lordships, and many other lands in the counties of Forfar, Perth, Kincardine, Fife, Aberdeen, Inverness, Banff, Lanark, Dumfries, Kirkcudbright, and Wigton. The family alliances were of a dignity suited to this high estate. Thrice did the head of this great house match immediately with the royal blood.

Such was the dignity of the Earl of Crawford, and such the extent of his power and the grandeur of his alliances in the thirteenth, fourteenth, and fifteenth centuries. Let us now contemplate the fortunes of two of the principal members of this illustrious race, in the course of revolving generations.

On the 9th of February, in the year 1621, died a prisoner in Edinburgh Castle, David, twelfth Earl of Crawford. Reckless, prodigal, and desperate, he had alienated the possessions of his earldom, so as to reduce the family to the brink of ruin. He had no sons, and to prevent further dilapidation, the agnates of the house determined, in solemn council, to imprison him for life. He was accordingly confined, the victim of his own folly and of this family conspiracy, in the castle of Edinburgh until his death. He left an only orphan child, the Lady Jean, heiress of line of the Earl of Crawford. This wretched girl, destitute and uncared for, was doomed to undergo the deepest humiliation. She received no education, and was allowed to run about little better than a tinker or gipsy; she eloped with a common crier, and at one period lived entirely by mendicity, as a sturdy beggar or "tramp." The case of this high-born pauper was made known to King Charles II. soon after the Restoration, and that monarch very kindly granted her a pension of a hundred a-year—then a very considerable sum—in consideration of her illustrious birth, so that she must have ended her days in pecuniary comfort, at all events; though it is probable that the miserable habits she had acquired precluded the possibility of the enjoyment of her amended position.

In little more than a century after the death of the spendthrift, imprisoned lord—in the year 1744, died at the age of eighty, in the capacity of *hostler* in an inn at Kirkwall, in the Orkney Islands, David Lindsay, late of Edzell, unquestionably head of the great house of Lindsay; and Lord Lindsay, as representative of David and Ludovic, Earls of Crawford. It would be tedious to explain how the earldom had gone to another branch, but such is the fact; and provided the claim to the Dukedom of Montrose brought forward by the present Earl of Crawford and Balcarres were admitted, the poor hostler would be one in the series of the premier dukes of Scotland.

One day, this David Lindsay, ruined and broken-hearted, departed from Edzell Castle, unobserved and unattended. He said farewell to no one, and turning round to take a last look at the old towers, he drew a long sigh and wept. He was never more seen in the place of his ancestors. With the wreck of his fortune, he bought a small estate on which he resided for some years; but this, too, was spent ere long, and the landless and houseless outcast retired to the Orkney Islands, where he became hostler in the Kirkwall inn!

The Earldom of Crawford is now most worthily possessed by the true head of the great house of Lindsay, the Earl of Balcarres, whose ample fortune enables him to maintain the splendour of its dignity, while his worth and high character add lustre to its name. His learned and accomplished son, Lord Lindsay, has recorded the heroic deeds and varying fortunes of his race in a work, every page of which reflects his pure and chivalrous nature, and which is enlivened by his charming fancy and playful wit, while his historical research has made it a most valuable or rather indispensable acquisition to the library of every Scottish gentleman.

St. Clair of Roslyn.

"Seemed all on fire that chapel proud
 Where Roslyn's chiefs uncoffined lie,
Each baron for a sable shroud
 Sheathed in his iron panoply.

"Blazed battlement and pinnet, high
 Blazed every rose-carved buttress fair:
So still they blaze when fate is nigh
 The Lordly line of high St. Clair.

"There are twenty of Roslyn's barons bold
 Lie buried within that proud *chapelle*,
Each one the holy vault doth hold,
 But the sea holds lovely Rosabelle."

No family in Europe beneath the rank of royalty boasts a higher antiquity, a nobler illustration, or a more romantic interest than that of St. Clair. Cradled in the baronial castle whose towers crown the brink of the most precipitous and wooded glen in the Lothians, and buried under the florid arches of the richly decorated chapel which crowns the adjacent bank, the Lords of Roslyn made Scotland ring with the renown of their deeds, which needed not to be enhanced by romance and poetry—for both are outdone by the vicissitudes of their fortunes.

The St. Clairs are descended from a noble Norman race, and came into Scotland in the days of King Malcolm Canmore. William St. Clair was the son of a great baron in Normandy, whom tradition has styled "Count de St. Clair:" and his mother is said to have been a daughter of Richard, Duke of Normandy. He obtained a grant of extensive estates in Midlothian, and was seated in the castle of Roslyn, which has ever since belonged to his descendants.

There were two families of the name settled in the neighbouring counties of Midlothian and East Lothian, of equal antiquity, but between whom we are unable to trace any connection by blood. St. Clair of Roslyn was distinguished by more splendid alliances and larger possessions; but St. Clair of Hermandston can scarcely be said to have come behind it in ancient nobility or in martial prowess.

During the days of the great struggle for national independence, the Lords of Roslyn were distinguished for their patriotism. In 1303, Sir Henry St. Clair was one of the principal leaders of the gallant band of 8000 men, who, issuing from the caves and romantic glens of Roslyn, defeated three English armies successively in one day, though they each mustered 10,000 strong. He, or his son, Sir William, obtained from King Robert Bruce a grant of all the royal lands in Pentland in 1317. It is probably in relation to this acquisition that the romantic story is told of the hunt of Pentland, where St. Clair is said to have wagered his head that his hounds, "Help," and "Hold," would kill a stag that had often baffled the

King's favourite dogs, before it could cross the March Burn. King Robert took him at his word, and staked Pentland against his head. The stag was actually in the March Burn when " Hold " stopped it, and " Help" turned it, and then they killed it, and saved their master's life and got him an estate.

Sir William St. Clair of Roslyn was the companion-in-arms of King Robert Bruce, and he had a worthy competitor for renown in his namesake and neighbour, Sir William of Hermandston, who fought so bravely at the battle of Bannockburn, that King Robert bestowed upon him his own sword, with which he had won that glorious day. It was long possessed in the house of Hermandston, and was inscribed with the French motto, *" Le Roi me donne St. Clair me porte."*

When King Robert died, Sir William of Roslyn had the honour of being one of the Scottish lords who were selected to accompany Sir James, the Lord of Douglas, on his romantic expedition, with his master's heart, to the holy sepulchre at Jerusalem. Their crusade was attended with all the circumstance of royal pomp and solemn chivalry, and their gallantry alone caused them to fall short of their pious and loyal purpose: for, passing through Spain on their way to Palestine, the Scottish knights could not resist the ardour which impelled them to join the chivalry of Spain in the battle against the Moors: and both the Lords of Douglas and of Roslyn perished on the bloody field of Theba, in Andalusia, in 1330.

The son of this crusader, who was also called Sir William, may be said to have founded the grandeur of the Sinclair family by a most illustrious alliance. He and his ancestors were, it is true, among the greatest of the feudal nobility; but, in consequence of his marriage with Isabella of Stratherne, he and his descendants became for several generations little less than princely. This lady was the eldest daughter and heir of Malise, seventh Earl of Stratherne, and Earl of Orkney and Caithness, and she inherited the right to her father's great Orcadian earldom, which she transmitted to her son.

The illustrious race of Scandinavian Earls, of which Isabella was the heir, was founded in the ninth century, by Earl Rogenwald, a great Norwegian chief, the common ancestor of the Earls of Orkney and the Dukes of Normandy, who were descended from two brothers, Eynar and Rollo, so that William the Conqueror and his contemporary, Thorfin, Earl of Orkney, were cousins in no very remote degree. The Earls of Orkney boasted the intermixture of a large share of royal blood. Earl Sigurd II., who was killed at the battle of Clontarf in 1014, was married to one of the daughters and co-heirs of Malcolm II., King of Scotland: so that the subsequent Earls of Orkney and their representatives are joint co-heirs with the reigning family of the ancient Scoto-Pictish monarchs. Earl Paul, who began to reign in 1064, married the granddaughter of Magnus the Good, King of Norway, who died in 1047. Margaret, Countess of Orkney, daughter and eventual heir of Earl Haco, in 1136 married Madoch, Earl of Athol, a prince of the royal race of Scotland, being nephew of King Malcolm III.; and her descendant,

Earl John, in the year 1300 married a daughter of Magnus, King of Norway, who died in 1289. The son of this marriage, Earl Magnus, whose reign commenced in 1305, had the same rank and dignity conceded to him in 1308, by Haco, King of Norway, that belonged to the princes of the royal family. His daughter, Isabella, carried the earldom of Orkney to Malise VI., Earl of Stratherne; and her son, Malise, the seventh earl, was father of another heiress, Isabella, who wedded William St. Clair.

Thus the princely earldom of Orkney came to be inherited by Henry St. Clair, Lord of Roslyn, who, in 1379, had his rights fully admitted by Haco VI., King of Norway, and was invested by him with the earldom; and his dignity of earl was immediately after recognized and confirmed by his native sovereign, Robert II., King of Scotland. ' Tradition says that this Henry St. Clair married Florentia, a lady of the royal House of Denmark.

The son and grandson of Earl Henry, successively Earls of Orkney and Lords Sinclair, married ladies of royal race, the granddaughters of two Scottish kings, Egidia, daughter of William Douglas, Lord of Nithesdale, by Princess Egidia, daughter of King Robert II., and Elizabeth, Countess-dowager of Buchan (widow of the Constable of France) and daughter of Archibald, fourth Earl of Douglas, Duke of Touraine, by the Princess Margaret, daughter of King Robert III. The St. Clairs continued to be Earls of Orkney, vassals of the crown of Norway, and recognized as Scottish earls by their native monarchs, until 1471, when the Orkney and Shetland Isles were annexed to the Scottish crown, on the marriage of King

James III. with Princess Margaret of Denmark. The object of that monarch was to humble the pride, and to diminish the overgrown power of William, third Earl of Orkney, of the line of St. Clair. He accordingly compelled him to exchange the lordship of Nithesdale for the earldom of Caithness, and the earldom of Orkney for the great estates of Dysart and Ravensheugh, with the castle of Ravenscraig, in the county of Fife.

In the full zenith of his power, William, third Earl of Orkney, united in his own person the highest offices in the realm: for he was Lord Admiral, Lord Justice General, and Lord Chancellor of Scotland, and Lord Warden of the three Marches. He built and endowed the beautiful chapel of Roslyn, which is still admired as the architectural gem of Scotland. He also greatly enlarged his castle of Roslyn, where he resided in princely splendour, and was waited on by some of the chief nobles of the land as officers of his household—Lords Dirleton, Borthwick, and Fleming, and the Barons of Drumlanrig, Drumelzier, and Calder. The daughter of this great potentate was wedded to a prince of the blood, Alexander, Duke of Albany, son of James II. The marriage, however, was dissolved, and its sole issue, a son, was made Bishop of Dunkeld, in order to cut short his succession.

There is a curious tradition connected with the chapel of Roslyn in relation to the noble race of its founder. Immediately before the death of one of the family, the beautiful building appears to be brilliantly illuminated. This superstition Sir Walter Scott conjectures to be of Scandinavian origin, and to have been imported by the Earls of the house of St. Clair from their Orcadian Principality to their domains in the Lothians. The many generations of barons of Roslyn are buried in the vaults beneath the chapel pavement, each chief clothed in complete armour.

As the family of St. Clair had attained to its highest power and eminence in the person of William, third Earl of Orkney, it may also be said from him to date its decline. I have already stated, that after the possession of the Orkneys and Shetland Islands for nearly a century, this Earl was compelled to resign them to the crown in 1471, having previously resigned his great lordship of Nithesdale. For these he obtained the very inadequate compensation of the Earldom of Caithness and the estates of Dysart and Ravensheugh, with the castle of Ravenscraig, in the county of Fife. The Earl died in 1480, enjoying the titles of Earl of Caithness, together with the inferior title of Lord Sinclair (which had also been held by his father Henry, along with his earldom), and possessed of very great estates, of which the principal messuages were Roslyn Castle in Mid-Lothian, and Ravenscraig Castle on the coast of Fife.

At the close of his life, the Earl made settlements of his large possessions, which were still more destructive to the prosperity of his family than the oppression at the hands of the King, of which he had been the victim. By splitting his estates into fragments, he speedily broke down the grandeur of his race; but it seems uncertain whether this was done under royal coercion or from mere parental caprice.

By his first marriage, with Elizabeth Douglas, Countess

of Buchan, grand-daughter of King Robert III., he had a son, William, who, while his father held his two earldoms, was styled " Master of Orkney and Caithness," according to Scottish usage, as heir to both, although in fact he succeeded to neither. His father, during his lifetime, gave him the estate of Newburgh in Aberdeenshire, and nothing more at his death. By his second wife, Marjory Sutherland, the Earl had a large family; and particularly two sons, between whom, in 1476, he most unjustly divided his whole inheritance, to the exclusion of his eldest son.

To the elder of the two, Sir Oliver, he gave the ancient family estate of Roslyn, and all his great possessions in the Lothians and in the counties of Stirling and Fife. To his younger son, named like his first-born, William, he conveyed the earldom of Caithness, with the King's consent, so that when his father died, he succeeded to that title with the estates annexed to it. This arbitrary arrangement has been a great puzzle to antiquaries. It is evident that the Earl meant entirely to disinherit his eldest son; but why the second, though most splendidly endowed, was left a mere Baron, not a peer, while the youngest was made an Earl, is matter of curious speculation. Some have conjectured that this arose from partiality to the third son; while others have surmised that Oliver was the real favourite, because he obtained by far the most valuable portion of the heritage, for the estates annexed to the Caithness earldom were in a remote county, and comparatively poor.

William, the disinherited eldest son, became Lord Sinclair, a title which had not been surrendered to the crown, and which had been held by three previous generations of the family. His life was spent in a struggle with his younger brothers, and he forced Sir Oliver to disgorge all the Fifeshire estates, while he was solemnly acknowledged by him and the Earl of Caithness to be their chief and the head of their house. He died very soon after this family arrangement was concluded, in 1488.

From these three brothers are descended the three great branches of the House of Sinclair or St. Clair, for the two forms of the name are indifferent, and have been used arbitrarily by different families of the name as a matter of taste.

From William, the youngest of the three, who had the higher title of Earl of Caithness, is descended the long line of holders of that Earldom, together with their numerous younger branches; and it is a very remarkable fact that this title has never been long held in any one direct line, but has gone four times to very remote collaterals—the most distant of all having been the grandfather of the present Earl.

The second son, Sir Oliver, was the ancestor of the Baron of Roslyn, of whom I am about to treat.

The eldest son, William, the disinherited master of Orkney and Caithness, was the ancestor of a long line of Lords Sinclair, concerning whom it may not be improper to say something before we proceed with the later Roslyn line. On his death in 1488, his son Henry was recognized by the King and Parliament of Scotland as Lord Sinclair. He was in reality the fourth Lord, although he is improperly reckoned the first, because he was the first of the family who held that title alone. He fell at Flodden in 1513.

His daughter Agnes, Countess of Bothwell, was the mother of the third husband of Queen Mary, who, when raised to ducal rank, selected the title of Orkney from regard to his maternal ancestry. William, second Lord Sinclair, was the leader of a romantic expedition, which he undertook in conjunction with his relation, John, Earl of Caithness, in 1529, during the stormy minority of King James V., with a view to recover the Orkney Islands as his family inheritance. He was vanquished and taken prisoner, and the Earl was killed.

The Lords Sinclair kept up the dignity of their former greatness by high alliances; as their successive intermarriages were with daughters of the Earl of Bothwell, Earl Marischal, Earl of Rothes twice over, Lord Lindsay, and Earl of Wemyss. John, seventh Lord Sinclair, died in 1676, without male issue, and with his affairs in considerable embarrassment. He was under great pecuniary obligations to Sir John St. Clair of Hermanston, a rich and ambitious man, the head of a very ancient family, but of an entirely different stock, having the engrailed cross blue instead of black, and being in no way descended from any of the Lords Sinclair. A marriage was arranged between this gentleman's eldest son and the seventh Lord Sinclair's only daughter and heir. Both husband and wife predeceased their respective fathers, and their son, Henry St. Clair, was heir-apparent both to his maternal grandfather, Lord Sinclair, and his paternal, Sir John St. Clair. On the death of the former, he inherited the Sinclair peerage, as eighth Lord in right of his mother; and although the undoubted heir male of the family, John Sinclair of Balgreggie, lived four and thirty years after, he never claimed the title, because it went in the female line.

Young Lord Sinclair, then a youth of seventeen, under the control of his paternal grandfather and uncles, obtained, through their means, a new patent of his peerage in 1677, from King Charles II., which totally changed the ancient line of succession, cutting out the female heirs of the body of the young lord, and settling the title on the family of St. Clair of Hermanston. Henry, eighth Lord Sinclair, died in 1723. His two sons, the Master of Sinclair, and General St. Clair, a distinguished diplomatist, had no issue; and his daughters were passed over in consequence of the new patent which was obtained in favour of the family of Hermanston, and according to which the present Lord Sinclair holds his peerage. He is not descended in any way from the original family, and is as complete a stranger to the old Lords Sinclair as if he was of an entirely different name. According to the Scottish saying, "He is not a drop's blood to them," although he holds their title by a capricious remainder in the new patent. But it should be observed that when that new patent of the title was obtained, the original peerage was not resigned to the crown, so it is presumed still to exist, although dormant.

Henry, eighth Lord, had several daughters. The eldest was the ancestress of Mr. Anstruther-Thomson of Charleton, who is heir-general and representative of the ancient Earls of Orkney and Lords Sinclair. The second daughter was the ancestress of Sir James Erskine, Bart., on whom the Sinclair estates of Dysart and Roslyn (which had been purchased from the last of the later barons of Roslyn by the Master of Sinclair) were settled by a special entail; and who moreover became second Earl of Roslyn on the death of his maternal uncle, the Lord Chancellor Wedderburne, Lord Loughborough, who had been created Earl of Roslyn, with remainder to his nephew, the heir of Roslyn Castle.

Thus the succession of the Sinclair family is curiously apportioned. The heirship of blood and lineal representation of the Lords Sinclair belong to Mr. Anstruther-Thomson, as descendant of the eldest daughter. The succession to the estates of Dysart and Roslyn has been conveyed, by special destination, to the Earl of Roslyn, the descendant of the younger daughter; and the title of Lord Sinclair has been claimed and awarded to the actual holder of that dignity, who is of a totally different family, and not even remotely connected with the original lords.

I must now follow the fortunes of the later Barons of Roslyn of the cadet branch.

Sir Oliver inherited his father's splendid domain in 1480; and as Lord of Roslyn Castle and all the great estates annexed to that princely manorial seat, he made a great figure among the Barons of Scotland, and held a prouder place than most of the lords of Parliament. His younger son, Oliver Sinclair, was the favourite of King James V., and was called "his great minion." The king utterly disgusted all his principal nobles by suddenly raising Oliver to the command of the army for the invasion of England in 1542, and the most lamentable disasters ensued; for these unpatriotic men refused to fight under him, and preferred the disgraceful alternative of a surrender to the enemy. The tidings of this shameful catastrophe broke the King's heart. He continued to exclaim, "O fled Oliver! Is Oliver taken? All is lost!" And he only lived to hear the further disappointing news, that his Queen had given birth to a daughter, the unfortunate Mary. Oliver Sinclair was taken prisoner to London, and soon released. He fell into obscurity, but his line continued for some generations, until its last female descendant carried the blood of Oliver, the king's unhappy minion, into the house of Dalhousie, and he is lineally represented by the ex-Governor-General of India. Sir Oliver had another son, who was Bishop of Ross, and a man of some note. It was he who began the long feud with Lord Borthwick, his neighbour, which endured during four generations. Tradition says that he threw one of the Borthwick family over the drawbridge of Roslyn Castle after dinner! The quarrel thus inhospitably commenced was continued about some lands which Lord Borthwick held of Roslyn as a vassal.

Sir Oliver was succeeded by his son Sir William, who in the civil wars of Scotland espoused the party of the Queen Dowager and Regent. He died in 1554, and the family difficulties began in his time, and went on increasing during the next two centuries, until they ended in the alienation of the castle and chapel of Roslyn, all that at length remained of the princely estates, to the elder line of Sinclair.

Sir William's son, of his own name, was appointed

Lord Justice General of Scotland in 1559, by Francis and Mary, and in 1568 he fought gallantly for the Queen at Langside, for which he was forfeited. And although his estates were afterwards restored to him, they were so deeply involved that he was compelled to sell one of the best of them—Herbertshire, near Stirling.

A romantic adventure happened to Sir William, which introduced the future Barons of Roslyn to singular allies. One day, when he was riding from Edinburgh to Roslyn Castle, he rescued a gipsy from the gibbet, and restored him alive and well to his own people. This excited the lasting gratitude of the wandering tribe, and they placed themselves under the special protection of the barons of Roslyn, who do not seem to have shrank from the connection. When the whole gipsy race in Scotland acknowledged Sir William as their patron, he allowed them, at certain seasons, to come and nestle under his wing, and he had two of the towers of Roslyn Castle allotted to them. About this time, also, commenced the connection of the barons of Roslyn with the renowned fraternity of freemasons, which lasted as long as the race continued to exist; a St. Clair of Roslyn being always at the head of the Scottish freemasonry.

During the time of his son, Sir William, who lived in the end of the sixteenth century, considerable additions were made to the ancient castle in buildings erected in the style of that period. He had a son, Sir William, who, being a Roman Catholic, was persecuted by the Presbyterians, and fled to Ireland. Other motives have been assigned for his precipitate departure, for, though he had a wife and numerous family, he carried off with him in his flight a beautiful girl of the lower ranks.

Father Hay, who was the stepson of one of the subsequent Barons of Roslyn, thus writes:—" His son (the son of the former Sir William), Sir William, died during the troubles, and was interred in the chapel of Roslyn, the very same day that the battle of Dunbar was fought. When my good father (that is, father-in-law or stepfather) was buried, Sir William's corpse seemed to be entire at the opening of the door of the vault; but when they came to touch the body, it fell into dust. He was lying in his armour, with a red velvet cap on his head, on a flat stone. Nothing was decayed except a piece of the white furring that went round the cap, and answered to the hinder part of the head. All his predecessors, the former barons of Roslyn, were buried after the same manner, in their armour. The late Roslyn, my good father (father-in-law), was the first that was buried in a coffin, against the sentiments of King James VII., who was then in Scotland, and several other persons well versed in antiquity, to whom my mother (the widow) would not hearken, thinking it beggarly to be buried in that manner. The great expense that she was at in burying her husband occasioned the sumptuary laws which were made in the following parliaments."

The Roslyn who was buried after this royal fashion was James St. Clair, a member of the Church of Rome, who had lived a great deal in France, where he enjoyed considerable distinction. His widow endeavoured to obtain redress from King James II. for the great losses which the family had sustained on account of their loyalty to

Charles I. But she had very little success, as the powerful minister, the Earl of Melfort, was against her. She, however, obtained considerable sums from parliament for the woods that had been destroyed. During the minority of her son Alexander, while this lady managed the family affairs, a very valuable seam of coal was discovered on the estate, which had, however, no permanent effect in arresting the ruin of the falling house.

About this time, in 1688, the beautiful chapel at Roslyn was defaced and desecrated by the Presbyterians. The fabric, however, is now in perfectly good order, much having been spent in its restoration. It is not at present used for public worship, but it is the never-failing object of intense admiration to all lovers of beautiful architecture, and its vaults are still the last resting-place of the members of some branches of the family.

Alexander St. Clair and William St. Clair were the two last Barons of Roslyn. Their affairs were in a very embarrassed condition. The estate had gradually dwindled to nothing, and all that remained to the last lord of Roslyn was the site of the splendid castle which contained the halls of his fathers, and that of the elaborately adorned chapel which attested their munificence.

William St. Clair, the last Roslyn, was weighed down by so heavy a load of debt from the old encumbrances which pressed upon him, that while yet in the prime of life, in 1735, he was obliged to sell the last remnant of his noble inheritance. He lived nearly forty years afterwards, and was a very well known member of Scottish society, until the year 1772, when he died without issue. With him expired the whole male line of Sir Oliver St. Clair, the founder of the later family of Barons of Roslyn. There exist, however, collateral representatives of the family in the female line.

But Roslyn Castle, although it was alienated by the last Baron of the junior line, is still possessed by the family; and, in fact, it reverted in 1735, to the eldest branch of the original house, who had been so unjustly deprived of it in 1476, two hundred and fifty years before. When William St. Clair of Roslyn sold his ancient castle in 1735, it was purchased by John Master of Sinclair, and the Hon. General St. Clair, sons of Henry, eighth Lord Sinclair, and grandsons of the heiress of the rightful elder line, which was disinherited by their common ancestor in order to enrich his favourite younger son.

Roslyn was then joined to Dysart, as part and parcel of the Sinclair estates, and is now the property of the Earl of Roslyn, who is the lineal descendant of the Master of Sinclair's younger sister, while Anstruther-Thomson of Charleton is the lineal descendant of the elder. The Earl of Roslyn has added some adjacent property to this most picturesque possession, and the castle and chapel are preserved by him, in excellent repair, as a noble monument of fallen greatness.

Stewart of Craigiehall.

"Scion of chiefs and monarchs, where art thou?"
BYRON.

WHILE the descent of some families from greatness to obscurity has been striking and sudden, others have fallen by slow degrees, and by a downward progress which has endured for generations. A branch of a race of illustrious Magnates flourishes for centuries in honour and affluence as a baronial and knightly house; it then sinks to the condition of moderate country gentry; it next subsides into the trader and petty magistrate of a small provincial town; and at length utterly dies out in poverty and obscurity.

Such is the not uncommon fate of a great family; and I am about to furnish an instance of it, which claims our interest not on account of any strange vicissitudes, but because it illustrates the gradual decay produced by the alienation of landed property. An hereditary estate, however small, associates the owner with the existing lords of the soil, and connects him with his ancestry in bygone times. But no sooner is this link broken than he sinks to an inferior station, and all his boasted ancestry is forgotten, or is, at least, regarded as an uncertain dream.

This is forcibly exemplified in the fate of a branch of the illustrious line of the Steward of Scotland, which came off as an early cadet of the Lords of Innermeath, flourished for centuries as Barons of Durisdeer and Knights of Craigiehall, then sank to be inconsiderable "Lairds" of Newhall, whence it dwindled into merchants of the petty town of Queensferry, and finally died out in the person of a poor country surgeon! Hence there are no remarkable vicissitudes of fortune. But, on the other hand, there is the instructive lesson of gradual decay, which teaches all landed proprietors that with loss of land, station also is lost; and that a baronial house will probably dwindle into the most profound obscurity in the course of a couple of generations, if deprived of all territorial distinction.

In the course of another quarter of a century this truth will be manifested in the children of the victims of the Encumbered Estates' Court in Ireland. We have already seen the heir of the D'Arcys of Kiltullagh traversing as a pious but poor clergyman the broad lands which once owned him as a master, and the heiress of the vast estates of Ballynahinch dying miserably on board an American packet! The House of Durisdeer existed in an age and country where the Encumbered Estates' Court was unknown; and therefore they have not been hurried to execution like Martin of Galway, and others, but have been suffered to perish by a more lingering decay.

It is a curious fact that neither the Bruces nor Stewarts can boast of a participation in the royal blood which entitled the holders of those noble names to a seat on the Scottish throne. After the marriage of Robert de Bruce with Isabella of Huntington, only one younger branch diverged from the parent stem, viz., Bruce of Exton, which almost immediately ended in a series of heiresses, who conveyed the royal blood and the inheritance to the ancient family of Harington, afterwards Lord Harington of Exton. Not one of the existing families of Bruce can even trace their descent from the original family before its intermarriage with royalty. There is, indeed, every reason to suppose that they possess a common origin with the royal Bruces; but it is impossible actually to prove it, further than by the complimentary expression bestowed by King David Bruce on Robert Bruce, the first of Clackmanan, of "Dilecto et fideli Consanguineo."

The case of the Stewarts, however, is different. Many of their great lines can be distinctly traced to younger sons of the successive Lords High-Stewards; and thus they can prove a common origin with the royal family. But none are descended in the male line from that family after it became royal, except through links of illegitimacy, like the Earls of Castle Stuart and Moray, who are sprung from James, son of Murdock, Duke of Albany; and the Marquesses of Bute, who trace their descent from King Robert II.

The family of Craigiehall is descended from Alexander, the fourth Lord High-Steward of Scotland, who died in the year 1283. He had two sons—I., James, his successor in the dignified office of Lord High-Steward of Scotland, and grandfather of Robert II., the first of the race of Stewart who ascended the Scottish throne; and II. Sir John Stewart of Bonkyl. The latter acquired his estate by marriage with Margaret, daughter and heir of Sir Alexander Bonkyl of Bonkyl; and on account of this alliance all the families of Stewart who are descended from him bear the buckles of Bonkyl, in addition to the paternal coat of Stewart.

Sir John of Bonkyl was a noble patriot, a brother-in-arms of the illustrious Wallace, and perished gloriously at the battle of Falkirk, in defence of the liberties of his country against the English, in 1298. No Scotsman should ever forget the title to honour and respect which the family of Stewart acquired before they began to reign, by their undeviating and zealous defence of the independence of their native land against the aggressions of the English. Whenever the banner of liberty was unfurled, it was sure to be bravely defended by the Lord High Steward and all the nobles of his race. And certainly there never was a more devoted patriot than Alexander, the Steward's son, Sir John of Bonkyl.

This noble knight is the patriarch from whom many distinguished branches of Stewart derive their descent. His eldest son, Alexander, was father of John Stewart, Earl of Angus. His second son, Alan, was ancestor of the Earls and Dukes of Lennox and of the later Stewart kings who ascended the throne of Great Britain. His fourth son was the ancestor of the Lords of Lorn and Innermeath, the Earls of Athol, Buchan, and Traquair, and also of the baronial family whose gradual fall I am about to notice.

Sir James Stewart, the fourth son of Sir John of Bonkyl, fell at the battle of Halidon Hill, in 1333. His son, Sir Robert Stewart of Innermeath, had two sons. I. Sir John, who became Lord of Lorn, and was ancestor to a long line of Earls of Athol. II. Robert, who had a charter of the lands of Durisdeer in 1388, and who fell at the battle of Shrewsbury in 1409. Robert Stewart of Durisdeer had a daughter, Isabella Stewart, who married Robert Bruce, the first of Clackmanan, ancestor of the Earls of Ailesbury and Elgin, and a son who succeeded him as Baron of Durisdeer.

I will not give a long list of the inheritors of his blood and honours. Suffice it to say, that the descendants of Robert Stewart of Durisdeer held baronial and knightly rank for many generations, and were seated at Rossythe Castle on the coast of Fife, and the shores of the Firth of Forth. It is stated that the mother of Oliver Cromwell, the Lord Protector, was the daughter of a younger branch of this family which had settled in the town of Ely.

The representative of Stewart of Durisdeer and Rossythe became possessed of the great estate of Craigie Hall, in the county of Linlithgow, by marriage with the heiress of the ancient family of Craig, of Craigie Hall, and his descendant Sir John Stewart, of Craigie Hall, bore for his arms quarterly 1 and 4, or a fess chequè azure and argent, in chief three buckles azure for Stewart of Bonkyl; 2 and 3, ermine on a fess sable three crescents argent, for Craig of Craigie Hall.

After several generations of Knights of Craigie Hall, this fine estate was sold in the seventeenth century to an opulent merchant in Edinburgh, named John Fairholm. This person purchased the estate of Craigie Hall from Sir John Stewart in 1643. His son, John Fairholm of Craigie Hall, had an only daughter and heiress, Sophia, born in 1668, and married in 1682 to William Johnstone, first Marquess of Annandale. She was the Marquess's first wife, and the only surviving issue of this marriage was Lady Henrietta Johnstone, married in 1699 to Charles Hope, created Earl of Hopetoun in 1703. Her second son, Charles, inherited her estate, and was the great grandfather of the present Mr. Hope-Vere of Craigie Hall.

When Sir John Stewart sold his principal estate, he still preserved a small adjoining property called Newhall, which was inherited by his grandson, Alexander Stewart. This gentleman married a lady of distinguished birth, a daughter of Sir David Carmichael of Balmedie. But misfortune continued to pursue his family. In the next generation Newhall also was sold, and came into the possession of a near relative, Dundas of Duddingston, and has finally been acquired by the Earl of Roseberry, and now forms a portion of his beautiful domain of Dalmeny Park.

Stewart of Newhall then retired to the neighbouring petty borough of Queensferry, where his family engaged in commerce, and for a generation or two held the position of principal merchants in that very obscure country town. The last heir of the family, Archibald Stewart, went out to the East Indies, with a view to seek his fortune. But his health failed, and he returned to his native town, where he established himself as a surgeon, and for many years gained a hard livelihood as a country practitioner, riding over the broad and fair lands which had owned his ancestors as lords, and gathering a few shillings per visit from the descendants of the vassals of his fathers. He died somewhere about the year 1830, leaving an unmarried sister, the last of his ancient and noble race.

It may be mentioned that Archibald Stewart, the surgeon of Queensferry, and direct heir of the wealthy and high-born knights of Craigie Hall, possessed the distinguished illustration of being coheir to the princely house of De Ergadia, Lord of Lorn, and the still greater honour of being one of the coheirs of the line of the royal Bruce. King Robert I. was twice married. By his first wife, the daughter of the Earl of Marr, he had one daughter, Marjory, the wife of Walter, the High Steward of Scotland, and ancestress of the long line of Stewart Kings. By his second wife, Elizabeth, eldest daughter of Richard de Burgo, Earl of Ulster, he had issue, his son and unworthy successor, King David II.; Margaret, wife of William, 4th Earl of Sutherland, and ancestress of the Earls of Sutherland; and Matilda, the wife of Thomas de Izac. The daughter of this marriage, Joanna de Izac, who was coheir of the royal blood of the Bruce, along with her cousins, Robert II., King of Scotland, and William, 5th Earl of Sutherland, married John de Ergadia, Lord of Lorn, the descendant and representative of a branch of the kings of the Isles. The Lords of Lorn had sided with the Baliols, and were the firm adherents of the English interest; and John, Lord of Lorn, was imprisoned and forfeited by King Robert Bruce. His son John was restored in 1346, and became the husband of that monarch's granddaughter,

Johanna de Izac. The issue of this marriage was two daughters. 1. Isabel de Ergadia, who carried the lordship of Lorn to her husband, John Stewart of Innermeath, and was ancestress to the long line of Stewarts, Lords of Lorn and Innermeath, and Earls of Athol. 2. Janet de Ergadia, who married Robert Stewart of Durisdeer, the brother of her sister's husband. She was ancestress of the Stewarts of Rossythe in Fifeshire, and of the Stewarts of Craigie Hall in Linlithgowshire; and one of her last descendants, coheir of the ancient Lords of Lorn and Princes of the Isles, as well as of the Kings of Scotland, was Archibald Stewart, surgeon in Queensferry.

This is not a fitting place for the discussion of questions of disputed genealogy. It may nevertheless be mentioned that there is, to say the least, a high probability that the heir male of Stewart of Cragiehall, if such there be, is also heir male of the great house of the Lord High Stewards of Scotland; in short, is "the Stewart."

Gargrave and Reresby.

"'Twere long to tell, and sad to trace,
Each step from splendour to disgrace."—BYRON.

THE story of the Gargraves is a melancholy chapter in the romance of real life. For full two centuries or more, scarcely a family in Yorkshire enjoyed a higher position. Its chiefs earned distinction in peace and war; one died in France, Master of the Ordnance to King Henry V.; another, a soldier too, fell with Salisbury at the siege of Orleans; and a third filled the Speaker's chair of the House of Commons. What an awful contrast to this fair picture does the sequel offer. Thomas Gargrave, the Speaker's eldest son, was hung at York for murder; and his half-brother, Sir Richard, endured a fate only less miserable. The splendid estate he inherited he wasted by the most wanton extravagance, and at length reduced himself to abject want. "His excesses," says Mr. Hunter, in his History of Doncaster, "are still, at the expiration of two centuries, the subject of village tradition, and his attachment to gaming is commemorated in an old painting, long preserved in the neighbouring mansion of Badsworth, in which he is represented playing at the old game of put, the right hand against the left, for the stake of a cup of ale."

The close of Sir Richard's story is as lamentable as its

course. An utter bankrupt in means and reputation, he is stated to have been reduced to travel with the packhorses to London, and was at last found dead in an old hostelry! He had married Catherine, sister of Lord Danvers, and by her he left three daughters. Of the descendants of his brothers, few particulars can be ascertained. Not many years since, a Mr. Gargrave, believed to be one of them, filled the mean employment of parish clerk at Kippax.

A similar melancholy narrative applies to another great Yorkshire house. Sir William Reresby, Bart., son and heir of the celebrated author, succeeded, at the death of his father, in 1689, to the beautiful estate of Thrybergh, in Yorkshire, where his ancestors had been seated uninterruptedly from the time of the Conquest, and he lived to see himself denuded of every acre of his broad lands. Le Neve states in his MSS., preserved in the Heralds' College, that he became a tapster in the King's Bench prison, and was tried and imprisoned for cheating in 1711. He was alive in 1727, when Wotton's account of the Baronets was published. In that work he is said to be reduced to a wretched condition. At length he died in great obscurity, a melancholy instance how low pursuits and base pleasures may sully the noblest name, and waste an estate gathered with labour and preserved by the care of a race of distinguished progenitors. Gaming was amongst Sir William's follies—particularly the worst species of the folly, the fight of game-cocks. The tradition of Thrybergh is (for his name is not quite forgotten) that the fine estate of Dennaby was staked and lost on a single main.

A Dethroned Monarch.

"Thy place is filled, thy sceptre wrung from thee."
SHAKESPEARE.

On a marble monument, in the church of St. Anne's, Soho, there is a slab placed to the memory of the King of Corsica, with this inscription by Horace Walpole:—

> "Near this place is interred
> Theodore, King of Corsica,
> Who died in this parish, Dec. 11, 1756,
> Immediately after leaving
> The King's Bench Prison
> By the benefit of the Act of Insolvency.
> In consequence of which
> He registered his Kingdom of Corsica,
> For the use of his Creditors."

> "The grave, great teacher, to a level brings
> Heroes and beggars, galley-slaves and kings;
> But Theodore this moral learned, ere dead,
> Fate poured its lessons on his living head,
> Bestow'd a kingdom and denied him bread."

The King of Corsica was by birth a Prussian, and by name Theodore Anthony Neuhoff. Early in the spring of 1736, an unknown adventurer, he was landed in Corsica, from an English vessel, with a considerable supply of arms and money, and he placed himself immediately at the head of the islanders, then in revolt against the Genoese. A successful campaign ensued, and on the 15th of the April following, Theodore was crowned King of Corsica, with the consent, and amid the acclamations, of the whole people. He held his court at Bastea, and distributed honours and rewards amongst his followers. The calm endured, however, but for a short period: the Genoese gaining ground again, it became necessary to seek for foreign supplies and foreign aid, and Theodore undertook at once the mission. Laying aside his kingly character, he assumed the habit of an Abbé, and proceeded to Livonia; but what success attended his efforts, we are unable to state; for, during several months after his arrival in that country, no one knew what had become of him.

The next year he appeared at Paris, but, being instantly ordered out of France, he journeyed to Amsterdam, and was there enabled, by the assistance of some merchants, to equip a frigate of thirty-two guns and one hundred and fifty men. But an evil destiny seems to have thwarted all his plans. Arrested by the Neapolitan government, he was detained a prisoner in the fortress of Cueta; and though eventually liberated, he does not seem ever to have made way afterwards. His exertions to assist his island subjects were unremitting: but disappointment and ruin were the only results. At last, broken down by fate, he retired to England—then, as now, the refuge of fallen politicians—but here, too, suffering and misery awaited him. Day by day his situation became more deplorable, and the closing years of his unhappy life were passed in the King's Bench prison, from which a general Act of Insolvency only released him to die.

"This prince," (I quote from Horace Walpole) "after

having bravely exposed his life and crown in defence of the rights of his subjects, miscarried, as Cato and other patriot-heroes had done before him. For many years he struggled with fortune, and left no means untried, which indefatigable policy or solicitation of succours could attempt, to recover his crown. At last, when he had discharged his duty to his subjects and himself, he chose this country for his retirement: not to indulge a voluptuous, inglorious ease, but to enjoy the participation of those blessings which he had so vainly endeavoured to fix on the Corsicans. Here, for some months, he bore with more philosophic dignity the loss of his crown, than Charles V., Casimir of Poland, or any of those philosophic visionaries who wantonly resigned them in order to partake the sluggish indolence and at length the disquiets of a cloister."

After comparing Theodore with James II., and giving him the preference, Walpole adds, "The veracity of an historian obliges me not to disguise the bad situation of his Corsican Majesty's revenue, which has reduced him to be a prisoner for debt in the King's Bench prison: and so cruelly has fortune exercised her rigours upon him, that last session of Parliament he was examined before a committee of the House of Commons on the hardships to which the prisoners in that gaol had been subject. Yet let not ill-nature make sport with these misfortunes! His Majesty had nothing to blush at, nothing to palliate in the recapitulation of his distresses. The debts on his civil list were owing to no misapplication, no improvidence of his own, no corruption of his ministers, no indulgence to favourites or mistresses. His life was philosophic, his diet humble, his robes decent; yet his butcher, his landlady, and his tailor, could not continue to supply an establishment which had no demesnes to support it, no taxes to maintain it, no excises, no lotteries, to provide funds for its deficiencies and emergencies."

Another quotation—one from a modern writer,* whose wit and fancy give a charm to all he writes—will appropriately end this strange eventful history:—

"Nearly forty years," says Dr. Doran, "after King Theodore was consigned to the grave in St. Anne's, an old man, one night in February 1796, walked from a coffee-house at Storey's Gate to Westminster Abbey. Under one of the porches there he put a pistol to his head, pulled the trigger, and fell dead. The old man was the son of Theodore, Colonel Frederick. The latter had been for many years familiar to the inhabitants of London, and remarkable for his gentlemanlike bearing and his striking eccentricities. He had fulfilled many employments, and had witnessed many strange incidents. Not the least strange, perhaps, was his once dining at Dolly's, with Count Poniatowski, when neither the son of the late King of Corsica, nor he who was the future King of Poland, had enough between them to discharge their reckoning. Distress drove him to suicide, and his remains rest by the side of those of his father. He left a daughter, who was married to a Mr. Clark, of the Dartmouth Custom House. A daughter, one of the four children of this marriage, was established in London at the beginning of this century,

* Dr. Doran, "Monarchs retired from Business."

where she earned a modest livelihood as an authoress and an artist. Her card ran thus:—

MISS CLARK,
Granddaughter of the late Colonel Frederick, son of
Theodore, King of Corsica,
PAINTS LIKENESSES IN MINIATURE,
From two to three Guineas.
No. 116, NEW BOND STREET.
Hours of Attendance from twelve in the morning
until four."

The O'Neills,

Chiefs of Slucht=Henry=Caoch, in Clanaboy.

"Gens antiqua fuit multos dominata per annos."

"O'Neill of the Hostages, Conn, whose high name
On a hundred red battles has floated to fame;
Let the long grass still sigh undisturbed o'er thy sleep,
Arise not to shame us, awake not to weep!"
Lament of O'Gnive, bard of O'Neill, of Clanaboy,
in the Sixteenth Century.

WHAT visions of the past of Ireland in the olden times, long, long ago, are recalled to memory by the royal name of O'Neill! How often have the aged bards and seanachies sat in the banquet hall, and by the funeral bier, and recounted in song and story the deeds of the heroes of the *Lamh derg Eirin!* Penetrating into the mists of time, far beyond the period generally assigned for the commencement of authentic history, they point out with exultation, in the dim vista, the prince schoolmaster, NIUL, of Scythia, fountain of the race. And a right noble origin it was—that trained student from the public schools of his royal father, King Phenius, at Magh-Senair; more illustrious by far than that of modern princes and nobles who proudly claim descent from some fierce warrior, who, after all, was but the herald of devastation and misery, not, as Niul, the harbinger of peace and civilization.

With affectionate care and minuteness, these same old chroniclers trace the voyages of the sons of Niul, by his wife the Egyptian Princess, Scota, from the time they leave Egypt until they reach Spain, in search of their "land of promise," the western isle; and these old bards paint, with all the glow and fresh warm tints of an eastern imagination, the mighty deeds and renown of the royal warrior, MILESIUS, King in Spain, and second great chief of the race of Niul. And from HEREMON his son, first monarch of Ireland, they unroll a long line of illustrious Kings and Princes, warriors, legislators, and men of learning.

NIALL THE GREAT, *Noigallach*, or of the "nine hostages," grandson of Mortough, is, however, the special object of the praise of the bards and seanachies, next to Conn of "the hundred battles." They point out, with pride and exultation, the glories of their beloved land of the Gael, under his rule, of his renown in war both at home and abroad, and of his triumphant train, graced by *nine Princes* of royal blood, as hostages from different states and kingdoms that he had conquered.

With the death of Niall's descendant, Malachy, who succeeded Mortough, "the great O'Neill," in 987, commences the decadence of the ancient dynasty—the royal and once powerful House of O'Neill,—and with it the fall of Ireland as a distinct and independent nation. At his death contending Princes of other races—the O'Briens and O'Connors—following the example so fatally set by the ambitious views of Brian Boru, contested for the sovereignty, and weakened the national resources and power. Eventually their pretensions were crushed by MURTOUGH MAC NEILL, a South Hy-Niall Prince, who closed his reign and his life in the year 1168, one year only preceding the Anglo-Norman invasion. He was the last monarch of the race of NIALL THE GREAT, whose posterity had thus *exclusively occupied the throne of Ireland for upwards of six hundred years.*

His heroic efforts, crowned ultimately with success, to redeem the falling fortunes of his house, and to restore the sceptre which had slipped from it, are deserving of all praise. His brief presidency in the Hall of Tara was but the flickering of that regal lamp, which had shone in Ireland full two thousand years as a beacon and light to the Gael, and which was extinguished at his death; for his successor, Roderick O'Connor, who assumed the crown, and resigned it to the English, was but partially acknowledged by the nation.

Any further notice of this ancient sept would be but to trace, step by step, its decadence and its fall—marking, from era to era, the heroic efforts of its successive chiefs, ill supported and frequently opposed by their countrymen, in unavailing struggles with the English, to avert its inevitable destiny. First, they were Monarchs in Ireland, then Princes, next Chiefs, now nobles of English creation, again Anglicised "squires," and finally, confiscated, crushed, and scattered, they became wanderers in, or exiles from the land of their inheritance. In that land, those who remained, except a few—and those few unimportant, save one—became literally "hewers of wood and drawers of water," where their great fathers reigned. Such is the destiny and decadence of the royal house of O'Neill!

In the twelfth century the family tree became divided into two chief stems, which threw out minor branches. The two leading lines are popularly known as THE O'NEILLS OF CLANABOY, descendants of Hugh Duff O'Neill, King of Ulster, and THE O'NEILLS OF TYRONE, descendants of his younger brother, Prince Neill Roe O'Neill. Of the latter house were Con Baccagh O'Neill, first Earl of Tyrone, who cursed those of his kinsmen who would build stone houses and live in the English fashion, and Shane a Diomus O'Neill, "John the proud," who waged war against Elizabeth, and, when he visited the Queen at her Court to arrange the terms of peace, astonished the good citizens of London, in his march through their streets at the head of his unshaven Galloglasses, or battle-axe guards, with long flowing hair, and saffron-dyed mantles. To this line belonged Hugh, Earl of Tyrone, the accomplished statesman and general, who also for many years was at war with the English Queen, and at Bealanaboy and other places foiled her best generals and worsted her choicest troops: submitting to James the First, and fearing arrest, he fled to Spain in 1607, and died at Rome, aged and blind. Of this same branch were Sir Phelim Roe O'Neill, whose reputed character for cruelties perpetrated in the "great rebellion" of 1641, was partially redeemed by his stern refusal on the scaffold in 1652, to save his life and preserve his estates by bearing false testimony against the ill-fated Charles the First; General

Owen Roe O'Neill, the gallant defender of Arras for the Spaniards, and victor of Benburb, where General Monroe and the flower of the English army were defeated, and Major-General Hugh Duff O'Neill, his nephew, who baffled Cromwell at Clonmel, and worsted Ireton at Limerick. But with the race of those illustrious men, patriots or rebels as they may be, who sustained by their brilliant deeds of arms the reputation of their house, I have now no concern; it is to a branch of the O'Neills of Clanaboy, the elder line, that the subject of my sketch relates.

HUGH BOY O'NEILL, "yellow Hugh," grandson of Hugh Duff, was king of Ulster in the thirteenth century, and recovered from the English their extensive territories in the counties of Antrim and Down, called after him "Clanaboy," which his descendants held until the reign of James the First; they had their chief seats at Edinduffcarrick, now Shane's castle, in the county of Antrim, and Castlereagh in the county of Down. Bryan Balaf O'Neill, fourth in descent from Hugh Boy, was so powerful as to impose a tribute upon the English of the adjoining districts called "Bryan Balaf's eiric," which continued to be paid or exacted, until put down by proclamation in the reign of Elizabeth. Sir Henry O'Neill, the descendant of his eldest son, Con, conformed, and saved out of the common wreck of the lands of the O'Neills during the confiscations of James the First, the present noble estates of Shane's castle, thirty thousand acres, which are in possession of the heir-general, the Reverend William O'Neill, while the heir male, Charles Henry O'Neill, Esq., barrister-at-law, who claims the honourable distinction of " The

O'Neill of Clanaboy," rents from the heir-general *sixty acres* of the lands of his ancestors.

The second son of Bryan Balaf, namely, Henry Caoch O'Neill, possessed that territory—part of Clanaboy—called after him, "Slucht Henry Caoch." Bryan O'Neill was the seventh in descent from Henry Caoch. The confiscations of James the First, and the "settlement of Ulster," by the introduction of "English and Scotch Protestants," had swept away his inheritance, and, like many of his kinsmen and others of proscribed houses in Ulster and other parts of Ireland, he became a soldier of fortune on the continent. He served for some time in Holland under the Prince of Orange; and on the rupture between Charles the First and his Parliament he tendered his services to the King, by whom they were gladly accepted. He was present under Lord Conway at the "rout of Newburn," where "the Scots," says the old chronicler Hooper, "having crossed the river, put the royal forces to the most shameful and confounding flight that was ever heard of, our foot making no less haste from Newcastle than our horse from Newburn —the Lord Conway never afterwards turning his face towards the enemy;" but he adds, "there were in that infamous rout at Newburn two or three officers of quality taken prisoners, who, endeavouring to charge the enemy with the courage they ought to do, being deserted by their troops, could not avoid falling into the Scots' hands, namely, Wilmot, who was commissary-general, and O'Neill, who was Major of a regiment, both officers of name and reputation, and of good esteem in the court with all those who were incensed against the Earl of Strafford, towards whom they were both undevoted." Major Bryan O'Neill and Wilmot had, however, fallen into the hands of old friends; for, as Hooper adds, " those gentlemen were well known to several of the principal commanders in the Scots' army who had served together with them in Holland, under the Prince of Orange, and were treated with good civility in their camp." Afterwards, at the treaty of Ripon, they were released, as thus quaintly told by Hooper :—" When they (the Scots) came to Ripon they brought them Wilmot and O'Neil with them, and presented them to the King by his commissioners, to whom they were very acceptable." After the King had raised at Nottingham, on the 26th of August, 1643, the royal standard, which was " blown down the same night it had been set up by a very strong and unruly wind," the royal army, on the 23d October following, under Prince Rupert, bivouacked on Edge-hill, and fought the famous battle of that name against the Parliament forces commanded by the Earl of Essex. In this battle Colonel Bryan O'Neill distinguished himself in the highest degree, leading on his dragoons, rallying them when broken, charging again into the serried ranks of the enemy, and breaking and pursuing them, but never losing sight of the King's person; for at that critical moment when the dragoons had pursued too far the routed horse of the Roundheads, and left his Majesty exposed to the fate that befel his predecessor Henry the Third, at the battle of Lewes, when in the hour of victory over his barons he was taken prisoner, O'Neill was among the small but Spartan band that guarded his Majesty's person. For his bravery on that occasion, the honour of an English Baronetcy was conferred upon him by his Majesty, on the 13th Nov. 1643, by the title of "Sir Bryan O'Neill of Upper Clanaboy." He was twice married; first, to Jane Finch, of the Earl of Nottingham's family, and secondly, to Sarah, daughter and co-heir of Hugh Savage, of Portaferry, Esq. By the latter marriage, he had Hugh, appointed one of the Justices of the King's Bench in 1687: this learned Judge married Martha, daughter of William Lord Howth, and left Bernard and Mary. The daughter married Charles O'Neill, Esq., of the Feeva, county of Antrim, and died in 1790, aged one hundred years; and her brother, Bernard, having also married, died in the year 1798, leaving two daughters. Sir Bryan O'Neill died about the year 1670, and left by his first marriage an only son, Sir Bryan O'Neill, second baronet, Baron of the Exchequer in 1687. He and his half brother, the Hon. Justice Hugh O'Neill, adhered to the cause of James the Second, and lost all the landed estates which their family had acquired after the previous confiscations. Sir Bryan, the second baronet, married Mary, daughter of Edward Plunket, Lord Dunsany, by whom he left an only son, Sir Henry O'Neill, of Kellystown, in the county of Meath, third baronet, who married twice; first, Mary, daughter of Mark Bagot, Esq., and secondly, Rose, daughter of James Brabazon, Esq., of the noble house of Meath, by Mary, daughter of Dudley Colley, of Castle Carbery, and aunt of Richard, Lord Mornington, grandfather of the Duke of Wellington.

By his first marriage Sir Henry O'Neill had Sir Bryan, fourth baronet, who died without issue, and Sir Randall, fifth baronet, who was surveyor of customs at Rush, in the county of Dublin, and died having had a son and a daughter, who both died unmarried. Sir Henry O'Neill, by his second marriage, left Sir Francis O'Neill, of Kellystown, in the county of Meath, sixth baronet, who married Miss Fleming, of the county of Louth.

And here I have to notice one of the many social wrongs inflicted by the penal laws in Ireland on those who happened to retain any remnant of property preserved from the various confiscations of James, Cromwell, and William, or obtained by subsequent acquisitions. Those laws happily no longer sully the pages of the Statute book, but as long as they remained, they legally disqualified from possessing real estate all persons of the proscribed faith; who were obliged in consequence to resort to the common expedient of getting leases in the names of those friends of the favoured creed whom they could trust. It was thus Sir Francis O'Neill held the lands of Kellystown. The lease was in the name of Mr. Brabazon of Mornington, and in the simplicity of his nature and the confidence of friendship, Sir Francis surrendered it to his landlord, for a new lease made *directly to himself*, on better terms. Casting aside the mask he had worn, his landlord caused the simple and too confiding baronet to be served with ejectment, and had him evicted; for his lease was void in law, under the "popery acts." Removing for temporary convenience, under pressure of the sheriff's warrant, to a small farm called Cradh, adjoining Dowth Hall, on the estate of Lord Netterville, Sir Francis O'Neill shortly after left it, and took the farm of Knockanmooney, opposite to

Kellystown, his former residence—the river dividing them. But here, encumbered with a large family,—he had fourteen or fifteen children,—he became embarrassed in circumstances, let his rent fall into arrear, was ejected for non-payment, sold out, and turned adrift once more.

Retiring into the village of Slane, Sir Francis O'Neill, sixth baronet, the descendant of a race of the Kings, representative of the dashing dragoon of Edge Hill, and the cousin of three Peers, Mornington, Dunsany, and Meath, rents a cabin of four apartments, and keeps in it a small huckster's shop and dairy, the produce of two cows, while his two horses and carts, last remnant of his stock, attended by his second son, John O'Neill, cart flour for hire from the mills of Slane to Dublin! In that humble cabin the aged and poverty-stricken baronet was visited in the month of May, 1798, by John, the first Viscount O'Neill, and his two sons, Charles and John, the late earl and the last viscount, on their way to Shane's Castle; for John, the first Lord O'Neill, princely in mind as he was exalted in station, never turned his face from a poor relation. On that occasion Sir Francis O'Neill took a melancholy pleasure in shewing to his lordship the last remnant of his family plate, a silver cream ewer and tablespoon, engraven with his crest, the hand and dagger, also the Patent of Baronetcy, with its large, old-fashioned wax seal, and his parchment pedigree, tracing his descent from the prince schoolmaster, Niul of Scythia and Egypt. And in a little outhouse or shed, open at three sides, in that humble yard, he also pointed out his broken carriage, emblazoned with his arms, *the red hand* of O'Neill, which was almost effaced and illegible from exposure to wind and rain. Fit emblem it was of the broken fortunes of his house! The noble Viscount did not live to fulfil the promise he then made to better the condition of this reduced gentleman of his house, for in a short month afterwards he was in his grave—barbarously and treacherously murdered at Antrim by the rebels of Killead. Sir Francis O'Neill himself, shocked by the event, and by the feeling that the last reed on which he depended was broken, soon followed, and in the year 1799 was placed beside his father, Sir Henry, in the grave, inside the ruins of the old church of Mount Newton. In a year and a half after his interment, his wife, the Lady O'Neill, was laid by his side.

It is almost needless to follow the fortunes of his children. One only retained the rank and position of a gentleman. His eldest son, Henry, when his father had began to fail in circumstances, went out to Spain to his relative, Colonel Con O'Neill, formerly of Carlyan in the Freeva, who procured a commission for him in his own regiment. The last letter received from him by his relatives in Ireland was dated in 1798. John, the second son, married Catherine Murtagh, who kept a small dyer's shop in West Street, Drogheda, and died in very humble circumstances indeed, about sixteen or seventeen years ago. Frances O'Neill, the eldest son of John, is now a working millwright in Drogheda. James, another son of Sir Francis, was a working baker in Dublin, and died about the year 1800.

Bryan, the youngest, and only surviving son of Sir Francis O'Neill, had an eventful life. Born in Kellystown, shortly before they left it, he went with his father to Cradh, Knockamooney, and Slane. Here he grew up in poverty, but fortunately received a fair mercantile education. He enlisted, when about eighteen years of age, in the Louth Militia, in which he rose to the rank of sergeant, and volunteered in 1812 into the 88th or Connaught Rangers, commanded by Colonel O'Malley, whose sister, Dora, had married John O'Neill, Esq., of Ballyshannon. He was promoted in 1813 to the rank of serjeant-major, which he held for seventeen years, until his discharge in 1830. He joined the 88th at Castlebar, went thence to Gibraltar and Portugal, and returning to Gibraltar, was sent to Cadiz, to strengthen the garrison there. He afterwards passed again into Portugal, where he was at the storming of Badajos, and the battles of Fuentez D'Onore and Rodrigo, and subsequently accompanied the army of occupation to France in 1816: he returned home in 1818, and in 1830 was discharged at Langard Fort in England, on a pension of two shillings and two pence a day. In all his campaigns he did not receive a single wound, or as he expresses it himself, "a single scratch," although he did his duty, in battle, as one of the "fighting eighty-eighth knew how to do it." In 1830 he was appointed by the corporation of the city of Dublin chief officer of the Newgate guard—a quaint-looking corps, dressed up in costume not unlike the Royal Artillery, who required a strict disciplinarian like Serjeant-Major O'Neill to preside over them. He was discontinued in this office at the break-up of the guard in 1836, when he took two houses in Cook Street, Dublin, in one of which, number 95, he now resides, with his eldest son, Francis O'Neill, a coffinmaker!

Sergeant-Major Bryan O'Neill, youngest son of Sir Francis O'Neill, the sixth baronet, is now in his seventy-fifth year, and is a tall and distinguished-looking man, in whose appearance and manners, notwithstanding his age and poverty, and the ordeal through which he has passed, may be traced the high lineage and noble blood of Clanaboy.

And thus I close this sketch of the decadence of a branch of the royal house of O'Neill, in which the mutability of fortune is signally displayed. The descendant of Prince Niul of Scythia and Egypt, of Milesius, King in Spain, of the royal author, Cormac Udfadha, of Con of " the hundred battles," and Niall the Great, of the chivalrous Niall Caille, and Hugh Boy, and Brian Balv, and Henry Caoch, and the gallant and dashing Colonel of Charles the First's dragoons at the battle of Edge Hill, the cousin of three peers and a duke, and the lineal descendant of a hundred kings, is reduced to the humble lot of a discharged pensioner of the crown, at two shillings and twopence a day, and occupies a room in a small shop in an obscure street, where his eldest son is a coffin-maker!

MacCarthy More.

"How chang'd! Those oaks that tower'd so high,
Dismember'd, stript, extended lie."

The decay of great families is generally to be traced either to personal extravagance or to attainder and forfeiture, consequent on political commotions: but in Ireland, the causes of decadence are manifold, in addition to those I have just alluded to. When it is remembered how perpetually that country has been the scene of civil strife, dynastic contests, and English confiscations, one can hardly believe that any of the old houses have survived, and continue, even unto this time, to be lords of some part of their original patrimony. Yet there are many such: the Geraldines, who

". . . . . royally once reigned
O'er Desmond broad and rich Kildare, and English arts disdained,"

still stand foremost in the Irish peerage, and have preserved, with national love and national accord, the first place among the Anglo-Norman races, ever since the day when Maurice Fitz-Gerald, the renowned companion in arms of Strongbow, set foot on Irish ground, at Wexford, in 1169. Of the other families established in Ireland at the same period, some few besides have succeeded in escaping destruction, and may be reckoned among the present nobles of the land; the principal of these are the De Burghs of Clanricarde, the FitzMaurices, the Butlers, the De Courcys, the St. Lawrences, the Talbots of Malahide, the Brabazons, the Prendergasts, &c. Among the native Irish, there are few traceable descendants of the minor dynasts now in the enjoyment of their ancient possessions, but, of the five royal families which divided the island, all, excepting the O'Melaghlins, who disappear at a very early epoch, may, I am inclined to think, be carried down to some existing representative.

M'Murrough, King of Leinster has for male heir, Kavanagh of Borris, co. Carlow, who possesses a splendid estate in the heart of Leinster. Of the O'Neills, one branch exists on the continent; the present Mr. O'Neill, of Shane's Castle, is heir general of the Princes of Clanaboy, and Mr. C. H. O'Neill, Barrister, Dublin, claims the high honour of being their male representative. The O'Briens were Kings of Thomond or North Munster. The Earls of Thomond derived their earldom, and the present Lord Inchiquin his barony, from the last monarch of their name, who resigned his crown to Henry VIII., and received those titles and a regrant of his estate as some compensation. The O'Connors, last monarchs of Ireland, have still an heir male in Connaught, and the MacCarthy-Mores, Kings of Desmond or South Munster, and the MacCarthy-Reaghs, Princes of Muskerry, are in all probability represented in the male line by Mr. MacCarthy of Carrignavar.

Of the minor dynasts the Ulster plantation has left few

or none in that province. In that part of Leinster which formed the old territory of the Pale, the O'Byrnes of Wicklow, protected by their mountains, were the last sept to preserve their independence. Lord de Tabley, their present chief, has laid aside his ancient warrior name, and cannot be counted amongst Irishmen; but a branch of the family still reside on a very valuable portion of their old lands at Cabinteely, on the borders of Wicklow and Dublin. The central district of Ireland, including the old kingdom of Meath, is better provided with true Milesian blood. O'Moore of Cloghan, chief of his name, was, until recently, seated in the centre of Leix; and though an English reader might take the surname of the late Earl of Upper Ossory to be Anglo-Norman, yet the fine estates of that nobleman, now held by the Right Hon. John W. Fitzpatrick, were his as heir to the younger branch of the clan Mac Giolla Phadruig. The Foxes of Foxhall in Longford have in like manner Anglicised O'Sionach, to which clan their family and estates belonged. Cavan and its borders in Meath were, and are partly still, the share of the O'Reillys, a Westmeath branch of which has taken the name of Nugent. In the province of Connaught, forfeitures and Elizabethan or Cromwellian blood are less common than in other parts of the island; and with the exception of the noble house of Browne, the formerly ennobled Eyres, the Knoxes, and perhaps, (despite the Sarsfield connectionship), I could add the Binghams, all the great proprietors derive the whole or the greater part of their blood and estates from ancestors of Milesian or Anglo-Norman descent, but chiefly the latter. Of the undoubted Milesians, I find Charles K. O'Hara, Esq. holding his ancient patrimony in Sligo, Sir Samuel O'Malley owning lands so bravely preserved by his celebrated kinswoman, Grace O'Malley, in the rapacious days of Queen Elizabeth; and Mr. O'Flahertie, of Lemonfield, become a peaceful neighbour of that town of Galway, whose timid merchants used to suffer so much from the turbulent clan from which he springs, that over their western gate appeared the prayerful inscription:

" From the ferocious O'Flaherties, Good Lord, deliver us."

Sir Richard O'Donnell's branch of the house of Tyrconnel is said to have settled in Mayo on the marriage of its founder with the heiress; the same cause, a richly-dowered heiress, certainly brought the O'Dalys from Burreen to Galway, a damsel in whose honour the charming air of Aileen Aroon is said to have been composed, having given them the broad lands of Carrownekelly, now the valuable estate of their lineal descendant, Lord Dunsandle. The eastern portion of Connaught was anciently the principality of the O'Kellys; and members of that sept, Mr. Kelly of Castle Kelly, in particular, still retain a large part of the lands which were held by that historical family.

In Munster, between the rapacity of the Desmond family at its first settlement, which devoured the substance of many of its Hibernian neighbours, and its immense power and influence just before its ruin, which induced most of the remaining ones to join and perish with it, the greater or princely families are not numerous. But many of the minor ones exist in affluence. The M'Namaras, or Sons of the Sea, so called from claiming a mermaid as their mother, are well represented by Lieut. Col. M'Namara, and by Mr. M'Namara of Ayle, in that, their original county. Mr. O'Loghlen, of Port, nephew to the late eminent Sir Michael O'Loghlen, is the direct descendant of the chieftains of Burreed. The O'Gradys have divided: and whilst one branch, under the name of Brady, still retains a beautiful park, a fine estate in their old territory at Schariff on the banks of the Shannon, a fair southern heiress (these heiresses seem ever to have been favourites in Ireland) tempted the other, at the close of the thirteenth century, across that river to the county of Limerick, where it has formed several influential families. The O'Grady of Kilballyowen is chief of the name; and a younger branch was raised to the peerage in the person of the late eminent Chief Baron Viscount Guillamore. The O'Quins also left Clare for Limerick, but at a more recent date. The estate of Adair, confirmed to them by the Act of Settlement, is now the picturesque residence of their representative the Earl of Dunraven. The chief branch of the O'Sullivans of Kerry is probably extinct; but some of the minor ones are extant; and the wild mountains that give him his title are still the property of one of their chiefs, Mac Gillycuddy of the Reeks. We find the O'Donoghues of the Glyns still in the same neighbourhood. Mr. Ryan, of Inch, is probably the chief, certainly a descendant, of the ancient sept of his name. And the district of which his estates form part was the ancient " O'Ryan's country;" whilst the O'Meaghers of Kilmoyler, and some other members of that family, are yet proprietors where their clan was once seated in Tipperary. But that county was too fertile, and too near the other possessions of the great rival houses of Ormonde and Desmond not to have been early appropriated by the Anglo-Norman conquerors, to whose descendants much of it and of its neighbouring counties of Kilkenny and Waterford still belongs.

The MacCarthys, to whom I have already alluded, were a regal and princely house: and, on the arrival of the English invaders in the twelfth century, were styled the Kings of Desmond and Cork. No family claims a higher ancestry than this. The curious in long genealogies will find in Keating's "History of Ireland" the whole pedigree, derived, through Heber, the fair son of Milesius, the Spanish hero, from the patriarch Noah himself! In all those civil contests and warlike encounters which shed so melancholy a hue over the annals of their ever-distracted country, the MacCarthys bore a distinguished part. From Cormac More, who lived in the beginning of the twelfth century, sprang two sons: Daniel, the elder, succeeded his father as "the MacCarthy-More," and Diarmid, the younger, founded the powerful house of Muskerry. The descendant of Daniel was created Earl of Glencare by Queen Elizabeth, in 1565, but as he died without legitimate issue, his honours died with him. His last collateral male representative was Charles MacCarthy-More, an officer in the Guards, who died in 1770. The dwindled possessions of this branch of the family became vested in his cousin, Herbert, of Mucruss. I have somewhere seen a curious anecdote regarding a late descendant of this illustrious race. One MacCarthy, a poor farmer in the county of Cork, who deemed himself, and perhaps correctly, the rightful heir of the Kings of Desmond, kept up, in his humble homestead, all the semblance of royal state that his lowly condition would permit. His simple meals were supplied to him at a table apart from the rest of his family, a custom invariably followed in the olden time, when the MacCarthy-More held regal sway in his Castle of Kilcoleman.

The descendants of Diarmid MacCarthy had a longer existence as magnates of the land. They held Blarney and a large portion of the county of Cork. The fourth Lord, Cormac, was a nobleman of distinguished valour, and a munificent patron of the church, of art, and of learning. The Castle of Blarney was erected by him, as also the splendid Abbey of Kilcrea. His successor, Cormac, had a fearful feud with James, Earl of Desmond, whom he defeated with much slaughter near Mourne Abbey, in 1521. The eighth Lord, Cormac MacTeige, according to Sir Henry Sidney, "the rarest man that was ever born among the Irishry," was appointed Sheriff of the county of Cork, after he had defeated Sir James, brother of the Earl of Desmond.

The power of the MacCarthys at this period may be conjectured from the fact that a force of three thousand fighting men were always at the call of the chieftain. This Cormac was politic enough to keep in favour with the English. To him James the First granted for ever the lordship, town, and lands of Blarney. Donogh, the tenth lord, took an early and decided part in the dreadful civil war which broke out in 1641. He was appointed one of the leaders of the confederated Catholics, and Lord Castlehaven reports that he used all his influence to bring the nation back to their obedience to the king and laws. In 1642 he appeared in Carberry at the head of a large force, led by his own feudatories, MacCarthy Reagh, O'Donovan, O'Sullivan, &c. He was opposed by Inchiquin, the chief of the O'Briens of Thomond, who defeated him. Soon afterwards, however, the king made him president of Munster. On the Restoration, he was created Earl of Clancarty, and a bill was passed which restored a large portion of his forfeited estates. Donogh, the third earl, joined James II. on his landing at Kinsale, and with the fortunes of James fell those of Clancarty. His property, which, on a loose calculation made in the middle of the last century, was supposed to be worth £150,000 per annum, was confiscated, and he was taken prisoner on the surrender of Cork, and driven into exile. The fourth Earl, Robert, indignant at the treatment his family had received, deserted the king's service as captain of the ship Adventure, and joining the Stuarts, never after returned to England. The French king granted him a pension of £1000 a-year, and he lived and died at his chateau near Boulogne, leaving two sons, who dying without issue, the family in the direct line expired.

So ended the chief line of this distinguished but turbulent race; like many others of their princely compeers, they sowed to the storm, and reaped the whirlwind. One eminent and recognised offshoot, MacCarthy of Carrignavar, continued to flourish long after the parent stem had withered away; but the ruthless spoliation of the

Encumbered Estates' Court has doomed even this last scion almost to destruction, and within the last few years condemned to sale the greater part of the small remaining remnant of the vast territorial possessions of the Lords of Muskerry. Male heirs, still, however, exist, and the castle of Carrignavar is preserved; but though thus, in a great measure, severed from their ancient patrimony, they will not soon be forgotten in the land of their ancestors. The veneration of the Irish peasantry for "the rale ould gentry" will long cling to the cherished name of Mac-Carthy.

The Maguires of Tempo,
co. Fermanagh.

"Maguire is leader of their battalions,
He rules over the mighty men of Monach,
At home munificent in presents,
The noblest lord in hospitality."

O'Dugan, 14th century.

The fame of "the three Collas," grandsons of the accomplished monarch Cormac Ulfadha, is celebrated by the old chroniclers in many a page of Irish story. With their invasion of Ulster, early in the fourth century, commenced the most sanguinary struggle on record. The old inhabitants—the brave Clanna-Rory—fought, with their traditional valour, for their very existence; their enemies, the Colla-Huais, for conquest and a settlement. Their last battle of Aghderg, in the county of Down, continued while "six suns rose and went down," and ended in the defeat and ruin of the Clanna-Rory. The renowned Red-branch Knights disappeared for ever from history, and their princely palace of Emania, whose construction formed one of the great epochs of Irish chronology, was destroyed, and not a trace of its long-celebrated glories was left behind.

From Colla-da-Chrioch, the youngest of the brothers, descended the Maguires, Princes of Fermanagh, and Lords of Enniskillen, who assumed the surname, in the ninth century, from Uidher, or "Guire," ninth in descent from Colla-da-Chrioch.

These Maguires kept right noble state in their princely halls in their castles of Enniskillen, Portora, and Monea in Fermanagh. They had their allamhs or bards, their hereditary brehons or judges, and other chief officers of state. When they marched to compel eiric, or join the muster of their dynast, the great O'Neill, King of Ulster, Mac Caffrey, their hereditary standard-bearer, unfurled the standard of *Mac Uidher* at the head of a thousand warriors. On the summit of the magnificent Culcagh, a mountain near Swanlinbar, on the borders of Cavan and Fermanagh, The Maguire was inaugurated as Prince of Fermanagh: and an imposing ceremony it was. No canopy but the blue vault of heaven, emblazoned with the glorious sun; multitudes of Clansmen clustered on the top, and the sides, and by the foot of the hill, the Chief himself stood on a stone chair of state: the laws were read to him by the Brehon, the oath administered, and the blessing given by the *Coarb* of Clogher, the white wand of sovereignty placed in his hand, the standard unfurled, and the slipper put on, when, amid the clang of bucklers, the music of a hundred harps, and the ringing cheers of thousands of the Clan Mac Uider, he was pronounced THE MAGUIRE.

Fermanagh was called in remote times "Maguire's country," where for twelve hundred years and more the

Maguires maintained their power as independent princes. Tributaries to the O'Neills, Kings of Ulster, and often allied to them by marriage, they proved ever stanch to their suzerains; the first to attend muster, and to rally under the royal standard of *Lamh-derg Eirin*, "the red hand of Ireland," was Maguire's contingent. In the roar of battle the voices of the stout men of Fermanagh were loudest, and their good battle-axes keenest in hewing through the dense masses of opposing foes.

Space will not permit more than a passing allusion to those brave chiefs, but from amongst them all, I cannot refrain from giving a brief outline of the career of the last Prince of Fermanagh, the gallant Hugh Maguire, in the reign of Elizabeth. His father's sister, Judith—a proud and stately dame—was mother of the great Hugh O'Neill, Earl of Tyrone. After the death of his father, he was harassed by the pretensions of Connor Roe Maguire, called "the Queen's Maguire," who joined the English and disputed the chieftaincy with him. When the Lord Deputy Fitzwilliam informed him that his country being now "shire ground," he must prepare to admit a sheriff to execute the Queen's writs, he answered characteristically, " Your sheriff shall be welcome, *but let me know his eiric* (how much his life is worth), *that if my people should cut off his head, I may levy it upon the country.*" Afterwards, in the year 1593, Captain Willis is found in his country as sheriff, but shut up with his *posse comitatus*, and besieged in a church by the Fermanagh people, where he was reduced to the last extremity until relieved by Hugh O'Neill, then an ally of the English. The forces of Fermanagh being in the field, did not lay down arms. Maguire led them southwards, and at Tulsk, in Roscommon, defeated Sir Richard Bingham, the governor of Connaught, and slew Sir William Clifford. Shortly afterwards he fought the battle of Athcullin, on the river Erne, against Marshal Bagnall, and forced Hugh O'Neill, who had charged across the river at the head of the English cavalry, to recross it, after being severely wounded. In 1594 he again defeated Sir George Bingham at the battle of Beal-atha-na-riscoid, or "yellow biscuits," on the river Erne, within four miles of Enniskillen, then garrisoned by English troops, and forced the garrison to surrender. In the following year, 1595, he entered, plundered, and devastated Brefney O'Reilly, the country of "the Queen's O'Reilly." When Hugh O'Neill rose in alliance with O'Donnell, Maguire joined his standard and never after left him. He was with O'Neill at the battle of Clontibret, where Sir John Norris was defeated; also at the battle of Killcloony, where the united armies of the Lord Deputy Sir William Russell and Sir John Norris were routed with the loss of six hundred men. He commanded O'Neill's cavalry at the battle of Mullaghbrack in 1596, and contributed considerably to the victory.

In 1597, while O'Neill was fighting the great battle of Drumfluich against the new Lord Deputy Burrough, Maguire was in Mullingar on the invitation of the O'Farrells, preying on and plundering the English of the Pale in that quarter. In 1598, he was by the side of O'Neill and O'Donnell, "Red Hugh," in the great victory obtained at Bealanaboy, where Marshall Bagnall and about three thousand of the English were slain, with many superior officers. In the next year, 1599, he joined O'Donnell in his expedition into Thomond, and parting him there for a time, attacked and took the Baron O'Brien's castle of Inchiquin, with the baron himself prisoner; and having swept all the surrounding country, rejoined O'Donnell at Kelfenora, laden with spoil. He was with O'Neill at the celebrated conference between him and the Earl of Essex at the ford of Ballacluish, near Dundalk. In the year 1600 he accompanied that chieftain as commander of his horse, in his great expedition into Leinster and Munster, to punish his enemies and reconcile and unite his friends, where at O'Neill's camp, on the borders of Muskerry and Carberry, the chiefs of Munster attended and gave eighteen hostages. Here the gallant Maguire closed his brilliant career and his life. One day in March, shortly before the festival of St. Patrick, he went out from O'Neill's camp, accompanied by Felim McCaffrey, his standard-bearer, and a small party of horse, and some foot, to reconnoitre the country towards Cork. Sir William St. Leger, Vice President of Munster, was informed of it by a spy, and placed a strong party in ambush in a narrow defile about a mile from Cork. On nearing the place, Maguire espied them, but nothing daunted, though the odds against him were fearfully great, he stuck spurs into his horse and dashed at the head of a small troop into the midst of his enemies. Singling out St. Leger, who shot him on his approach with a pistol, he cleft his head through buckler and helmet, leaving him dead on the spot, and cut his way through the ranks of opposing horsemen—

five of whom he killed with his single arm, and escaped; but gashed and cut fearfully about the head, as he was, by the sabres of his foes, the brave Maguire did not proceed far until he fell exhausted, and on the following day delivered up his gallant spirit to Heaven. O'Neill and the other Irish chiefs mourned his loss, and laid him in a southern grave. He was the last prince of Fermanagh, for none of the chiefs of it after his time possessed the power or property of their ancestors sufficient to sustain the rank.

On the death of the gallant Hugh, his brother Constantine became The Maguire, and joined O'Neill, whose cause he sustained until the submission of the Earl in 1603. Afterwards, in 1607, when O'Neill and O'Donnell meditated their flight from Ireland, it was Con Maguire, aided by O'Brien, who brought the Spanish ship to the harbour of Lough Swilly, in which they and their friends embarked; Maguire himself died soon after at Geneva, while preparing to go to Spain.

After this event the entire of Fermanagh was confiscated by James the First. In the redistribution of lands Bryan Maguire obtained two thousand acres of Tempo-dassel, and Connor Roe, the "Queen's Maguire," thirteen thousand three hundred acres. The son of the latter, Bryan Roe, was created Baron of Enniskillen, and by his marriage with a sister of the celebrated General Owen Roe, O'Neill was father of Connor Lord Maguire, who was attainted, and his estates confiscated, for being concerned in the rebellion of 1691: he was conveyed to the Tower of London, and after a lengthened imprisonment, was brought to trial, and condemned, hanged, and beheaded at Tyburn, in February,

1644. The title, nevertheless, was assumed by his son and descendants, the last of whom, Alexander Maguire, called the eighth baron, was a captain in Buckley's regiment in the Irish brigade in the service of France.

Several chiefs of the Maguires are mentioned during the Cromwellian and Williamite wars; and many of them became distinguished officers in the French and Austrian armies.

The descendants of Bryan Maguire of Tempo, "senior of the race," contrived to retain the lands granted to him by James the First, through every after-vicissitude, until the commencement of the present century, when the property passed from the late Constantine Maguire, Esq., chief of his race and last inheritor of Tempo, into the hands of a Belfast merchant.

Mr. Constantine Maguire was a gentleman of refined education and polished manners. After leaving Tempo, he resided chiefly at Toureen Lodge, near Cahir, on a small estate he had in the county of Tipperary, where he lost his life in a mysterious and barbarous manner. On Saturday, the 1st of November, 1834, Mr. Maguire and a lady of his family were out walking on the lawn, adjoining the high road in front of his mansion. After a short time his companion left him, and proceeded towards the house to order breakfast. She had scarcely reached it when she heard a shot fired. Running back she saw two men escaping from the lawn at full speed, and found Mr. Maguire stretched on the grass, a lifeless and mangled corpse. A ball had passed through his heart, and his head was literally smashed and battered to pieces, apparently with the butt-end of a musket. The murderers escaped, and, notwithstanding the offer in the Dublin Gazette of a large reward, no trace of them was ever discovered. Like the kindred assassinations, which took place afterwards in Ireland, of the second Lord Norbury and Mrs. Kelly, the murder of Mr. Maguire has remained shrouded in mystery.

Upon the death of Mr. Constantine Maguire, his younger brother and heir male, the celebrated duellist, Bryan Butler Maguire, popularly known as "Captain Bryan Maguire," became chief of his race, but inherited no part of the ancient patrimony.

The life of Captain Maguire was an eventful one, and contained as many startling incidents as would supply materials for half-a-dozen modern novels. He wrote and published his Memoirs in 1812, but his subsequent career, to which I shall by and by refer, was still more singular. In 1799, when very young, he obtained a cadetship in the East India Company's service, and joined the 8th Regiment of native infantry at Cochin, formerly a Dutch settlement on the coast of Malabar. Here he is found, with some other Irish officers, incurring the enmity, and it seems also the "jealousy," of the Dutch gentlemen, who prohibited their daughters from "dancing with the gentlemen of the army," and at public assemblies and balls the novel spectacle was exhibited of "unmarried ladies dancing with their own relations, and wives with their husbands." Both parties being bent on mischief, it was not long until their bellicose propensities were developed. Captain Maguire, who seems to have been the chief object of Dutch animosity, was attacked, sword in hand, in a public billiard-room "by a Captain

Thuring of the *Minerva*." Maguire defended himself with "a large black billiard cue," forced his antagonist out of the room, and fractured his scull, of which he died in a few weeks after, at Andengo. The governor now interfered, and the officers not on active service were ordered to rejoin their regiments. Maguire and his friends embarked on board the *Deria Dowla*, and landed at Callicut, where his companions and he parted, and he set out in an open boat for Bombay, a distance of three hundred miles. Finding this small craft unequal to so long a voyage, Maguire formed the bold resolution of cutting out a vessel from the roads of Goa. His six servants—Lascars, stout, resolute fellows—entered heartily into the project, and, in a dark night, laid him alongside a Portuguese vessel half laden. Boarding in silence, they closed down the hatches on the crew, thirteen in number, and stood out to sea. As they neared Port Victoria, a pirate vessel hove in sight, and bore down on Maguire, who, nothing daunted, fired into the enemy his only gun, "an iron four-pound swivel, crammed with iron balls rolled up in an old worsted stocking;" which "so astonished the pirate that he sheered off," and Maguire reached Bombay in safety. But here, again, his evil genius followed him in the shape of two of his old Dutch acquaintances of Cochin. They had him arrested and tried before the Recorder, Sir James Mackintosh, "for waylaying and assaulting" them. A "scene in court" took place at the trial. The judge was secretly cautioned to be on his guard, as Maguire intended to shoot him when delivering sentence. The prisoner was searched in open court, but the charge of attempting to assassinate the judge turned out to be groundless. A verdict, however, was given against him, for the attack on the Dutchmen, and he was sentenced to twelve months' imprisonment. On another occasion, he and some friends were returning in the evening from the woods, after a "jollification," when one of them "incautiously discharged his gun into the tent of Major G—— ;" the ball passing in rather close proximity to that gallant gentleman's head, Maguire and another of the party were tried for malicious shooting. The former defended himself in court in a speech of much tact and ability, and took occasion to repudiate the charge, industriously circulated against him, of being a "professed duellist." He was acquitted, but soon after got into another affair, which compromised his position in the army. He became the bearer of two written challenges to an officer of the Bombay European regiment, who brought him to a courtmartial; and the articles of war being very severe against duelling, Maguire was cashiered after eight years' service. On his way home, the fleet was detained a short time at St. Helena. One day, during his stay there, Maguire entered a public room, in a tavern, where a number of officers were enjoying themselves rather freely, the band-master of the regiment being seated at a piano. The officers ordered the intruder out in a *brusque* manner, which he politely declined ; when they vociferated, "Throw him out of the window!" Maguire coolly presented a pistol. The officers, headed by Major Mac D——, advanced on him sword in hand. Retreating to the wall, he protested that, in defence of his life, he would shoot the first man who crossed a line he had marked. Major Mac D—— still rushed on, when Maguire fired, and shot him dead on the spot. Instantly putting the discharged pistol behind his back, he cocked and presented it as a second one loaded, at the rest, who fled. He was tried on the charge of murder, and acquitted, but put on board by the authorities. It was not long after he had reached London before he got into another serious squabble. Seated one evening in a box in the Golden Cross Tavern, Charing Cross, two gentlemen were speaking near him in a loud tone. One of them, a Mr. T——, told the other he had "intimidated a big Irishman at the play the night before; that he had several affairs with men of that nation, and always found them to be empty swaggerers." Maguire's temper was roused at this disparagement of his countrymen, and he called on the gentleman to retract the calumny. The other refused, when Maguire threw his glove in his face. A meeting was immediately arranged, the parties to fight with swords until one was killed. They adjourned to an adjoining room, and placed four candles in it, one at each corner. They then stripped and sparred for some time. Maguire stood on the defensive, to ascertain his adversary's mode of fighting, and in the course of six minutes received three slight wounds, from which the blood flowed copiously. He then made a " desperate display of skill," and in less than three seconds ran his sword through the body of his adversary, who fell on the floor, bathed in blood. The gentleman's wound was bound up, and fortunately proved not to be mortal.

After this, Maguire is found involved as principal or

second in numerous "affairs of honour," up to the year 1812, when he published his Memoirs. These transactions were duly chronicled in the police office reports and newspapers of the day. In one of those cases, Captain Maguire writes to the friend of his antagonist, " I protest to God that I *will follow him all over the world until I make him explain.*"

But it would take a work in itself of considerable magnitude to record all the eccentricities, strange adventures, and vicissitudes in the life of Captain Bryan Maguire: I will not stop to narrate how he was shot through the lungs by an attorney, who, awkwardly enough, insisted on firing across a table, and how neither died, though dangerously wounded; nor will I record his frequent *rencontres* with bailiffs in their attempts to arrest him for debt; nor his extraordinary escapades when arrested and confined, as, for instance, his distilling alcohol in an old iron kettle, (transformed by his ever-fertile genius and mechanical skill into a portable still), and his keeping his fellow prisoners in a perpetual round of inebriation, to the amazement of the unconscious governors, whose vigilance prevented the possibility of the smuggling into the prison of spirituous liquors. I must not, however, omit mention of his shooting practice at break of day, from the windows of his lodgings in St. Andrew's Street, Dublin, at the cross on the " Round Church;" or of his retreat from the officers of justice to the county of Wicklow, where, located in an old thatched cabin on the brink of a hill, he threw up a fortification of earthworks, and mounting an old brass field piece, defied his enemies, while he levied voluntary contributions from the neighbouring farmers, who were rather pleased with his outlaw mode of life, acting as an independent chief among them in open defiance of the law.

The good citizens of Dublin will not fail to remember how in the evenings, about four o'clock, the captain was to be seen, bearded like a pard, promenading up and down Sackville Street on the single flag path which adorned the outer edge of the footway on the post office side, with a "huge Irish blackthorn" in hand, and how every person on his approach gave way and stepped aside upon the muddy footway.

These strange freaks, which in the present day would necessitate a lengthened visit to a prison or an asylum, were then viewed, among a certain class of Irish sporting gentlemen, as harmless eccentricities, and the amusements of an accomplished "fire-eater," in his lighter moments.

But eccentric follies and vain-glorious feats, sooner or later, must terminate. As time wore on, Captain Maguire became entangled in a heavy Chancery suit for his wife's fortune, which he never realized, and he became reduced, step by step, to the extreme of poverty, eking out a precarious subsistence from the casual contributions of a few friends. Writing to one of these, on the 28th of May, 1830, he says, "I request to see you, without delay, if possible. My son George is dying. I am unable to go to you. I am served with notice by the landlord, and have neither house nor home to go to." His son George, a fine intelligent lad of twelve years old, did die, and the unfortunate parent, who, whatever may have been his faults and follies while in the heyday of youth, health, and prosperity, had at least the strongest natural feelings, would not part with the remains of his child, but embalmed his body with his own hands—for he had acquired a knowledge of the art in the East and placed the case in his bed-room, where he kept it for some years. Writing again, in the month of February, 1831, about the Chancery suit, which made but slow progress, under the rules of procedure in those days, he observes, "It compels me at this season of the year, and the roads so bad, to send my son (Charles), ragged and nearly barefooted, to you with this. * * * Margaret died of starvation while the suit proceeded." And on the 27th of June, 1831, he writes again to the same party, "Nothing but the very deplorable state to which you have seen me reduced would make me trespass on you for the trifle I mentioned, to purchase some medicine to soften the dreadful cough I have—being shot through the lungs once—the cough may end fatally with me if it is not attended to. * * * I say from my heart may God defend every unfortunate mortal that is situated like yours truly, B. B. Maguire."

When the news of the assassination of his elder brother was communicated to him, Bryan Maguire, the once dashing officer and dare-devil, the chief of the proud lords of Fermanagh, was found in a large old-fashioned wastehouse at Clontarf Sheds, denuded of every comfort. The room he occupied had for furniture neither drapery nor carpet, but a single deal table, a chair and an old form. On the floor was a mattress of the poorest description, on which he lay, with barely any covering, day and night, for his wearing apparel was in pawn; his gun and a brace of pistols, last remnant of his former self, hung over the chimney-piece, and the embalmed body of his eldest son still rested in a shell in the corner. His second and only remaining child, Charles Maguire, a fine, strong, enduring boy of about fourteen years of age, a mere drudge and servant-of-all-work to his father, was his sole companion. In the next year, 1835, Captain Maguire was ejected from this his last asylum, at the instance of one who had, in other and better days, professed himself to be his friend, and who is now no more. The unfortunate man did not long survive his eviction, but died in a few months afterwards, somewhere about Finglas, and not a stone marks the spot where he sleeps in death. Charles Maguire, his sole surviving child, remained with him to the last, and then went on board a merchant vessel as a common sailor, and was never more heard of.

But although the race of Tempo has become extinct, it is gratifying to record that a healthy branch of the old tree still flourishes in the family of Maguire, now represented by Edward Maguire, Esq., of Gortoral House, barrister-at-law, a justice of the peace for the county of Fermanagh; in that county as well as in Leitrim, he is possessed of a fair landed estate, and on his Fermanagh property stands the picturesque and ivy-clad ruin of one of the castles of his ancestors, princes and chiefs of the MacUidher.

The Fall of Desmond.

"The knights are dust,
Their good swords rust;
Their souls are with the saints, I trust!"
COLERIDGE.

THEY were a gifted as well as a brave race, those Desmonds. They and the present ducal Geraldines of Leinster derived from a common ancestor: they were contemporaries in their accession to the dignity of Earls, and twins in renown, influence, and vastness of territory. Gerald, the fourth earl, was called "the poet," and that deep susceptibility of the beautiful, which is the vital spring of the poetic nature, was, unluckily for him, inherited by his grandson, Thomas, the sixth earl. Wearied and benighted, one ill-starred evening, on his return from hunting, he took refuge in the Abbey of Feale in Kerry, the dwelling of a tenant, named William MacCormack. The Earl "came, saw, and," if he "conquered," became no less the conquest of MacCormack's lovely daughter Catherine. He married her, and the consequence was loss of title and estate: his uncle, James, forcibly usurped both, and Desmond, after several fruitless attempts to regain his birthright, died an exile at Rouen, in 1420, King Henry V. himself, it is said, honouring the funeral obsequies with his valorous presence, though he had overlooked the wrong. Moore has thus gracefully sung this ill-fated love story:—

THE DESMOND.

"By the Feale's wave benighted,
  No star in the skies,
To thy door, by love lighted,
  I first saw those eyes.
Some voice whispered o'er me,
  As the threshold I cross'd,
There was ruin before me,
  If I loved, I was lost.

"Love came, and brought sorrow
  Too soon in his train;
Yet so sweet, that to-morrow
  'Twere welcome again.
Though misery's full measure
  My portion should be,
I would drain it with pleasure
  If poured out by thee.

"You who call it dishonour
  To bow to this flame,
If you've eyes, look but on her,
  And blush while you blame.
Hath the pearl less whiteness
  Because of its birth?
Hath the violet less brightness
  For growing near earth?

"No! Man for his glory
  To ancestry flies;
But Woman's bright story
  Is told in her eyes.
While the monarch but traces
  Through mortals his line,
Beauty, born of the Graces,
  Ranks next to Divine."

In our days such a proceeding as the uncle's usurpation would be simply impossible, but *then* the Sovereign of England, either occupied by foreign wars or engaged, as in the struggle of the Roses, with claimants to his own throne, was perfectly content that might should take the place of right, so that the adherence of the former could be thus secured and his own authority in Ireland remain undisturbed. Lascelles correctly states in his " Res Gestæ Anglorum in Hiberniâ" (p. 27), "that the influence of the great lords, that of the Earl of Kildare in particular, was superior to the laws;" and the Irish government itself violated its own Statute of Kilkenny, which, with other enactments, made marriages with the Irish high treason, and forbade the tyrannical exaction called *coyne and livery*, to which it had itself recourse. In the reign of Richard III., too, Gerald, Earl of Kildare, Lord Deputy, actually passed an act of Parliament that the men of the town of New Ross might *reprize themselves against robbers*, which means, says Sir William Betham (*Feudal Dignities*, i. 379), that persons robbed might rob the innocent to indemnify themselves for having been previously plundered.

James, the usurping Earl of Desmond, whom Henry VI. appointed Constable of the Castle of Limerick (of whose massy strength a portion yet remains), procured half the vast county of Cork from Robert Fitz-Geoffry Cogan, in addition to his other previous broad domains, and was succeeded by his son Thomas, eighth Earl, who from the possession of these vast estates, and the lofty seat of Lord Deputy of Ireland, fell into a prison, and ended his life on the block in 1467, leaving a successor, himself another example of the vicissitudes to which his family was doomed. After flourishing for twenty years in riches, honour, and power, he was basely murdered by his own servants, aged only twenty-eight.

But the crowning adversity, as also another instance of the usurpations tolerated by the Sovereign of England in Ireland, is presented by Gerald, the sixteenth Earl, the "*Ingens rebellibus exemplar.*" He dispossessed his elder brother of the title and inheritance, thus becoming Lord of a territory extending over a space of one hundred and twenty by fifty square miles, and producing forty thousand gold pieces annually, at a time when money was twenty times more valuable than it was in 1804. Defeated at the termination of his ten years' rebellion against the English crown, he became reduced to the greatest distress, " and," says Camden, in his annals of Queen Elizabeth, "in no place safe, shifted from place to place." For a considerable period he remained wandering among the bogs and mountains, with the utmost difficulty succeeding in warding off actual starvation. At Kilguaigh, near Kilmallock, in the county of Limerick, and in the depth of winter, he and his Countess, Eleanor Butler, daughter of Lord Dunboyne, once escaped the search of the royal adherents only by flying from the miserable hovel which served as their place of concealment, and hiding themselves, sunk up to the throat, in a "lough" of water. Having at last crept into the rugged wilderness of the Kerry mountains, Desmond was congratulating himself on a comparative security, when hunger compelled some of his followers to plunder a few cattle. They were pursued by the owners, guided, it is said, by the treacherous son of a woman who had been nurse to the earl, and the cabin in which the unfortunate Desmond lay, was discovered; here, in the cold dawn of the 11th of November 1583, one of the pursuers, first fracturing the Earl's arm by a sword cut, dragged the aged nobleman out of the hovel, and severed his head from his body. This bloody trophy was sent to Queen Elizabeth, and set up on the Tower of London, or, as others say, on London Bridge. His vast estates were parcelled out among "Undertakers" from England.

Thus expired the great house of Desmond; for though, upon the death of Earl Gerald, James Fitzgerald, son of his wronged elder brother, assumed the title and was recognised as such by the Irish, as indeed was his right, his father having never joined in the rebellion so tragically suppressed; the Queen rejected his petition for restoration to his honours, probably because the estates had been bestowed upon others. This drove him also into rebellion. From his sufferings and privations he was called the "*Sugaun*" Earl, and died a prisoner in London. But James, son of Earl Gerald, the "Ingens exemplar," had been recognised by the Queen as Earl, in order to extinguish the "*Sugaun*." This he did, but was abandoned by the Irish in consequence of his having been brought up in the Protestant faith, while a prisoner in England. He soon returned thither, and died, some say by poison, and John Fitzgerald, brother of the "*Sugaun*" earl, having entered the service of the King of Spain, by whom he was allowed to live in a position very unbefitting his birth or the magnanimity of a monarch, died, leaving one son,

Gerald, created by the Spanish king Count of Desmond. To this barren honour, however, was that Monarch's favour limited; the Count pined in poverty, and at length, in disgust, entered the service of the Emperor of Germany, where he ended his career as became the last of his dignity, for being governor of a fortress, he died, in 1632, of the privations and sufferings consequent on his valiant and inflexible refusal to surrender to a besieging force. Thus was hushed the last of those clarion voices which, at the head of a battle of Gallowglasse and Kerne, had so often startled the ears of their foemen with the slogan of "Shanet Aboo."

> "Peace to each manly soul that sleepeth;
> Rest to each faithful eye that weepeth;
> Long may the fair and brave
> Sigh o'er the hero's grave."

The illustrations of decadence which I have adduced in the foregoing pages are but a small instalment from the materials which offer, and still leave this melancholy chapter of family history far, very far, from being exhausted. But not to encroach overmuch upon the patience of my readers, I will give, for the present, only two or three more examples of these strange vicissitudes.

A high and potent family were the UMFRAVILLES of Northumberland, men of the strong hand and the stout heart—qualities which in the old time gave men the mastery over their fellow-creatures. The patriarch of their race, "Robert with the beard," lord of Tours and Viex, like so many others of his fortunate countrymen, accompanied William the Conqueror in his expedition upon England; and, like them, too, reaped an ample portion of the general plunder. Ten years after the battle of Hastings, he obtained from his royal master a grant of the valley of Redesdale, in Northumberland, with all its castles, woods, and franchises, to hold of him and his heirs for ever, by the service of defending that part of the country from wolves and the king's enemies by "the sword which the said King William wore at his side when he entered Northumberland, and which he gave to the said Robert." But, alas for the instability of all human greatness! this illustrious family, dignified with the titles of baron and earl, was on its wane ere the Russells had yet risen into importance upon the spoils of the church. The last but one of their male descendants in the direct line kept a chandler's shop at Newcastle, but failing in this humble occupation, he was glad to accept the office of keeper of St. Nicholas' workhouse, in the same town, where he died, and left his widow with a son and daughter utterly destitute. Fortune, however, at this dark moment, before turning her face from them for ever, shed a passing gleam upon their extinction. Their sad story came to the ears of the Duke of Northumberland,*

---

* Another anecdote of the munificence of the House of Northumberland I cannot omit here.

At the commencement of the first revolution in France, the Abbé de Percie was obliged to fly from his living in Normandy to this country. Soon after his arrival in London, he was hustled who generously allowed a small pension to the widow, and after educating her son, procured for him a midshipman's appointment. In due course of time, John Umfraville rose to the rank of captain; but he left no issue, and with him expired the illustrious race of Umfraville.

Nothing has more contributed to these startling vicissitudes than the civil wars so long and bloodily maintained between the houses of York and Lancaster. As either party rose or fell in the scale,—and such mutations were not few,—it inflicted or suffered persecution and the worst of cruelties. Death, exile, and pauperism were the constant results to the defeated. Of this, we have a lively picture in the history of Philip de Comines, who narrates how " in the wars between these two contending houses (York and Lancaster) there had been seven or eight memorable battles in England, in which threescore or fourscore per-

in New Street, Covent Garden, and robbed of twenty guineas, which he had received but a few minutes before, at Herries' Bank.

With the remainder of his little property he went to Bath, where that small remnant was soon expended. In this dilemma, he was reminded of his relationship to the noble English family of the Percys, and as the Duke of Northumberland was at that time at Bath, he was advised to apply to his Grace for relief. The Abbé immediately wrote to the Duke, who returned a polite answer, requesting a few days for investigation. In the interval, his Grace communicated with Lord Harcourt, at whose house the Duc D'Harcourt resided; and inquired whether the Abbé De Percie was really of the family of the De Percies of Normandy. Soon after, the statement having been found correct, the Duke transmitted to his newly-discovered kinsman a gold box with a bank-note, inclosed in it, for one thousand pounds, and a general invitation to his table, which was from that day open to the refugee abbé.

sons of the blood royal of that kingdom were cruelly slain. Those that survived were fugitives and lived in the Duke of Burgundy's court; all of them young gentlemen (whose fathers had been slain in England) whom the Duke of Burgundy had generously entertained before his marriage (with King Edward's sister) as his relations of the house of Lancaster. Some of them were reduced to such extremity of want and poverty before the Duke of Burgundy received them, that no common beggar could have been poorer. I saw one of them, who was Duke of Exeter—but he concealed his name—following the Duke of Burgundy's train, bare-foot and bare-legged, begging his bread from door to door. This person was the next of the house of Lancaster; he had married King Edward's sister, and, being afterwards known, had a small pension allowed him for his subsistence. There were also some of the family of the Somersets, and several others, all of them slain since in the wars."

From these data the quaint annalist deduces the very comfortable moral that "those bad princes and others who cruelly and tyrannically employ the power that is in their hands, none, or but few of them, die unpunished, though perhaps it is neither in the same manner, nor at the same time, that those who are injured, desire."

Like, but at the same time unlike, is the fate of the family of the Hungerfords,—like, because we again see unbounded affluence sinking into utter poverty; and unlike, because fortune is altogether blameless in the affair. If the family was brought to decay and ruin, it was not owing to any of the adverse tricks of destiny against which no human prudence is able to defend itself; their decadence was wholly and solely attributable to the boundless extravagance of one of their members, who was surnamed, and not without good reason, THE SPENDTHRIFT—Sir Henry Hungerford. This agent of ruin to his descendants inherited a property which must have been immense, since it appears that he sold at one time eight-and-twenty manors, his income being no less than thirty thousand pounds per annum. Such a fortune would at first sight appear to be inexhaustible by the most profuse extravagance, but happily, most happily for the world, this is not the case. If nature has provided poison in the shape of misers to accumulate, she has not forgotten to supply the antidote in spendthrifts that squander; thus the balance of society is kept even, and the general harmony is preserved by the very means which the short-sighted on either side are most disposed to call in question. The enormous fortune in the hands of this individual, had it so remained, would have been a pent-up water, producing good to no one; as he scattered it, though with indiscriminate profusion, it was a beneficent shower, fertilizing where it fell. To him is attributed the demolition of the family mansion in London, upon the site of which now stands Hungerford Market. Sir Henry's bust did, and perhaps still does, exist under a niche in the wall, with the following description:—

"Forum, utilitati publicæ per quam necessarium,
Regis Caroli secundi innuente Majestate, propriis
Sumptibus erexit, perfecitque D. Edvardus
Hungerford, Balnei, Miles, Anno MDCLXXXII."

I may place this act of genuine munificence as a set-off to the extravagance which could squander five hundred guineas upon a wig to decorate his person on the occasion of a court ball. It must, however, be distinctly understood that my remarks as to his liberality apply only to the old, and not to the present market, which is indebted to him for nothing more than its site.

During three and-thirty years this singular personage, though so incompetent to manage his own affairs, sate in parliament to assist in managing those of the nation. By the end of that period he had completely dissipated his noble inheritance, and was compelled for nearly as long a term to subsist upon the charity of his friends and relations. It has indeed been said that he was made one of the Poor Knights of Windsor, but his name does not appear to have been enrolled amongst them. Be this as it may, so little did the total wreck of his fortunes affect either his health or happiness, that he lived to the unusual age of one hundred and fifteen years, dying in 1711 :*

"My parks, my walls, my manors that I had,
Even now forsake me ; and of all my lands,
Is nothing left me but my body's length."

By a yet greater declension, the last direct heir of Conyers, of Horden, a race at one time so celebrated, was brought in his old age to the workhouse; the noble

* The male line of Hungerford is extinct in England, but direct descendants of the old and illustrious stock may still be found in Ireland, the present representatives of the two existing branches being THOMAS HUNGERFORD, Esq., of Inchidony, co. Cork, and THOMAS HUNGERFORD, Esq., of Cahirmore, also in the county of Cork.

blood of the senior line* of the Rokebys in Yorkshire ebbed out with a carpenter during the last century; and at the beginning of the present the heir of the eminent and ancient family of CASTLETON, and the twelfth baronet of the name in succession, was a breeches-maker at Lynn, in Norfolk. "The Universal Magazine," of 1810, thus records his decease:—

"Died at Lynn, aged fifty-eight, Mr. Edward Castleton. He was the last lineal descendant of Sir William Castleton, of Hingham, Norfolk, who was created a Baronet in 1641: the family and title are therefore now become extinct. He died a bachelor, and never resumed the baronetcy. He for many years followed the very humble employment of breeches-maker in Lynn, but latterly lived on a small patrimonial inheritance."

The loyalty of the Roches should have preserved them from suspicion. In a petition presented to the Lords of Council in 1614, it is stated that in Tyrone's rebellion three of the sons of Lord Roche were slain, and many of his people. The castle of this stout cavalier maintained a brave defence against the beleaguering army of Cromwell during the Parliamentary war; and the famous Countess of Derby was not singular in displaying the heroism so remarkable in a female breast, for Lady Roche proved that her fidelity to her sovereign was superior to regard for her own safety. She refused to yield up the castle, and sustained a siege

* A junior branch of the Rokebys, sprung from the marriage of Benjamin Rokeby (5th son of Thomas Rokeby, of Barnaby, slain at Dunbar, in 1650) with Rebecca Langham, of Arthingworth, in Northamptonshire, have always held, and still hold, the position of a county family of distinction.

for several days with great spirit; but a battery having been brought to bear on the walls from a place since called Camp Hill, she found the place untenable, and was forced to capitulate. Though the Lord Roche might have retained his estates on submitting to Cromwell, he refused to break his allegiance, and confiscation deprived him of his possessions. He retired to Flanders, where he obtained the command of a regiment, and might have lived in comfort, if not affluence, but the pay which should have supported his family was contributed to assuage the exile of his sovereign; and how was he repaid?—"Put not thy trust in Princes," saith the proverb. Charles II. was restored to the throne of his fathers, but was Lord Roche to the castle of his? The following letter, addressed from the Earl of Orrery to the Duke of Ormonde, dated June 14th, 1667, recommending Lord Roche and his destitute family to his Grace's favour, is the fullest answer:—"It is a grief to me to see a nobleman of so ancient a family left without any maintenance; and being able to do no more than I have done, I could not deny to do for him what I could do, to lament his lamentable state to your Grace." Lady Roche, of the second or third generation from this gallant cavalier, was seen begging in the streets of Cork!

The last story to pass before us in this genealogical diorama is not less singular than any that have preceded it: but to understand it rightly, I must reverse the witches' charm in the case of Banquo's progeny, and evoke the shadows of the dead in lieu of tampering with the images of the future.

"Michael Palæologus," says Gibbon, "was the most illustrious, in birth and merit, of the Greek nobles. Of those who are proud of their ancestors, the far greater part must be content with local or domestic renown, and few there are who dare trust the memorials of their family to the public annals of their country. As early as the middle of the 11th century, the noble race of the Palæologi stands high and conspicuous in the Byzantine history; it was the valiant George Palæologus who placed the father of the Comeni on the throne; and his kinsmen or descendants continue, in each generation, to lead the armies and councils of the State. The purple was not dishonoured by their alliance; and had the law of succession and female succession been strictly observed, the wife of Theodore Lascaris must have yielded to her elder sister, the mother of Michael Palæologus, who afterwards raised his family to the throne."

Michael Palæologus was crowned Emperor in 1260, and in the following year Constantinople was recovered. With the next fall of that famous city, its capture by Mahomet II. in 1452, ended the imperial house of Palæologus. At that memorable siege, Constantine Palæologus, the last Greek emperor, who "accomplished all the duties of a general and a soldier," fell by an unknown hand, and with him fell the empire over which he ruled. The Palæologi —the illustrious race so honourably commemorated by Gibbon—furnished eight emperors to Constantinople, and were the last of the ten dynasties, exclusive of the Franks, that reigned over the Greek empire. Mighty, indeed, were these Palæologi; mighty in power, dignity, and renown: yet, within less than two centuries from the heroic death of the Emperor Constantine, their direct descendant, Theodore Palæologus was resident, unnoticed and altogether undistinguished, in a remote parish on the Tamar, in Cornwall.

The parish was Landulph, about two miles from Saltash, a locality already associated with the Courtenays, another family of Byzantine celebrity. The ancient church of Landulph has many curious memorials; but there is one monumental brass of surpassing interest, inscribed with these words :—

"Here lyeth the body of Theodoro Paleologvs
Of Pesaro in Italye, descended from ye Imperyall
Lyne of ye last Christian Emperors of Greece,
Being the sonne of Camelio ye sonne of Prosper,
The sonne of Theodoro the sonne of John ye
Sonne of Thomas second brother to Constantine
Paleologus the 8th of that name and last of
Yt lyne yt raygned in Constantinople bntill sbb
Deued by the Tvrks. Who married with Mary
Ye daughter of William Balls, of Hadlye in
Sobffolke, Gent., and had issue 5 children,
Theodoro, John, Ferdinando, Maria and Dorothy,
& departed this life at Clyfton ye 21th of
Janbar, 1636."

This inscription is surmounted by the imperial arms of the Greek empire.* The family of Theodoro Palæologus

---

* In 1811, the tomb in which Theodoro Palæologus was buried was accidentally opened, and a body was there found in a single oak coffin, in so perfect a state as to determine that he was in stature far beyond the common height, and that his features

continued to reside at Clifton, near Landulph, for some time after the date of the monumental brass. The daughter Maria, thereon commemorated, died at Clifton, in 1674, and her sister Dorothy, who married William Arundell, Esq., and who is styled in the parish registry of marriages at St. Mellion's, where the ceremony took place, as "Dorothea Paleologus, *de Stirpe Imperatorum,*" resided in the neighbourhood of Landulph up to the time of her death in 1681.

Of Theodoro's sons, the eldest, named after his father, was at one time a lieutenant in Lord St. John's regiment, and died without issue; the second, John, fell at Naseby, fighting under the royal banner; and the third, Ferdinando, escaped after that same disastrous fight in which he was also engaged *ex parte regis,* to the island of Barbadoes, where he inherited an estate from his grandfather Bales, and where he married and settled, calling his distant home "Clifton Hall," in remembrance of his native Landulph. There he closed his life in 1678, leaving an only son, Theodore Palæologus, who died soon after, young and unmarried. Thus expired the male line of the Palæologi! But many a long year after, so late as the last war of independence in Greece, a Deputation was appointed by the Provisional Government to enquire whether any of the

were oval, and his nose very aquiline—all family traits. He had a very white beard, low down on his breast.

For this interesting anecdote, and much curious matter connected with the subject of this reference to the extinct imperial race of the Palæologi, I am indebted to John Thomas Towson, Esq., an accomplished antiquary and scholar.

family of Palæologus existed. This deputation proceeded to Italy, and various countries, where the Palæologi had become refugees, and, amongst other places, to LANDULPH ; but, as I have shown, no male Palæologus existed, or else the descendant of Theodoro, the humble resident of the Cornish village, might perchance have ascended the restored throne of Greece.

These stories of vicissitude and decay tell a mournful tale of the instability of all things human : royal and imperial dynasties—noble and gentle families—the proudest warrior and the ablest statesman " fret their hour upon the stage, and then are heard no more."

> " Whole ages have fled, and their works decay'd,
>   And nations scatter'd been ;
> But the stout old ivy shall never fade
>   From its hale and hearty green.
>
> " The brave old plant in its lonely days
>   Shall fatten upon the past :
> For the stateliest building man can raise
>   Is the ivy's food at last."

LANDMARKS OF GENEALOGY.

I AM well aware that to many the genealogical tree appears to be little better than a barren trunk, producing no fruit, or none of any value. Such, however, is not my conviction. If it be a natural and laudable feeling for the living in glory in the fame of their dead ancestors—if such recollections serve as a spur to good, and a check to evil to ourselves, Genealogy is a valuable and important science; if truth of persons as well as of facts be all-essential to history, if without the accuracy so obtained the actors of one age are liable to be confounded with those of another, to the obscuring of facts themselves, then again is Genealogy a valuable and important science. And can any one doubt that such is the case even in its fullest extent? Can any one, for a moment, doubt the influence—the beneficial influence—exercised upon most minds by the noble pride of lineage? What else is Genealogy, even in its driest form, denuded of all story—what else is it but the record of persons, as history is more peculiarly the record of events? In their more perfect shapes, the two are seen to blend with, rather than to encroach upon each other, History relieving the dryness of Genealogy by the attractive narrative of events, and Genealogy, by its minute description of persons, imparting a deeper, and, as it were, a more dramatic interest to History. Biography, too, perhaps the most pleasing branch of literature, owes a heavy debt to my favourite pursuit. What would it be but for the Genealogist's labours ?

If I have not exaggerated—as I trust I have not—the uses to be drawn from genealogical pursuits, little apology will be needed for the following essay, which may, perhaps, add something, however little (derived from my peculiar course of study), to the general stock of knowledge. No do I believe that Genealogy will prove, upon a closer acquaintance, so barren of amusement as it is by some imagined. On the contrary, I have no doubt that, reversing the effect of the desert mirage, while it seems from a distance to promise nothing but arid sands, it will be found on a nearer approach to be a pleasant land, wherein neither streams nor flowers, nor green leaves are deficient.

One of the greatest impediments a genealogical inquirer encounters at the onset of his researches, arises from a want of acquaintance with the public and private records necessary to assist him on his dubious and perplexing way. The perusal of mouldering deeds and crumbling parchments, the discovery of facts long gone by and forgotten, and the investigation of events and connections, trivial at the period of their occurrence, but all-important in future times to pedigree elucidation, must ever require the most determined energy and perseverance : but still, though toilsome may be the labour, it becomes comparatively light, and the prospect of final success far more certain when a knowledge is acquired of the principal archives and auhorities wherein are contained the evidences of family history. To supply the requisite information, and to conduct the reader over paths little frequented, and ground almost untrodden, I propose to indicate the various landmarks which may safely guide him to his journey's end, by affording a brief and concise description of the numerous important records which abound in public and private repositories; and which, when once indicated, can be easily referred to. I must here acknowledge the debt I owe to Mr. Grimaldi's " Origines Genealogicæ," for a vast amount of information with reference to the genealogical resources of England.

First in antiquity is the celebrated DOMESDAY BOOK, so called either from there being no appeal from its authority, or from its place of preservation (Domus Dei) at Westminster. This survey of all the lands in England, except the four Northern Counties, made by William the Conqueror, consists of two volumes written in Latin, and was completed in 1086. It was deposited in the Charter-House of Westminster Abbey in 1096, and still remains there in excellent preservation. Connected with this venerable authority are four other MSS., called, I. THE EXON DOMESDAY (preserved in Exeter Cathedral); II. THE INQUISITIO ELIENSIS; III. THE WINTON DOMESDAY; and, IV. THE BOLDON BOOK (a survey of the County Palatine of Durham); all of which, as well as the Domesday Survey itself, have been printed by order of the House of Commons, accompanied by full indexes of persons, places, and things, and may be consulted in all the public libraries. These records contain the name and title of each person of importance in the kingdom nearly eight centuries ago, the situation and extent of his estate, and, occasionally, his parentage and children.

The MONASTIC CHARTULARIES were parchment or vellum books, comprising copies of all charters referring to the property of the religious houses: for, however the spiritual merits of the monks may be canvassed, their energy in the preservation of their secular estates is undisputed; and these, together with the monastic Leiger books, Registers, Necrologies, Calendars, and Chronicles, contain much important genealogical matter, and, in some instances, entire pedigrees of eminent families, benefactors to the communities. In the collections made by the monks are to be found rolls of names of kings, nobles, and warriors; and among these I may especially mention the Great Tournament Roll, preserved in the College of Arms, representing the Tournament of Henry the Eighth, with portraits of himself and his courtiers; and the Crusade Roll of the time of the second Henry, exhibiting the names and emblazoned arms of 200 eminent knights of the last crusade. The most curious, however, of these documents is the ROLL OF BATTLE ABBEY, a record of the names of the principal Norman soldiers, kept by the monks of the monastery which was founded on the field of battle where Harold was slain.*

> * "Dicitur a bello Bellum locus hic, quia bello
> Angligenæ victi, sunt hic in morte relicti :
> Martyris in Christi festo cecidere Calixti:
> Sexagenus erat sextus millesimus annus
> Cum pereunt Angli, stella monstraute cometâ."

Much doubt has been thrown upon the accuracy of the Roll of Battle Abbey, so far at least as it may be regarded as the mus-

Two ancient manuscript copies of the Roll are in the British Museum (*Lansd. MSS.* 215, and *Harl. MSS.* 3763), and printed copies may be found in Leland's Collectanea, and Holinshed's and Stow's Chronicles, as well as in Fuller's Church History.

Some few chronicles, chartularies, and registers have been printed; but the most extensive published collection is in Dugdale's Monasticon, wherein many thousands are transcribed from the original grants, leiger books, or muniments of the respective monasteries. The Harleian and Cottonian Libraries, in the British Museum, comprise the largest quantity of these important documents; and in the

ter-roll of the Norman chiefs who survived the field of Hastings, there being more than suspicion that its holy guardians felt slight qualm at interpolation, when by that means they could propitiate the favour of some anticipated wealthy benefactor, or gratify the vanity of some potent steel-clad baron. "It was no unworthy pride," says Mr. Warburton, "that would introduce a little of the Norman sap into the family tree. And if to effect such an object, history be sometimes twisted, and heraldry suborned, let us look with indulgent eyes. Even at this day, in a country where titles command so much respect from the general worth of those who bear them, Norman blood is the proudest boast, and Norman features the proudest distinction." Be this as it may, the Roll of Battle Abbey is, at all events, one of monkish times, and has always been held in high estimation by the ancient chroniclers. Grafton calls the list he publishes, "The Names of the Gentlemen that came out of Normandy with William, Duke of that provynce, when he conquered the noble Realme of England: the which he states that he took out of an ancient Recorde that he had of Clarenceux King of Armes." And Stow asserts that his catalogue is transcribed from "A table sometime in Battaille Abbey." Guilliam Tayleur, too, a Norman historian, who could not have had any communication with the monks of Battle, has also given a copy of the muster-roll.

Augmentation Office, which was formed for their custody, an abundance is still preserved of great interest and value, with indexes for the benefit of the public. Private libraries, too, especially those of Cambridge and Oxford, possess some of these church records. Considerable, however, as the list is of those that have been preserved, it is painful to learn from John Bale, who wrote in 1549, that " the books of monasteries were reserved by the purchasers of those houses to scour their candlesticks, and to rub their boots; some were sold to grocers and sopesellers, and some were sent over the sea to the bookbinders, not in small numbers, but at times whole ships full. A merchant bought two noble libraries for forty shillings."

Of the genealogical utility of the monastic records no doubt can exist; and all the eminent writers on the subject of family history, Dugdale, Collins, &c., bear testimony to their value. In the claim to the Barony of Dacre, made by Margaret Fenys, *temp.* Queen Elizabeth, there was received as evidence, " a pedigree taken out of an old book, remaining now with my Lord William Howard, sometime belonging to the Priory of Lanercost."

ANCIENT CHARTERS and TITLE DEEDS afford direct proofs of a genealogy, as they set forth the description of the party, making the instrument his seal of arms, and occasionally some recital referring to his father, mother, wife, children, or other relations. The British Museum has a most extensive collection of " Cartæ Antiquæ" (*i. e.* deeds and writings dating from the Saxon period to the reign of Henry VIII.), royal charters, foundation charters, and private deeds. The Tower of London, the

Bodleian Library at Oxford, the Augmentation Office, the Duchy of Lancaster Office, Carlton Ride, the archives of our Cathedrals, the Chapter House at Westminster, the Archiepiscopal Palace of Lambeth, and the State Paper Office, all contain numerous royal and public charters, and a variety of deeds and endowments. Those at Oxford begin from the Saxon period of history, and relate, many of them, to the widely spread possessions of the Templars and the Knights of St. John of Jerusalem. The cartæ antiquæ of the Tower consist of forty one ancient rolls of inrolments of grants, from the time of the Saxon King Edgar to that of Henry III., made principally to ecclesiastics. A calendar of them, with an index locorum, was printed by Sir J. Ayloffe, in 1772, and in the office is an index virorum. The Lansdowne MSS. have an abstract of them, and full copies are in the Lincoln's Inn Library, and in the Harleian collection. In private families, long possessed of hereditary estates, the cartæ antiquæ are numerous beyond all idea. The repositories of the Howards, Cavendishes, Manners's, Talbots, Shirleys, Digbys, Percys, Seymours, and many others, contain thousands and tens of thousands of these important records. One single chartulary of the Percys comprises nearly two thousand transcripts. The House of Marr in Scotland, whose nobility ascends to the remotest period, establishes the fact by a charter of the year 1171.

Next come the MONUMENT, the TOMBSTONE, and the COFFIN PLATE, the last sad memorials of this world's evanescent greatness, recalling to the antiquary and the historian the lives and merits of those " who were of fame, and had been glorious in another day." But it should be borne in mind, that errors in dates, and even in names, sometimes occur in these inscriptions. Of this, the epitaphs to Sterne and Goldsmith afford remarkable evidence; in the latter a mistake of no less than three years occurs. "In the claim to the Berners barony," says Mr. Grimaldi, in his most learned and admirable work, 'Origines Genealogicæ,' "evidence was adduced before the House of Lords to prove that the time of the death of a party was *not* as engraved on the monument. Many causes contribute to this incorrectness: executors are not always well informed on the subject; frequently all transactions relating to funerals and monuments (of eminent men especially) are under the direction of an undertaker, a person seldom very careful or very learned; he again hands over half his orders to the stonemason, a man of less learning; and if (as is the case) we daily see the most absurd orthography in epitaphs, there is less reason to impute infallibility to the same chisel when carving dates, though the stranger, fortunately for the sculptor's reputation, can be no critic there."

Much important information may be derived from COFFIN PLATES, especially regarding families of rank or of long residence on manorial estates. The sepulchre of the Brydges, Dukes of Chandos, supplies ample data for a full and authentic pedigree of that distinguished house; and the "Memorials of the Tufton Family" are, to a certain extent, derived from the Coffin Plates found in the vaults of the Earls of Thanet. The earliest funeral monuments are those bearing the names of Romanized Britons in Cornwall and Wales; and in the cathedrals of St. Albans, Westminster, Winchester, and others, may still be seen inscriptions eight centuries old. But the times of Henry VIII. and CROMWELL, so fatal to church architecture and monastic records, were alike destructive of the stately monument and the venerable tomb. Inscriptions in which taste and vanity were competitors for perpetuating their votaries in the Temple of Fame, and which would have handed down invaluable information to the herald and genealogist, have thus perished, and the memory of many of the good and eminent of former days, as recorded in their epitaphs, can only be gathered from the copies of ancient monuments preserved in the Harleian, Cottonian, and Bodleian libraries, from the County Histories, and from the various works on the subject published within the last two hundred years, such as Weever's Funeral Monuments, Le Neve's Monumenta Anglicana, and Gough's Sepulchral Memorials.

THE GREAT ROLL OF THE EXCHEQUER, well known as the PIPE ROLL, contains an account of the revenue of the Crown, beginning in the fifth year of the reign of King Stephen, and continued to the present time. It is a document of great interest and utility, to which nearly every ancient pedigree is indebted. In it may be found a perfect list of the sheriffs of the different counties, and almost every name of note of English history. Transcripts of some of the early Pipe Rolls are in the British Museum, and much valuable matter, carefully digested, may be found in the important collection bequeathed by Mrs. Madox to the National Repository. As an instance of the genealogical utility of this celebrated record, we may instance the case of the Russell pedigree, which commences by stating that "this illustrious family hath been for many ages possessed of a large estate in the county of Dorset, as is manifest from the account of the sheriff in 1202, when John Russell gave fifty marks for licence to marry the sister of a great man called Daun Bardolf." This sheriff's account, proving John Russell's existence, marriage, and estate, is obtained from the Pipe Roll, and the particulars of these parties exist on no other record.

The POST MORTEM INQUISITIONS were inquests held by a jury of the county, summoned by the escheator, to inquire of the death of every one of the king's tenants, of what lands he died seised, who was his heir, &c. These returns, the Inquisitiones Post Mortem, sometimes called escheats, commencing with the third year of the reign of Henry III., and terminating 20 Charles I., are preserved in the Chapter House, in the Rolls Chapel, in the Duchy of Lancaster Office, and at Carlton Ride, Carlton Terrace, London, and assist materially all genealogical researches. The same may be said of the "Proceedings in Chancery," a productive source of family history.

The PLACITA ROLLS, or the Pleadings in the several Courts, and the Judgments on them, contain proofs of heirs, their ages, and pedigrees, classified according to the several courts. "They give," says Mr. Sims, in his admirable 'Manual of the Public Records,' "the most important information upon every subject respecting which men wage legal war with each other; and among these subjects are most especially to be enumerated the claims to lands, honours, and baronies." Mr. Sims gives in his very important work a minute analysis of the PLACITA

Rotuli, and Parliamentary Records; and to those who have occasion to refer to any of those important sources of information, I cannot do better than to direct them to 'the Manual,' as the surest and safest guide.

I now come to the principal, and often the only records by which families in the middling class of life can trace any descent prior to the introduction of parochial records, for the Inquisitions, of which I have just spoken, were only taken on the tenants in capite,—I refer to WILLS and ADMINISTRATIONS. Few, if any, documents contain so great an amount of genealogical details; for the testaments of men of property almost invariably name two, and frequently three or four, clear descents, and refer to relations and kindred who could never otherwise be attached to the pedigree. The Will Offices, therefore, of the different dioceses, as well as those of the Courts of Peculiars, are the great sources whence the modern genealogist must derive his materials; and in all cases, one of his first proceedings should be a reference to such of these important documents as may be likely to throw light upon the subject of his investigation. Made at a solemn and impressive moment, and with a feeling of the sanctity of the instrument, they are scarcely ever inaccurate or false, and in perusing their details, we seem to hear again the voice and words of the departed, telling his own story and referring to facts of other times, with all the truth and certainty which personal knowledge can alone impart.

The principal Will Offices are, I. DOCTORS' COMMONS, St. Paul's, London, in which may be found the Wills proved within the Archbishopric of Canterbury. II. YORK, the jurisdiction of which extends over the counties of York, Chester, Lancaster, Cumberland, Westmoreland, Northumberland, Durham, and Flint. III. CHESTER, which includes the whole county of Chester, and parts of the adjacent counties of York, Lancaster, Cumberland, Westmoreland, and Flint. IV. LINCOLN, to which are attached Leicestershire, Beds, Huntingdonshire, and Bucks, with parts of Hereford and Derby. V. LICHFIELD and COVENTRY, which comprises Staffordshire and Derbyshire, and the greater part of Warwickshire and Shropshire. There are besides the Will Offices of Bangor, Bath and Wells, Bristol, Chichester, Ely, Exeter, Gloucester, Hereford, London, Norwich, Oxford, Rochester, St. Asaph, and Winchester.

The next best clues the investigator has to the right elucidation of genealogy, are the Parochial Registers of births, marriages, and burials. These documents seem to have begun about the middle of the sixteenth century, shortly after the dissolution of the monasteries, and the dispersion of the monks, who had been until that time the faithful recorders of those events.* Many causes, and none more than the civil war and the usurpation of Cromwell, have combined to render incomplete the series of these national registries: but still, despite of their occa-

* In 1538, the 30th Henry VIII., a mandate was issued by the Vicar-General for the keeping of registers of baptisms, marriages, and burials, in every parish; before which date there were no parochial records; thenceforward, however, with the exception of the much-to-be-lamented hiatus caused by the troubled times of Charles I. and the Protectorate of Cromwell, a period of nearly twenty years, these documents have been regularly preserved.

sional deficiency, they are invaluable for the particulars they afford. While on the subject of parochial records, we may perhaps be excused a brief reference to one of the most notorious and ruinous abuses that ever existed in London—the system of FLEET MARRIAGES. These alliances were solemnized by regularly ordained clergymen, residing within the Fleet Prison or its rules, and generally confined for debt. Future generations will possibly discredit the extraordinary accounts of these proceedings that are handed down; but the following is an extract from the *Gentleman's Magazine* for 1735, copied by that work from the *Grub Street Journal*, bearing all the impress of truth: " A female correspondent who signs ' Virtuous,' complains of the many ruinous marriages that are every year practised in the Fleet, by a set of drunken, swearing parsons, with their myrmidons, that wear black coats and pretend to be clerks and registers to the Fleet, plying about Ludgate Hill, pulling and forcing people to some peddling alehouse or brandy-shop to be married; even on a Sunday, stopping them as they go to church. Not long since, a young lady was deluded and forced from her friends, and by the assistance of a very wicked, swearing parson, married to an atheistical wretch whose life is a continual practice of all manner of vice and debauchery. Another young lady was decoyed to a house in the confines of the Fleet by a pretended clergyman; Dr. Wryneck immediately appeared, and swore she should be married, or if she would not, he would have his fee, and register the marriage from that night. The lady, to recover her liberty, left her ring as a pledge that she would meet him the morrow night."

Among remarkable marriages celebrated in the Fleet, we may mention that of John Twistleton, Esq., father of Lord Saye and Sele, in 1735, and that of Henry, first Lord Holland, to the daughter of the Duke of Richmond, in 1744.

Such of the Fleet Registers as could be discovered and obtained, have been purchased by Government, and deposited at the Bishop of London's office, in Doctors' Commons.

Marriages at the May Fair Chapel were almost as notorious as those of the Fleet, and so numerous did they become, that 6000, it is said, took place in one year; a circumstance that hastened the passing of Lord Hardwicke's Act. At this chapel, on the site of which now stands Curzon Chapel, the Duke of Kingston was married to Miss Chudleigh, as was the Baroness Clinton to the Hon. Mr. Shirley, and the Duke of Hamilton to the beautiful Miss Gunning. The registers form three folio volumes, closely and clearly written, and now remain with the parish books at St. George's, Hanover Square.

With reference to this subject, the books containing entries of the grants of marriage licenses must not be forgotten, as very important genealogical guides, for, connected with them, are the original affidavits made by the applicants, which give the names, descriptions, residences, and ages of the parties to be married, the church where the ceremony was to be performed, and sometimes the parents' names. These licenses, of a date subsequent to the Reformation, with the affidavits, are to be found in the registries of the several archbishops and bishops.

I will next pass to another and perhaps the safest and most available Repository of Genealogical information, the

COLLEGE OF ARMS (Benet's Hill, St. Paul's, London), in which is deposited the most valuable series of pedigrees in existence, including the Heralds' Visitations and numerous other genealogical documents, which are described in "the Report on Public Records," 1837, p. 106. At the present time, the College of Arms has attained a high degree of efficiency and authority under the heraldic government of Sir Charles Young, *Garter*. On the interesting science of Heraldry, I have given in this volume a brief essay, showing its great importance with reference to family history, and its especial value as a kind of index to genealogy: I will therefore confine myself at present merely to the HERALDS' VISITATIONS, the most comprehensive of all the sources of heraldic and genealogical knowledge. These heraldic records contain the pedigrees of the landed proprietors of the time entitled to bear arms, and were compiled by virtue of a commission under the privy seal, issued to the two provincial Kings of Arms, authorising and commanding each of them, either personally or by deputy, to visit the whole of his province as often as he should think fit, to convene before him all manner of persons who pretended to the use of arms, or were styled esquires and gentlemen, and to cause those thus summoned to show by what authority they claimed the distinction. In furtherance of their arduous and ofttimes invidious duties, great and almost unreasonable powers were granted to them. They had full power and licence, not only to enter, upon reasonable request and at reasonable hours of the day, into all churches, castles, houses, and other places, to peruse therein all arms, cognizances, crests, and other devices, and to record the same, with the descents, marriages, and issue, in Register Books,—which are now so well known as the Visitations,—but also to correct and reform all bearings unlawfully usurped or inaccurately adopted, and in certain cases to reverse, pull down, and deface the same. The mode of procedure was this : on arriving at the place wherein the Visitation was to be holden, the provincial king issued a warrant, directed to the high constable of the hundred, or to the mayor or chief officer of the district, commanding him to warn the several knights, esquires, and gentlemen, particularly named in such warrant, as well as all others within his jurisdiction, to appear personally before him, at the house and on the day specified, and to bring with them such arms and crests as they then bore, together with their pedigrees and descents, and such evidences and ancient writings as may justify the same in order to their being registered. On the day appointed, the provincial King or his deputy attended, and so long as the laws of chivalry were honoured and esteemed, general attention and respect were paid to these summonses : attested pedigrees were submitted to the heralds, and thus were produced the important registrations of which I am speaking, and which have preserved to the present period many a line of descent that would otherwise have been irretrievably lost. With the lapse of years, however, the estimation in which the Visitations were held gradually died away, and after the Revolution of 1688 all the efforts of the decayed Court of Chivalry were unavailing to continue their operation. One of the circumstances that tended most effectually to their destruction was the incompetence and dishonesty of the persons who were deputed by the heralds to collect information. True it is, that when these illicit proceedings were discovered, the delinquents suffered fine and imprisonment, and we have on record a curious document which alludes to a far severer punishment; being a warrant from the Earl of Essex, Earl Marshal, to Robert Tresswell, Somerset herald, dated Dec. 31, 1597, signed by Dethick, Camden, and Segar, and directed to all justices of the peace, constables, and headboroughs, authorising the apprehension of one W. Dakyns, "a notable dealer in arms and maker of false pedigrees, for which fault, about xx years past, he lost one of his ears."

The Visitations made under the early commissions are in many instances a narrative, and (as may be supposed in their commencement) meagre in detail, sometimes containing little more than notes of arms of the gentry, and the Founders and Priors of monasteries, and seldom exhibiting more than the lineal descending line of the family; subsequently they assume a more important form, affording full and accurate statements of pedigrees, and supplying collateral details. The various entries are in most cases attested by the signatures of the heads of the house, and occasionally by persons on their behalf.

The earliest of the Visitations, recorded in the College of Arms, took place in 1529, comprising the counties of Gloucester, Worcester, Oxford, Wilts, Berks, and Stafford, and at intervals of about twenty-five years, they continued to be made until their final discontinuance, towards the close of the seventeenth century. The originals of these records are, with some exceptions, in the College of Arms. Various transcripts, however, exist, and the library of the British Museum is surpassingly rich in its collection of heraldic MSS. That great national institution, now so ably presided over by Antonio Panizzi, Esq., contains some of the original Visitations, and copies of most of the others, and the care with which they are indexed, and the facility afforded by the attention and valuable assistance constantly and unreservedly afforded by the intelligent Librarians at the Museum Reading-Room, render the consultation of these important documents a matter of not the slightest difficulty to the veriest neophyte in heraldic research. In some of the libraries at Oxford, Cambridge, especially in Queen's College in the former University, and in Caius College in the latter, and in many private collections, such as the splendidly rich one of Sir Thomas Phillipps, Bart., at Middle Hill, co. Worcester, these documents may frequently be met with. I annex the dates of the various visitations, printing, within brackets, each of those of which there is not a copy in the British Museum:—

BEDFORDSHIRE: 1566, 1582, [1586], 1634, [1669]. BERKS: 1531, 1566, [1597] 1623, 1664. BUCKS: 1566, 1574, 1634. CAMBRIDGESHIRE: 1575, 1590, 1619. CHESHIRE: 1533, [1566], [1569], 1580, 1591, 1612, [1663]. CORNWALL: 1530, 1573, 1620. CUMBERLAND: 1615, [1665]. DERBYSHIRE: 1569, 1611, [1634], 1662 DEVON: 1531, 1564, [1572], 1620. DORSET: 1530, 1565, 1623. DURHAM: 1575, 1615, [1666]. ESSEX: 1552, 1558, 1570, 1612, 1634, [1664]. GLOUCESTER: [1530], [1569], 1583, 1623.

HANTS: 1530, 1552, 1575, 1622. HEREFORD: [1569], 1586, 1634. HERTS: 1572, [1615], 1634. HUNTINGDONSHIRE: 1564, [1566], 1613. KENT: [1530], 1574, 1592, 1619, 1623, 1663. LANCASHIRE: 1533, 1567, 1613, [1664]. LEICESTERSHIRE: 1563, 1619. LINCOLN: [1562], 1564, 1592, [1634]. LONDON: 1568, 1634, [1664]. MIDDLESEX: [1572], [1634], 1663. MONMOUTH: [1683]. NORFOLK: 1563, 1589, 1613, [1664], [1668]. NORTHAMPTON: [1564], [1617], 1618. NORTHUMBERLAND: 1575, 1615, [1666]. NOTTS: 1530, 1569, [1575], 1614, [1662]. OXFORD: [1530], 1566, 1574, 1634. RUTLAND: 1618. SHROPSHIRE: [1569], 1584, 1623, [1663]. SOMERSET: [1531], 1573, 1591, 1623. STAFFORDSHIRE: [1528], 1563, 1583, 1614, 1663. SUFFOLK: 1561, 1577, 1611. SURREY: 1530, 1552, 1572, 1623, 1662. SUSSEX: 1530, 1574, 1633, [1662]. WARWICK: 1563, 1619. WESTMORELAND: 1615, [1664]. WILTS: [1530], 1565, 1623, WORCESTER: [1530], 1569, [1634]. YORKSHIRE: 1530, [1552], 1563, 1574, 1584, 1612, 1665.

Other heraldic records of great value are FUNERAL ENTRIES AND CERTIFICATES, documents which contain attested accounts of the time of death, of the place of burial, and of the marriages, issue, and frequently the collateral branches of the several persons whose funerals were attended by the Officers-of-Arms or their deputies, illustrated with the armorial ensigns of the deceased. The entries in the funeral certificates are so full and authentic, that they prove of the most essential service in the deduction of pedigrees. They were taken by virtue of an order of the Earl Marshal, issued in 1567, wherein it was enjoined that every King of-Arms, Herald, or Pursuivant, acting at a funeral, should lodge in the office of Arms a certificate signed by the executors and mourners present. With the decline of heraldic influence, consequent on the Revolution of 1688, these funeral entries fell into disuse, but there are certificates dated as late as 1717.

THE FOUNDERS' KIN PEDIGREES, also registered in the College of Arms, exhibit the descent of individuals from certain Founders of colleges or fellowships, who have directed a preference to be given to their own kindred, such as Bishop Wykeham at New College, Sir Thomas White at St. John's, and Archbishop Chichele at All Souls'.

Thus far I have referred to the principal heraldic documents elucidating family descent. An immense mass of information besides is supplied by the genealogical MSS. preserved in the Harleian and Cottonian Miscellanies and in the additional MSS. at the British Museum, and in the collections of Vincent, Glover, Le Neve, Brook, &c., in the College of Arms.

In connection with the subject of family bearings, I may not inappropriately, perhaps, refer to family entries in Bibles, letters, and manuscripts. These documents are so familiar to every one, that no description is required; but although their importance is universally acknowledged, it is surprising how irregularly the entries are generally kept. Every family should preserve a record of births, marriages and deaths; and thus the confusion and litigation in which the inheritance of titles and property are frequently involved would never occur. Those that already possess old Bibles containing these entries and family

MSS. cannot be too careful of them; for, owing to the destruction of many parish registers, they may, in all probability, contain the only proofs in existence by which their descents can be traced. Letters,* and the innumerable documents treasured up in families, afford very valuable assistance to pedigrees, and have at all times been used and received in evidence.

Another important repository of genealogical information must not be left unnoticed,—the Registers of the Universities, the College Admission Books, and the Matriculation Papers, affording, as they do, the Christian and surnames of the student, and of his father, the latter's station in life, his residence, the student's birth-place, his age, and school wherein he received his education. At Cambridge, the Matriculation Papers commence in 1544, twenty years before those of Oxford.

Among PRINTED BOOKS, in elucidation of "Peerage" history, the most valuable are "Dugdale's Baronage," "Collins' Peerage," "Archdale's Irish Peerage," "Edmondson's Baronagium," "Banks' Extinct Peerage," and "Courthope's Historic Peerage." For pedigrees of the Landed Gentlemen, the genealogist will find his chief guides the

* Prior to the reign of Henry V. specimens of English correspondence are rare; letters previously to that time were usually written in French or Latin, and were the productions chiefly of the great or the learned. The letters of learned men were verbose treatises, mostly on express subjects; those of the great, who employed scribes, from their formality resembled legal instruments. We have nothing earlier than the 15th century, which can be termed a *familiar letter*. The material, too, upon which letters were written, up to the same period, was usually vellum; very few instances, indeed, occurring, of more ancient date, of letters written on common paper.—*Grimaldi*.

COUNTY HISTORIES—a series of works which forms a branch of literature peculiar to England. The first labourer in the field of topographical research was the indefatigable Leland, and his " Itinerary " may with truth be considered the foundation stone of English topography. He was succeeded by the learned Camden, and after him came Dugdale, (the Prince of genealogists), Dodsworth, Erdeswick, Burton and Plott. The earliest County History is " Dugdale's Warwickshire." At present the Collection of English County Histories includes Ashmole's " Berkshire ; " Lipscombe's "Bucks ;" Ormerod's " Cheshire," (a magnificent work, of great authority) ; Carew's " Survey of Cornwall," and Polwhele's History of the same county, and also Gilbert's ; Nicholson and Burn's " Cumberland and Westmorland ; " Glover's " Derbyshire ;" Pole, Risdon, and Westcote's " Devon Collections ; " Hutchins' " Dorsetshire ;" Surtees' " Durham," (worthy of being placed next to Ormerod's Cheshire) ; Morant's " Essex ;" Atkyns' and Rudder's " Gloucestershire ; " Duncumb's " Herefordshire ;" Clutterbuck's " Herts ;" Hasted's " Kent ;" Corry's and Baines' " Lancashire ;" Nichol's " Leicestershire ;" Blomefield's " Norfolk ;" Baker's " Northamptonshire ; " Hodgson's " Northumberland ; " Thoresby's " Thoroton's Notts ;" Blore's " Rutlandshire ;" Blakeway's " Sheriffs of Shropshire ;" Collinson's and Phelips' " Somersetshire ; " Shaw's " Staffordshire ;" Gage's and Suckling's " Suffolk ;" Manning and Bray's " Surrey ;" Dallaway's and Horsfield's " Sussex ;" Dugdale's " Warwickshire ;" Hoare's " Wiltshire ;" Nash's " Worcestershire ;" Hunter's " Deanery of Doncaster" and " Hallamshire," (both the productions of a learned, able, and indefatigable antiquary); Whitaker's "Loidis and Elmete," "Deanery of Craven;" "Parish of Whalley;" and "Richmondshire;" Oliver's "Beverley;" Graves' and Ord's "Cleveland;" Watson's "Halifax;" and Poulson's "Holderness." Lysons' "Magna Britannia," a very able and useful work, refers only to the Counties of Bedford, Berks, Bucks, Cambridge, Chester, Cornwall, Derby, and Devon. There are besides numerous local books, such as Gregson's "Fragments of Lancashire;" Lysons' "Environs of London;" Savage's "Carhampton;" Gage's "Hengrave;" Ord's "Cleveland;" and Grainge's "Vale of Mowbray;" which give a great deal of local matter and genealogical detail not elsewhere to be found. In addition, I may, perhaps, be allowed to add, as a source of genealogical information, my own work on "The Landed Gentry."

The repositories of genealogical information in Ireland, though far from being as rich in materials as the English, claim a higher antiquity.

The genealogical pretensions of the Milesians or ancient noblesse of Ireland, rival those of the Imperial house of Austria, or the Ducal family of Arcot, whose pedigrees, it is said, reach back to the Deluge. The Scoto-Milesians trace their descent to the same epoch; and in many of the older pedigrees, the compilers, not content with the remoteness of Noah, pass on to the father of mankind,—Adam himself!

The Milesians were most particular in preserving and recording the genealogies of their families. The office of

"Antiquary," somewhat analogous to that of the modern English herald, was created to preserve a knowledge of historical events, and genealogies of families. The compilations of the antiquaries were duly examined in the Fez or National Assembly, and were recorded in the great register or Psalter of Tara. This practice of registering events and genealogies continued to be observed till a late period; and was kept alive in Christian times by a succession of Monastic chroniclers, to whom we owe those various volumes of Psalters and annals with which the ancient literature of Ireland abounds. The larger part of the genealogical contents of those numerous and voluminous works are collected and compiled in five great works in folio, which contain detailed pedigrees of Irish families; but, without the services of those great masters of the Gaelic, Dr. O'Donovan and Eugene Curry, the ponderous Works of the learned Seanachies and Scribes of ancient Irish Literature will be "sealed books" to the English reader. These Works are, I. The BOOK OF LEINSTER, containing about 300 pages, which was compiled about the year 1150, and is to be found in the library of Trinity College, Dublin. II. The BOOK OF BALLYMOTE, about 600 pages, compiled in the year 1391, now in the Royal Irish Academy. These two works are written on ancient vellum, and in the Irish character. III. The LEAVAR LECAIN, about 700 pages, compiled in the year 1416; a beautifully written paper copy of it in clear, bold, and legible modern Irish characters, is now in the library of the Royal Irish Academy. IV. The BOOK OF PEREGRENE O'CLERY, one of the four masters, compiled about the year 1650, and now also in the Royal Irish Academy.

And V. The Book of Duald Mac Firbis, compiled in the year 1650, and continued in part down to the year 1666. There is a very accurate and complete paper copy of it in the Royal Irish Academy. These works contain the sources of genealogical information, concerning the native families of distinction, or ancient *noblesse* of Ireland prior as well as subsequent to the Anglo-Norman invasion, extending down to the middle of the seventeenth century.

The Anglo-Irish sources of genealogical learning in Ireland since the English *regime* are chiefly to be found among the public records, deposited in the repositories of the official departments. They are, generally speaking, arranged in sub-divisional compartments, in the order of the reigns of the different sovereigns of England.

The first and most legitimate source of genealogical information is to be found among the records of the office of Ulster King of Arms, Dublin Castle. Twenty-four large folio volumes, in manuscript, of tabular pedigrees of the nobility and gentry of Ireland, of Irish, English, and Scottish descent, with their arms, form the official registration of Genealogies. These were compiled from public and private sources, and registered at various times. Two of these books are peculiarly interesting and valuable; one written by Roger O'Ferrall at the beginning of the 18th century, which traces the Pedigrees of Irish families with all their ramifications and collateral descents from the three sons of Milesius, Heremon, Heber, and Ir, and his uncle Ith; and the other by the Chevalier O'Gorman, a little later, which is equally interesting. Most of the Irish pedigrees commence in the remotest ages. The genealogies of the Anglo-Norman families in general extend no further than the battle of Hastings, starting from the Norman Conquest. Among the other important sources of genealogical information in Ulster's office are the following: I. "VISITATION BOOKS," which contain Pedigrees and arms of the nobility and gentry, and were taken by the Ulster Kings of Arms, on their Visitations of Counties, under Commissions; II. "LORDS' ENTRIES:" these consist of volumes of Pedigrees, and arms of the peers of Ireland, made pursuant to an order of the Irish House of Lords of the 12th August, 1707, for the purpose of facilitating proof of their descent, and right to sit and vote. III. "BARONETS' BOOKS," which contain the Pedigrees and arms of the Baronets of Ireland, under a royal warrant dated 30th September, 1789, for correcting and preventing abuses in the order of Baronets. IV. "FUNERAL CERTIFICATES," or attested returns of the names, arms, time of death, place of burial and marriage, and issue of the nobility and gentry, whose funerals were attended, according to ancient custom, by the officers of arms or their deputies, from the year 1595 to about the year 1698. V. "BOOKS OF PEERS," being lists of Peers as they sat in Parliament at various periods, and also of creations of peers, baronets, and knights from the time of Queen Elizabeth to the present time. VI. "BOOKS OF ROYAL LICENSES," containing entries of the Royal Licenses for changes of names, and arms, and other incidental matters. VII. "BOOK OF REGISTRATION OF GRANTS OF ARMS" to various persons from the time of Edward VI. to the present time.

These are the ordinary records of the office, but there are beside many volumes of manuscript ordinaries, and collection of arms—Books containing the arms of the ancient nobility of Ireland, that is to say, creations by the Kings of England, whether as Lords, or Kings of Ireland, and Pedigrees and arms of the Peers of England—Copies and abstracts of various matters relative to genealogical and antiquarian research — also copies of Visitations of some of the English Counties—Vellum Rolls and numerous paper Rolls of Pedigrees of ancient families in Ireland. The Library of Ulster's office has also been enriched through the liberality of the government, by the purchase of a considerable portion of the late Sir William Betham's valuable collection of MSS.

The Ulster King of Arms, as Keeper of the Tower Records, Dublin Castle, has likewise in his custody numerous documents which are ancillary aids to the genealogies of families. These consist of Plea Rolls of the several courts, of Parliament, and of the Crown, from the year 1246 to 1625 ; Rolls of Pleas, and of the Crown, before Justices in Eyre, and gaol delivery—Rolls of the Pipe, or public accounts of the Exchequer from the year 1240 to 1,760— Rolls of Sheriffs' Accounts—Attornments of Estates—Recognizances—Recusants' pardons—Books of orders and decrees of the Exchequer on matters of public revenue, and tenants to the Crown—Advowsons—Presentations to church benefices—Charters of towns and boroughs—Inquisitiones post mortem—Grants of offices—Settlements and other deeds arranged in Counties—Commissions—Kings' letters, &c.—Also records of the Houses of Lords and

Commons of Ireland, including the whole of the published and unpublished statutes of Ireland—Also transcripts of proceedings of the late Record Commission, consisting of books of reference to grants of manors, lands, tenements, fisheries, advowsons, tithes, ferries, markets, and other hereditaments, passed by patent under the great seal of Ireland—Also claims of suffering loyalists in 1798—and papers and returns connected with the yeomanry—and the census of 1831. In these several records of the Dublin Tower numerous references occur to names and descriptions of persons of every degree and calling, and are therefore of very considerable genealogical importance.

The other records, auxiliary to genealogical information, are those of the PAYMASTER OF CIVIL SERVICES, Custom House, Dublin, and consist of Books of Survey of forfeited estates—Regrants of forfeited lands—Rent Rolls of Crown lands—The Registrar of forfeited estates—the Down Survey and Maps—returns of Ecclesiastical preferments—of the Census of 1831, and emendation of it in 1834, and Census returns of 1841.

The REGISTRY OF DEEDS OFFICE, HENRIETTA STREET, contains original memorials of deeds, wills, and other instruments connected with landed estates from the year 1708. The PREROGATIVE REGISTRY, in the same building, contains original Wills, commencing about the year 1530—entries of grants of probate and administration, marriage licenses — pleadings and depositions relating to contested Wills—regal Visitations—faculties for clergymen to hold pluralities of livings, and for appointment to the office of Notary. DIOCESAN REGISTRIES, in the different Dioceses throughout the Kingdom, contain records somewhat similar to those in the Prerogative Registry. A great portion of them will be transferred under a recent Statute to the Prerogative Registry, Dublin. Connected with the ecclesiastical registers are the records of the CATHEDRALS. There are a few in the Cathedrals of Clogher, Leighlin, Limerick, Killaloe, Tuam, and Killala. Christ Church, Dublin, contains several thousand in number, which consist not only of those connected with the Cathedral, but of many matters outside, and of general interest. The UNIVERSITY OF DUBLIN has a most numerous and valuable collection of manuscripts, and is particularly rich in the history, antiquities, and topography of Ireland, and the genealogy of families. Many of the records of the council, of parliament, of the courts, of ecclesiastical houses, and of Birmingham Tower, Dublin Castle, have in the course of time found their way there, and render the collection very general, and varied, and of much value. The COLLEGE OF ARMAGH contains some MS. papers, namely, Rent Rolls, and surveys, and maps relating to the Church lands of the Diocese. THE KING'S INNS' SOCIETY, DUBLIN, contains records relating to the Benchers, and officers, Barristers, Attorneys, and Students, as they became connected with it. MARSH'S LIBRARY, Dublin, has several manuscripts, some of which might also be profitably consulted. In the ROYAL DUBLIN SOCIETY there is a numerous collection of manuscripts, relating to the civil and ecclesiastic affairs of Ireland and other matters, through which are interspersed much genealogical information. The ROYAL

Irish Academy is peculiarly rich in genealogical lore. There are, besides those books of Irish pedigrees already noticed, various other rare and valuable works, in which are to be found matters of pedigree, and biography of families. *The Borough Towns of Ireland* have also records of a local nature, which contain much useful information. But the records of the Courts of Law and Equity are by far the most numerous, and contain the most extensive materials for genealogy. The COURT OF CHANCERY Records consist of the Pleadings, Bills, Answers, Affidavits, Depositions, Reports, and Decrees, which set forth minute details of family affairs, connected with the descent and settlement of property and adjustment of rights; also Inquisitions, Convent and Catholic Rolls, letters of guardianship, Commissions of various kinds,—of lunacy, and of the peace, licenses and pardons—The Palatinate Rolls of Tipperary—Parliament Rolls—Cromwell's Rolls, election writs of Commoners, grants of offices, of lands, and a variety of other miscellaneous matter. The Law Courts of the Queen's Bench, Common Pleas, and Exchequer, have records of judgments, Rolls of Attorneys, and other matters of general interest. In the QUEEN's BENCH are records of outlawry and attainder.—On the Crown side, enrolments of Indictments and presentments.—In the EXCHEQUER, numerous Inquisitions, Outlawries, Memoranda Rolls, Certificates of persons transplanted into Connaught in the time of Cromwell, Inquisitions on surrenders of Monasteries, and estates of attainted persons, Certificates granted to adventurers and soldiers, the " Red Book of the Exchequer,"—Informations or bills for discovery of Estates, by "Protestant discoverers," and answers thereto; and in the COMMON PLEAS, records of fines and recoveries to bar estates tail, names of persons who took "the oaths," Tipperary palatinate records and extracts of outlawry.

The other sources of genealogical information are the records kept by the Clerks of the Crown for the Circuits— the city, town, quarter sessions, manor, and other Courts of inferior jurisdiction. The Manor Courts have been abolished by a recent act of Parliament. Lastly, much information may be gleaned from the last civil confiscation by the Encumbered Estates' Court. In the numerous volumes in manuscript of books of sale will be found the names of the owners, and of the three or four thousand purchasers, and of the lands purchased. If the Judges of the present Landed Estates' Court could be prevailed on to unlock and unseal the muititude of tin boxes of title deeds and abstracts of title to those estates deposited in the registry of the Court, a vast quantity of genealogical information and materials for the histories of families, and former proprietors of estates in Ireland, would be disclosed.

The general landmarks of Genealogy already noticed in the observations respecting the English sources, are equally common to Ireland, namely, monuments, tombstones, coffin plates, parochial registers of births, marriages, and burials—grants of marriage licenses, heraldry, entries in Bibles, letters and manuscripts, registers of Dublin University, college admission books, and matriculation papers. There are also in private collections numerous manuscripts and pedigrees of families of a valuable and interesting kind, scattered throughout every part of the kingdom.

SCOTLAND has always claimed and merited a high character for genealogical knowledge. Unfortunately, there never was in that country any "Heralds' Visitation;" and, to render this want the more severely felt, a fire, about the beginning of the last century, consumed a considerable part of the records of the LYON Office. Consequently the heraldic office in Edinburgh can date its information only from a very modern epoch. The records of the Lord Lyon's department consist of DIPLOMAS OF ARMS, and REGISTRATIONS OF PEDIGREES; but, from the reason just named, and perhaps from other causes, they are not so complete or valuable as one would suppose, considering the general appreciation of ancestral pride so common to all well-born Scotchmen. The other genealogical sources of information in Scotland, are—

I. The GREAT SEAL, and PRIVY RECORDS, (much to the same purport and effect as the English), the former beginning shortly after 1300, and the latter in 1498: their natural productiveness in pedigrees I need not expatiate upon.

II. The EXCHEQUER ROLLS, beginning about the same period as the Great Seal Record, with some transcripts of an earlier date. What remains of them thence downwards is very curious and valuable, illustrative of history as well as of pedigree, and is not so known to the world as it ought to be.

III. THE RETOURS, or INQUISITIONES POST MORTEM, both as to estates, and individuals *personally* (under the name of *General Retours*), containing also services or retours in cases of *tutory*, it being ordained by an old Scotch Act of Parliament, that the nearest agnate, or heir male of a pupil or minor, should be assigned the guardianship. From this the utility of these Retours in questions of male propinquity and pedigree is quite evident. These Records, to which there are printed indexes, come pretty fully down from about 1600 to the present moment, while there are few preserved of an earlier date.

In these Retours, Scotland has an advantage over England, where inquisitiones post mortem ceased more than two centuries ago.

IV. SCOTCH ACTS OF PARLIAMENT: the last full edition, in large folio volumes, was published by order of Government in the present century. Strictly they may be said to begin as a Record *per se* in 1424, from Vol. II.; but an earlier volume, a *talis qualis* one, and rather of a cumbrous and not very digested character, derived from extraneous sources, carries the parliamentary proceedings further back under title of Vol. I. All the above containing various confirmed grants to persons high and low, with lists of the nobility, and occasionally their creations, are very important, and often serviceable in pedigree and descent.

V. COMMISSARY OR CONSISTORIAL RECORDS, containing proceedings in the case of divorce, legitimacy, and executry, with records and testaments; they can only be said properly to commence from the era of the Reformation in 1560, and not fully even then. Before that period, they, together with Records of Bonds and obligations, being under the exclusive custody and authority of the church, were lodged in the chapter houses of the Cathedrals, and together with nearly all those lamented edifices, some of them, it is said, of great interest and beauty, fell a prey to the ruthless and mistaken zeal of the Reformers, at the instigation of Knox and his adherents, being then involved in one common destruction by fire and otherwise. It was Knox, I have always thought, and not Edward I., who caused such a loss of old Scottish muniments.

I may here, likewise, notice the ANNALS and REGISTERS of the UNIVERSITIES, which supply the names of the students who enter, and of those who graduate, with their filiations and connections: of these, the records of SAINT ANDREWS are the oldest and most abundant, commencing early in the 15th century. In these University documents occur the names of members of many of the noble and baronial families of Scotland, several unknown before; and hence they are very valuable in pedigrees of the first rank, while they may be appealed to as elucidatory of the early starting in life of Scotchmen who became famous in the literary world both at home and abroad. These Records have not suffered from the common ecclesiastical destruction. The Glasgow ones, too, beginning after the middle of the 15th century, are well kept, and probably the corresponding ones of Aberdeen.

VI. PARISH REGISTERS OF MARRIAGES, BAPTISMS, and DEATHS:—of these most useful landmarks, I am not aware of any in Scotland before the Reformation, and they are but meagre even afterwards. Regularity is not to be expected in a satisfactory state till about 1700, and there are subsequent lacunæ.

It is very material to add here, that all the preceding Records, by late public Acts and arrangements, have been transferred to, and now lodged in, that most extensive and valuable edifice, Her Majesty's GENERAL REGISTER HOUSE for Scotland.

Being thus brought together, the Records are much more accessible and useful in genealogical investigation, and for other purposes. There is in the Register Office a Record, bulky enough, entitled that of "Bonds and Obligations," exemplifying legal agreements and transactions of all kinds between persons, and beginning from about the middle of the 16th century, and continuing downwards. This Record has often been found extremely useful, so far as it goes, in questions of pedigree and descent. Further still, every Court and Jurisdiction in Scotland had such Records of Bonds and Obligations, and these documents are still kept within the sphere of their respective localities, and not transferred to Edinburgh. And when I add to the preceding that even still more important Record (kept in her Majesty's General Register House, Edinburgh) of the *res gestæ*, procedure and judgments of the Supreme Court, between various persons, and involving questions of every kind, including family descent and representatives, I have exhausted the chief public resources of genealogical information in North Britain.

The private CHARTER CHESTS of the Scottish Nobility and Landed Gentry afford most valuable genealogical materials, and throw light on the obscurity of pedigrees, which can in no other way be obtained.

THE DOUBLE SOJOURN OF GENIUS AT BEACONSFIELD.

"Glimpses of glory ne'er forgot,
That tell like gleams on a sunset sea."
                                    MOORE.

THE secluded locality of a small town or rural district having seldom much of event to record, resembles, in the quietude of its course from age to age, the calm descent, through generations, in retirement, of many an untitled family of landed possessions and honourable position. An incident common to both locality and family temporarily disturbs the tranquillity of either, and brings the resemblance closer still. Such incident is the advent of a great man, to give publicity for the present and fame for the future. The effect of this on lineage is well known; it is no less striking as to locality. The birth, or even the coming to reside within its precincts, of a genius brings the small town or country spot before the world, and when that genius passes away, the memory of his merits earns for it a reputation of lasting endurance. The locality, like the lineage, may become retired and humble again, but while it remains, the glory of its great man rests with it; it is enriched with the legacy of his fame. Thus is the little more than hamlet of Stratford-on-Avon of undying note to all civilization; and thus is the barren rock of St. Helena

"The proudest sea-mark that o'ertops the wave."

Seldom, however, does this fortunate sojourn of genius fall to the same small place more than once. Of its so happening, there are a few rare examples; and among them the little town of Beaconsfield is perhaps the most singular instance—so singular that we are induced to give the following, we trust not uninteresting, details about the place, and the two great Edmunds who have made it famous.

Beaconsfield, situate in the county of Bucks, three-and-twenty miles by road from London, holds the rank of a market town, and has the reality of being one of the most picturesque country villages within the neighbourhood of the metropolis. It stands on an eminence, from which its lighted beacon, in former ages, could be seen far and near, and thus it obtained its name of Beacon's-field. The most proximate railway station to the place, that of Wooburn Green, is more than two miles from it; and, with the exception of a single omnibus travelling three times a week, there is, we believe, no public road conveyance to it. Consequently Beaconsfield is lonely, and little frequented by the general run of holiday and Sunday tourists; it possesses none of those smart villas of all forms and no forms of architecture, quasi Grecian and quasi Gothic, grave and gay, which clustering in their varied gracefulness, crowd and somewhat cocknefy most of the suburban localities within a circle of twenty-five miles from London.

In Beaconsfield the houses are chiefly red brick stately dwellings of a bye-gone century; and, owing to a peculiar combination of circumstances, the fine seats close around it are either deserted, in ruins, or but seldom inhabited. Yet, amid this solitude and desolation, what a beautiful English village it is!—with its four streets or avenues grass covered, and trees growing in them, with its numerous quaint old domiciles and gardens, and its grand domains, rich in magnificent foliage, embracing the town on all sides. Fair it truly is, and though abandoned, it is not uncourted. The common flock of wayfarers come not, we have said, to Beaconsfield, but it boasts of visitors of a higher class—of those pilgrims who bend their steps in reverence towards the shrines of departed genius, and who love to linger near the landmarks that are left of men who were giants in their time. After Stratford-on-Avon, the holy of holies in literary remembrance, and Twickenham, which Pope has made immortal; there is nowhere in England such another memory as that which decorates in chief the verdant retirement of Beaconsfield—the memory of Edmund Burke. Here did he reside during the whole of his political career; here is his grave, and hither, wending his way up the green acclivity, may now and then be seen the traveller, either native, or from France or Germany, or still more distant parts, a visitor to the Medina of him whose eloquent wisdom was the first to sound amid the crash of revolution, and to summon Europe to the defence of civilization and order. But we pass with too ready fondness to the memory of Edmund Burke. Let us begin with an earlier sojourn of genius in

Beaconsfield, which has left a memory there, not so venerable, it is true, as that of Edmund Burke, yet most pleasant to dwell upon—a memory which, with strange tenacity, attaches to the place far more closely, and with far more visible marks than even the memory of Burke. The genius we allude to was Edmund Waller, the first lyric poet of his time, and the worthy precursor of Robert Burns, and Tom Moore, and the other great lyrists that were to succeed. Beaconsfield was the favourite and constant residence of Waller in his lifetime, and it is in death his last earthly resting-place. Edmund Waller and Edmund Burke, two remarkable men of two remarkable ages, both orators and politicians, but in all else how different! The very contrast gives a pungency to the double biography which a visit to Beaconsfield thus recalls. With the reader's permission, we will now view each of these famous men, especially in connection with that home of their choice, which to this day enjoys the twofold reputation of their double sojourn. Let us begin with Edmund Waller.

Edmund Waller's stately tomb in Beaconsfield churchyard tells us, in most graceful Latinity, that he was of the poets of his time easily the prince: that when an octogenarian, he did not abdicate the laurel he had won in his youth, and that his country's language owes to him the possible belief that if the muses should cease to speak Greek and Latin, they would love to talk in English. This epitaph records the truth. Waller may claim rank among our greatest poets, and he had the rare faculty of never varying in his talent, and of writing just as ably at all periods of his life, whether in youth, manhood, or age.

He was the first who gave that soft, silvery tone to English verse, which Pope afterwards brought to perfection; and there are a terseness of style and an elegance of thought in all his compositions, which few of our other poets have equalled, and none have surpassed. Take, for instance, some of the passages from his love songs, such as—

> "Amoret! my lovely foe!
>   Tell me where thy strength doth lie?
> Where the power that charms us so?
>   In thy soul, or in thine eye?"

or

> "They that never had the use
> Of the grape's surprising juice,
> To the first delicious cup
> All their reason render up;
> Neither do, nor care to know,
> Whether it be best or no.
>
> "So they that are to love inclin'd,
>   Sway'd by chance, not choice or art,
> To the first that's fair or kind,
>   Make a present of their heart.
> 'Tis not she that first we love,
> But whom dying we approve."

Or the following stanzas, which lose nought in juxtaposition with that famous passage of Byron, beginning "So the struck eagle,"* which embodies the same idea at more length, but with less correctness.

---

* Byron's well-known lines are as follow:—

> "So the struck eagle, stretch'd upon the plain,
> No more through rolling clouds to soar again,
> View'd his own feather on the fatal dart,
> And wing'd the shaft that quiver'd in his heart;

Waller's stanzas are to a lady singing a song of his composing—

> "Chloris, yourself you so excel,
>   When you vouchsafe to breathe my thought,
> That, like a spirit, with this spell
>   Of my own teaching I am caught;
> That eagle's fate and mine are one,
>   Which, on the shaft that made him die,
> Espied a feather of his own,
>   Wherewith he wont to soar so high."

Waller the poet must be ever respected. Waller the man was a curious compound: he was an aristocrat and a cavalier, and yet, led by family connection, he oft sided with the opponents of King Charles, and was the stanch friend of Oliver Cromwell. He was a good family man, a loving husband, and a kind father, yet he never addressed a line of verse to either of his wives, or to his children, nor, though thoroughly domestic, did he ever write about his own home. The objects of his amorous effusions were all of royal or noble rank and condition, all ladies of title. First came the now ever-memorable Sacharissa, his chief flame, who was the Lady Dorothea Sidney, the daughter

> Keen were his pangs, but keener far to feel
> He nursed the pinion which impelled the steel;
> While the same plumage that had warmed his nest
> Drank the last life-drop of his bleeding breast."

It may be here observed, that it would be barely within the bounds of possibility, for the eagle to be sufficiently alive to be thus contemplating with an arrow quivering in his heart. Waller avoids the objection by merely describing the shaft as making the bird die, no doubt from lodging and festering in a less immediately mortal part.

of Robert Sidney, second Earl, and sister of Philip Sidney, third Earl of Leicester. Waller was a widower when he courted her, and when she rejected him, and married the Earl of Sunderland, he quietly stopped his strains, and sought in the Peerage for some other beauteous theme of his poetic admiration. He wrote charming lines to "my Lady Carlisle;" to Amoret, who was the Lady Sophia Murray; to Galatea, who was the Lady Mary Fielding; and to my Lady Morton, when an exile in France like himself; and he went as far as to address the Queens of England and France. But these ladies had all places in his Quixotic affections inferior to that of the Lady Dorothea Sidney, "the matchless Sidney, that immortal frame of perfect beauty," as he called her. "Had Dorothea," exclaims Waller, while wandering in the lovely groves of the seat of the Sidneys at Penshurst,—"had Dorothea lived when mortals made choice of their deities, this sacred shade had held an altar to her power." Again he writes to her, the Lady Dorothea, alluding also to her great uncle, the matchless knight, Sir Philip Sidney,—

> "Thyself a Sydney! from which noble train
> He sprung, that could so far exalt the name
> Of love, and warm our nation with his flame;
> That all we can of love or high desire
> Seems but the smoke of amorous Sidney's fire."

Waller had Sacharissa's portrait for constant contemplation infixed in the wainscoat over the mantel-piece of his sitting-room, at his seat at Beaconsfield. That picture which he declared, "wonders so distant in one face disclosed," remained in the place he put it, until recently torn away and sold. Alas! for the gothic hand that took it down.

One cannot conclude this reminiscence of Waller's courtship of Sacharissa, without observing how strongly it goes to prove a remarkable fact—the greatness of a poet's power. Here was a lady, who was daughter of an earl, sister of two earls, wife of an earl, mother of an earl, and sister also of Algernon Sidney. Yet, with all this, what would have remained of her now, if the gentle poet, whom she disdained in her pride, had not granted her a distinction which time cannot destroy? Where are her other coronetted brothers and sisters? Passed into utter oblivion, from which not even the fame of Algernon Sidney could save them. Just like them, the Lady Dorothea would be to posterity a thing unknown, but that the poet's eye, in its glance from heaven to earth, lighted on her beauty; his imagination bodied her forth, and his pen gave name and habitation to those mere airy nothings, her sounding titles and her fleeting charms. What birth and rank could not do, this poet did. The coronet that nobility procured for Sacharissa was but of dust: the wreath that Waller's poetic sovereignty bestowed on her is immortal.

Waller was a courtier and a wit, a gay frequenter of the coffee-houses and taverns, and a rich exquisite of his time; yet he preferred to all else in the world his seat of Hall Barn, at Beaconsfield, its verdant seclusion, its domestic comforts, and its rural pleasures. Like what we shall tell directly of Burke, Waller loved to see friends around him, and he entertained hospitably. Like Burke, he had many of the great people of his day among his guests. Lords and ladies of the Commonwealth, and of King Charles' court, were welcomed in their turn. Among men of literary note, Evelyn, Roscommon, and Dryden were his friends; and at Waller's table, Cromwell, his relative, would unbend and lay aside all puritan restraint. "Cousin Waller," he would say, when his usual reserve was alluded to, "I must talk to these men (the Puritans) in their own way." Exiled in France for a serious, though over-blamed act of political intrigue, Waller, though living richly at Rouen, and at Paris, and enjoying the society of Corneille, St. Evremond, and Voiture, and of the English royalists, sighed for his home at Beaconsfield. Cromwell's pardon brought him back, and his panegyric of the Lord Protector is the finest poem he ever wrote. Yet, at the Restoration, Waller addressed another panegyric to Charles II. "Master Waller," said the King to him on his coming to court, "those verses you wrote on Cromwell are, they tell me, far better than those you have written on me." "Sire," was the apt and courtier-like reply, "poets always excel more in fiction than in truth." Such was Edmund Waller, a dubious politician, yet noted for his stern parliamentary eloquence; a fanciful lover, yet attached not fancifully, but soberly and stanchly to his own two wives and his children; a foppish cavalier, yet imbued with a strong round-head love of English liberty; a writer of love songs, but never trenching, as too many of the poets of his time did, on the bounds of morality or religion. Posterity must forget his faults in his greatness and his purity as a poet. Beaconsfield, through his choice, first became a place of note. Its earliest fame was Waller, and his memory hangs round it still. The visitor will find many a mark and memorial of Waller there. The poet's magnificent seat of Hall Barn, Beaconsfield, built by himself, but improved by his son, still remains. The Waller family left it only a few years ago, when it became the property of another distinguished man, whose sojourn was also a sojourn of genius at Beaconsfield, the late Sir Gore Ouseley, Bart., and at his demise it passed into other hands. In its now uninhabited condition, dismantled of its furniture, signs of the past may be discovered on the premises, and in the picturesque domain adorned with classic temples and obelisks. There the peculiar armorial ensigns of the Wallers meet one everywhere, the walnut tree crest with the royal escutcheon of France belonging to it, the origin of which was this :—The Waller family, it should be understood, is one of the oldest in England. A Sir Richard Waller, of the time of Henry V., was a distinguished warrior, and he took prisoner at the battle of Agincourt the principal and the most chivalrous combatant among the French, Charles of Orleans, who, by the way, married the widowed Queen of Richard II., and who, by another wife, was father of Louis XII. Charles was a perfect gentleman and a graceful poet. He remained for twenty-four years in the friendly custody of Sir Richard Waller, at his castle in Kent, and the idea may not be too far-fetched, that from this princely bard the Wallers may have imbibed that taste for verse which has made many of them poets even to this day, for Dr. Waller, of Dublin, is of the race. Henry V. marked his approval of Sir Richard's conduct in taking the French prince, by granting to him and his descendants the crest with the royal escutcheon as above mentioned, and the motto, "Hic fructus virtutis." This crest and motto, among many poetic emblems, are to be found continually repeated in the house and grounds of Hall Barn; and thus, over the whole house, to use the words of the poetic Charles of Orleans himself, " Le temps a laissé son manteau."

The churchyard of Beaconsfield presents the fine monument to Edmund Waller we have already mentioned. It was the work of filial affection, having been raised by Waller's son at a costly expense. Of late it has become much decayed, but funds are now sought by the Rev. John Gould, B.D., Rector of Beaconsfield, to effect its restoration. May his praiseworthy object meet with success. The poet well deserves a sacred memorial, who could, when in his extreme old age, and close upon his death, write such lines as these:

> "The seas are quiet when the winds give o'er:
> So, calm are we when passions are no more;
> For then we know how vain it was to boast
> Of fleeting things, so certain to be lost.
> Clouds of affection from our younger eyes
> Conceal that emptiness which age descries;
> The soul's dark cottage, battered and decayed,
> Lets in new light through chinks that time has made;
> Stronger by weakness, wiser men become,
> As they draw near to their eternal home;
> Leaving the old, both worlds at once they view,
> That stand upon the threshold of the new."

Let us now pass over some seventy years, and come to Beaconsfield's later and greater repute—the sojourn of genius there in the person of Edmund Burke.

Edmund Burke, through his mother's family, that of the Nagles, claimed kindred of Edmund Spenser, the author of the Faerie Queene, and the earliest school of his youth happened to be near the ruins of that Kilcolman Castle where Spenser wrote his famous poem. Here, among the lovely scenery of the spot, it is said Edmund Spenser's boyish namesake, England's future orator, loved to wander, picking up from the peasantry all those marvellous anecdotes and legendary tales which had not a little to do with the Faerie Queene, and which instilled in him much of that innate and eastern imagery which afterwards gave such splendour to his eloquence. Here also Edmund Burke first imbibed that craving for a country life, which clung to him through his whole existence. His next school-days, under his excellent Quaker master Shackleton, were passed in another rural locality, Ballitore, in Kildare. Here, too, it was his delight to roam on holidays in the fields; and with that mind that was ever bent on the acquisition of knowledge, to obtain his earliest insight into agriculture, of which he shewed such apt and practical experience when he became a Buckinghamshire country gentleman. Burke, whilst at Dublin University, evinced his rural taste by translating into English verse, from the second Georgic, Virgil's famous panegyric of a country life. Burke's lines display wonderful fervour and facility for a youth of sixteen, as the following passage will shew:

> "How happy, too, the peaceful rustic lies,
> The grass his bed, his canopy the skies;
> From heat retiring to the noontide glade,
> His trees protect him with an ample shade;

No jarring sounds invade his settling breast,
His lowing cows shall lull him into rest.
Here 'mong the caves, the woods and rocks around,
Here, only here, the hardy youth abound;
Religion here has fixed her pure abodes,
Parents are honoured, and adored the gods;
Departing Justice, when she fled mankind,
In these blest plains her footsteps left behind."

In a few years after this, Burke had come to London, had at five-and-twenty written a book that was to be a classic in our language, the "Essay on the Sublime and Beautiful," and had become the literary ally and close friend for life of Dr. Johnson, Garrick, Goldsmith, and Sir Joshua Reynolds: he had married the wife whom he ever continued to love with the fondest devotion; he had joined the party and government of the virtuous Lord Rockingham, and he had in a single night achieved his political fame by one of the finest pieces of eloquence that ever rang upon the ears of Parliament. Behold Burke then a great man, with the eyes of Europe upon him: he is also what he perhaps liked as well: he is a country gentleman. The seat of Butler's Court, or Gregories (as it was at different times called), at Beaconsfield, was his property, and he has here commenced that charming rural course of life which made his home so perfect and so happy. Burke delighted in society, and could not live without it. Warm in heart and buoyant in spirits, boundless in his knowledge and information, taking interest in every thing great or small, grave or gay, quite a cavalier in courtesy and in his notions of attention to the fair sex, Burke had an attraction about him, that fascinated all within his reach and influence. He loved, and was beloved by wife, children, and friends; his servants clung to him with constant affection, and the very beggar, that received his alms, had pleasant remembrance of the gentle word that would accompany the donation. And how Burke doted on that home. "Every care," would he say, "vanishes the moment I enter under its roof." Burke, at this seat, the value of which he nearly doubled by his own agricultural skill, exercised in his happier days a continual hospitality, not excessive or wasteful, but intellectual, lively and generous. Among his visitors were some of the greatest that England then possessed—men whose names, either in politics or literature, were to live for ever. Foremost among them was his friend and patron, Charles Wentworth, second Marquess of Rockingham, who, if not all-powerful as a prime minister, was the soul of honour, and was certainly among the wisest, the best, and the most amiable of England's premiers. There were also Lord Fitzwilliam, Rockingham's nephew, and the Duke of Portland, Burke's neighbour at Bulstrode, and Sir George Savile, Lord George Cavendish, and Admiral Keppel, and Flood, and Fox, and Sheridan. And then the literati. *Primus,* or, at any rate, the proudest *inter pares,* came Dr. Johnson. The potent Doctor admitted that Burke was the only man whom he feared in argument, or to whom he would strike his colours; notwithstanding which he was attached to him cordially. There was also that mysterious and constant friend, William Burke, M.P., (distantly related to Edmund, we believe, not as a Burke, but in the female line), to whom

Edmund owed his introduction to Lord Rockingham, and whom Mr. Jelinger Symons' recent clever book—a book, alas! soon followed by the death of its author—maintains to have been the author of the Letters of Junius. Then there was Burke's other loving and ever-devoted friend, the warm-hearted, unsophisticated, inimitable Oliver Goldsmith: and there were Sir Joshua Reynolds, author and painter; Garrick, author and actor; Arthur Murphy, historian and dramatist; and Dr. Burney and his daughter, Miss Burney, whose novel of Evelina, Edmund Burke sat up a whole night to read. Of minor statesmen, aristocrats, authors, and wits, a host used also to be flocking to Beaconsfield. Burke was himself the life of this continual concourse of rank, beauty, and talent. Politics were laid aside, and wit, mirth, and good humour reigned supreme. Various anecdotes represent the statesman-orator entering with glee into the sports and amusements of the social crowd about him, even to sharing in the jokes and games of children. He would, it is said, after a learned argument with the graver of his guests, go to join with equal intent in some suggested improvement of a boy's kite. He was the chief instructor of his own son, that darling object of his hope and pride; he prepared him for the University and Parliament, forming one whom he fondly looked to be greater than himself. But hospitality, domestic affection, and social converse were not the only charms of Burke's house at Beaconsfield. Charity gave it ever greater elevation and fame. The poor for miles round were the constant object of Burke's sagacious kindness and care: he established for them a school and saving fund, and various benevolent institutions. His charity, too, had, on more than one occasion, been of national value, since it was his wont (in the words of Mackay's famous song) "to help young merit into fame." The country owes to Burke's benevolence the painter Barry, and one greater still, whose introduction to prosperity happened thus. A starving poet, on the brink of ruin, was led by Providence to knock at Burke's door; he sent in a letter, asking Burke to save him. That appeal was listened to at once: the applicant was received, sheltered, and promoted: these facts and his subsequent success are of common and general knowledge. The bard was Crabbe, and Burke's act of humanity will go down to posterity coeval with the poet's verse. "The memory of Edmund Burke's philanthropy," writes his friend Shackelton, "*immortale manet.*"

Let now a few more years pass over Burke's home at Beaconsfield, and how changed and sad, and yet how worthy of contemplation the scene! The host of Gregories is struck down by a giant affliction. His only child, his idolized son, who was to him the life of his life, has died at the very onset of his career; and the father's grief, to use his own words, is one that cannot be comforted. Yet amid this sorrow, and the mortal sickness that his sorrow has engendered, Edmund Burke is as good and great as ever. His hospitality has only changed its object. The joys of the social circle of friends can charm no longer, but he has discovered another channel for his bounty. He has called around him the royalist refugees who had escaped destitute from the murderous revolution then going on in France. He has provided shelter for many of them, either in his own house or in its neighbourhood. He has induced the government to alleviate the wants of all of them. At Penn, three miles from Beaconsfield, he has founded a school for the children of the emigrants, which continued to flourish long after his death, until the restoration of royalty in France rendered it no longer necessary. The chief exile himself, the then unthroned representative of a line of kings, Louis XVIII., might be seen at the gate of Gregories, come to thank the lord of the mansion for what he had done for his people. Would that the Bourbons could always remember the service then rendered to them and their followers. Burke's political influence is now more powerful than ever. He has roused England and the greater part of Europe to sustain the cause of order, and from all sides he is looked to for advice. William Windham, the Minister at War, is his constant visitor. Wilberforce (who was present) describes one of these consultations of the government, by the side of Burke's dying couch. The attention, he writes, shewn to Burke by all that party, was just like the treatment of Ahitophel of old. It was as if one went to inquire of the oracle of the Lord. Edmund Burke died of a broken heart in 1797; and though more than sixty years have passed since then, Beaconsfield bears still visible marks of that incurable sorrow. The mansion of Gregories was no more cared for by its owner, and was sold from the family by his widow. What was an hereditary house to him who in his grief refused a peerage, with the title of Lord Burke of Beaconsfield? An accidental fire has since destroyed the dwelling, and one can scarcely trace, with no other landmark than a few ruined offices, the site of the mansion in the now deserted but still beautiful grounds. A decayed stable alone remains, with the very stall in it where Windham, when he rode down, big with the fate of nations, would put up his white horse. The humble tablet in the church marks Burke's burial there, instead of in Westminster Abbey, as it would have been but for the direction in his will. "My body I desire to be buried in the church at Beaconsfield, near to the bodies of my dearest brother and my dearest son, in all humility praying that, as we have lived in perfect unity together, we may together have a part in the resurrection of the just."

Burke's Grove, a noble plantation, remains in the rear of the mansion, as when Edmund used it as his favourite walk; and there are some at Beaconsfield who can remember his sad and stately figure gliding there to and fro, pondering, no doubt, over the loss he had sustained. This is elegantly alluded to in a poem recently written by a Beaconsfield author.

> "Oft to this sweet secluded spot he came,
> Far from the busy world and noisy fame,
> And sought amidst its solitudes to rest
> His wearied mind on Nature's quiet breast,
> When o'er his life's bright tide all darkly fell
> Death's shadow!—and the mourner sighed farewell
> To hope and joy. Ambition's course was run,
> The father's heart was buried with his son."

As with Waller, endeavours are making, under the auspices of the Rev. Mr. Gould, the Rector of Beaconsfield, to have there some suitable memorial of Edmund Burke. The attempt has met with encouragement, and it is to be hoped may eventually succeed. Edmund Burke, however, has not been fortunate in monumental honours; there is no public open air commemorative mark of him in England, nor, blushingly be it said, in Ireland either. Moore's statue, under the auspices of the Earl of Carlisle, has been lately raised in Dublin; Goldsmith's, pursuant to a suggestion of the same gifted nobleman, will soon be also erected there. Should not Burke's be the next proposed? Burke, in thought, word, and act, had Ireland ever near his heart, and he it was whose first act of power, when in office, was to procure for her that independence, the credit of which fell entirely to his able coadjutors in the struggle, Charlemont and Grattan. Yet what matters it that Waller and Burke should have no monumental trophies, beyond what still exist in their own beautiful and now lonely Beaconsfield? Are they not of the stamp of those who live, not in marble only, but in the minds of men, and whose works and memories are more lasting than brass, mightier than the pyramids, and indestructible by time or tempest? Are they not among those who never wholly die? Truly indeed has Pope said, "Nor yet shall Waller yield to time:" and with equal truth, has Grattan eloquently observed, "Edmund Burke's immortality is that which is common to Cicero or to Bacon, that which can never be interrupted while there exists the beauty of order or the love of virtue; and which can fear no death except what barbarity may impose on the globe."

RECOLLECTIONS OF ENGLISH COUNTIES.

"Many a land that is famous in story."
                                    SCOTT.

No country in the world contains so much of interest, to be seen at the expense of such little toil and time, as our own English land; almost every nook and corner has some point of attraction, some association on which the mind may pleasingly dwell; here, the ancient feudal castle, full of story, erst the stronghold of the Norman Baron, or of the bold adherent of the White or Red Rose; there, the border tower, with legend, and chronicle, and ballad around it, producing the same effect on the mind that the ivy does, when it coils and clusters about the mouldering ruin. In one county, the venerable Abbey recalls the piety, and learning, and munificence of the early ages; in another, the old royalist mansion tells of a loyalty that defied "the rebel Commons;" while in a third, a humble farmhouse is rendered famous by the hospitality and shelter afforded to a fugitive prince. Truly do those ancient Manor Houses of every style and design, moated, gabelled, or embattled, and those dateless churches, beneath whose grey walls repose the great and good of many generations, evidence that we inhabit an "old country," one full of remembrances, domestic and national. It is pleasant to live where so many illustrious men have lived, to admire the same vales, and woods, and streams, which so many poets have sung, and to dwell in scenes hallowed as the birth-places of Englishmen who have achieved immortality in literature, science, or martial fame. Washington Irving well expresses this idea :—

"Who can walk with soul unmoved among the stately groves of Penshurst, where Sydney passed his boyhood; or can look without fondness upon the tree that is said to have been planted on his birthday; or can ramble among the classic bowers of Hagley; or can pause among the solitudes of Windsor Forest, and look at the oaks around, huge, grey, and time-worn, like the old castle towers, and not feel as if he were surrounded by so many monuments of long-enduring glory? It is then, when viewed in this light, that planted groves and stately avenues, turreted castles and cultivated parks, have an advantage over the more luxuriant beauties of unassisted nature; it is then that they teem with moral associations, and keep up the ever-interesting story of human existence."

It was a remark of another distinguished American, Mr. Everett, who was at one time the United States' envoy in this country, "We have everything great in America. We have great rivers, great mountains, great forests, and great lakes; but we have no olden buildings, no castles or houses of an ancient aristocracy, and no monasteries. To see these, we must visit the land of our fathers."

There is something equally just and beautiful in these affectionate tributes to the old country, and the more such kind and ennobling feelings spread amongst the Americans, the better it will be for themselves. Abstractedly, there is no great value in uninhabitable ruins; and no doubt a mere utilitarian would look upon the finest Gothic cathedral as a mere stone receptacle for bones and dust; but somehow there is a feeling, in all save the obtusest of us, that will be heard in spite of utilitarianism, and we shall invariably find that whatever tends to connect us in idea with the past and the future, tends also—and in a greater degree than anything else, save revealed religion—to make us conscious that we belong not wholly to earth or to the present, but are portions of immortality. He who narrows his thoughts and wishes to the time being, may certainly reap some practical advantage from this limited application of his faculties, but it will be at the expense of higher and better feelings, just as the man who spends the whole of his life in pointing needles or tempering pen-knives, may acquire skill in that particular art, but in so doing becomes eventually as narrow as his occupation. The more we free our minds from the idea of time and space, which are only words of limit, the nearer we approach to the understanding of the infinite—to that which has neither beginning nor end—and nothing does this so effectually as the abstracting ourselves from the present in the consideration of the past. It may, however, be objected to us, as Horatio objected to Hamlet, " this is to consider too curiously;" but instead of imitating the philosophic Prince in our answer, which would lead us into the wilds of metaphysics, we will rather beg our readers to accompany us in a short ramble amongst the Halls and Castles of those who have helped to make the name of England so illustrious. In doing this, it is not our purpose to pay the least attention to geographical proprieties; limping time will have to toil after us in vain while we fly from place to place, for no better reason in the order of our march than their happenng thus to rise upon the recollection.

The antiquities of this country may for the most part be traced either to war or religion—to the turbulent though chivalrous barons, or to the monks, whom it is the fashion of modern ignorance to include in one sweeping censure, as if the embers of learning, art, and science had not been kept alive by them in the Monasteries, when, but for their industry, the mailed heel of kings and nobles would have trampled them out altogether.

We question much if any county in broad England is more deserving of notice than WARWICKSHIRE. True, it has not a minster like York, nor a university like Oxford, nor tin mines like Cornwall, nor has it ever been suspected like Devonshire of producing silver; ·neither can it boast like Derbyshire of Devil's Punchbowls, or shivering mountains with stalactite caverns in their bosoms; but for all that, in its own quiet, unobtrusive way it offers many points of interest to those who delight in beautiful scenery, or in the recollections of other times. If, for instance, the Avon be not so broad as the Thames, nor so wild as the Severn when it quarrels with the sea—as it not unfrequently does—still it has a charm both for natives and foreigners in its connection with the name of Shakespeare, that sets it above all other English rivers; and Charlecote Park, memorable as having been the scene of the poet's early delinquencies, where he stole deer, "but did not kiss the keeper's daughter," an omission which Sir John Falstaff in his case seems to have thought rendered the affair altogether venial.

In addition to these claims upon our notice, cannot Warwick show the remains of the once gigantic Kenilworth? Small remains we must needs confess, but to which many an innocent traveller has made his pilgrimage, deluded by that arch wizard Walter Scott—he should have been christened Michael—expecting in the simplicity of his heart to find something like the Kenilworth built up a second time in what may truly be called the magic volume, for even that potent tome, which William of Deloraine abstracted from under the sleeper's head, could not have had greater powers of enchanting. Is there not also the wonder-working Spa of Leamington, which realizes the fable of Medea's kettle, and makes the old, if not quite young again, yet almost as good as young? And is not Warwick renowned beyond all measure by its two valiant earls, by Guy who slew "Colbrand, the giant," that same mighty man; and by the no less formidable champion, who made and unmade monarchs at his own pleasure, Warwick, " proud setter up, and puller down of kings ?" And, moreover, is not the impregnable castle—impregnable in those days—which he inhabited, well worthy of a day's journey, if it were only for its access and external appearance? Built upon a rock at the foot of which flows the Avon, it is approached by a broad winding path hewn out of the solid rock, so that for a hundred yards or more, expectation is kept upon the stretch by the total shutting out of all prospect beyond these enormous walls of living stone that rampart you in on either side. As you draw near the end of this sombre and mysterious avenue, first one massive tower appears, then a second, then a third, and next the whole castle bursts upon the sight in all its ponderous magnificence. Never did the spirit of feudalism find a more appropriate dwelling.

Is there not also the quaint old-fashioned town of Coventry, with its pretty legend of the Lady Godiva, which some learned antiquaries have taken as much pains to demolish as if it had been a drop of poison virulent enough of itself to corrupt the whole well of truth? Why, in the name of dulness, do they not set about proving that little Thomas Thumb is a great lie, that the heroic Jack never climbed up a beanstalk, and that there is no such thing in rerum naturâ as a phœnix? But let them talk and write as they please; "in spite of spite," Lady Godiva still continues every third year to ride in pageant through the city. And long may she do so! Genius of dulness! We are not sure to be cheated out of all the illusions of our childhood, to be deprived of all those beautiful beliefs which hang like green leaves about the tree of life, and which being torn away, the trunk stands bare and unsightly as a birch in December.

Abounding as Warwickshire does in situations of surpassing loveliness, no marvel that its broad expanse can boast of some of the finest seats in England. Independently of those to which we have already alluded, there are Ragley, Pakington, Grendon, Wroxhall Abbey, Eatington, Stoneleigh, Whitley Abbey, Grove Park, Shuckburgh, Wroxton Abbey, Arbury, Alscot, Guy's Cliffe, Atherstone, Birbury, Studley Castle, Clopton, Moxhul, Stivic, Newbold Hall, Compton Verney, Ansley, and Merevale. The county families of distinction are those of Grevile, Conway, Shirley, Lucy, Chetwynd, Dugdale, Newdegate, Leigh, Wilmot, Hartopp, Shuckburgh, Mordaunt, Craven, Verney, Bracebridge, Dilke, Adderley, Skipwith, and West.

But to turn our pilgrim's steps to other shrines; let us visit old BEAUCHIEFF ABBEY. This monastic relic is in the extensive parish of Sheffield, a name which in the present day is so inseparably connected with the idea of plated goods and cutlery, that few will be able to imagine that it was ever the site of heroic deeds and baronial castles. Even the name of Hallamshire is seldom if ever heard beyond the locality to which it applies. Yet this was not always the case. There was a time when this district was the favourite residence of lordly barons, though of such days the traces are but few, and those few rapidly decaying, and giving place to the more useful, but certainly less picturesque, purposes of modern life.

Beauchieff Abbey was founded in 1183 by Robert Fitz-Ranulph, the powerful Lord of Alfreton, of Norton and of many other places in the county of Derby, and it seems in a short time to have become highly popular. And well it might. The spirit of religion in those days was sincere and fervent, besides which, the people, who had hitherto been called upon to support such institutions in parts far away from them, had now all the advantage that belongs to the presence of a landlord, who consumes on his estate what his estate produces. Other benefactors were found to continue the work which had been so well begun: and in course of time the Monks of Beauchieff became a rich and important community. At the general ruin, however, of the monasteries, the site was granted to Nicholas Strelley, and here now stands in a lovely vale, at a short distance from the scanty remains of the old Abbey, one of the best specimens of Elizabethan architecture now existing, the residence of Mr. Pegge Burnell, Strelley's direct descendant.

Another great Monastic foundation was WHITBY ABBEY, in Yorkshire—"high Whitby's cloister'd pile"—but its beginnings, like the tiny springs from which mighty rivers flow, were small indeed. Three poor monks set out, towards the close of the eleventh century, from Evesham Abbey for the north, with the pious intention of restoring monastic institutions in Northumbria. They travelled on foot, with a little mule to carry their books and priestly garments, and they wended their way onward, slowly, but cheerfully. Inadequate must have appeared, in human estimation, the means possessed by these lowly brethren for the mighty task they had undertaken, but a Divine guidance directed their steps, and prospered their endeavours. Having sojourned for a brief period at Newcastle-upon-Tyne, they journeyed on, and built themselves huts among the ruins of the ancient Abbey of Whitby, and erected a temporary place of worship. Here they gathered together a goodly number of followers, and became the founders of that holy community, which, subsequently, held such puissant sway in "Whitby's broad domains."

Sir Richard Cholmley, who eventually obtained possession of this dissolved monastery's lands, was a distinguished soldier, and fought with great gallantry in Scotland. He loved pomp, and generally had fifty or sixty servants about his house; nor would he ever go up to London without a retinue of thirty or forty men. His hair and eyes were black, and his complexion so swarthy, that he was usually styled "The Black Knight of the North." To his son and successor, Sir Francis Cholmley, the mansion of Whitby Hall owes its erection.

With less of antiquity to recommend it, but with the advantage of modern refinement, and present habitation, is DUNCOMBE PARK, with its castle of Helmsley, remarkable in a county full of fine seats, for the varied interest of the scenery, and the numerous treasures of art which it contains:—

"And Helmsley, once proud Buckingham's delight,
Slides to a scrivener or a city knight."

If, using the privilege of the seven-leagued boots, we step from Duncombe Park into Craven, we shall stumble on ESHTON HALL, which finds such honourable mention in the bibliographical pages of Dibdin, and will be long remembered as the residence of a distinguished patron of literature, Miss Richardson Currer.

But the grandest place in Yorkshire is CASTLE HOWARD, a princely mansion, four miles from Malton, erected by Charles, the third Earl of Carlisle, on the spot where once stood the old castle of Hinderskelf: it is more extensive than Blenheim, and is not altogether the work of one architect, nor is it from one design. The north front was built by Sir John Vanbrugh, and consists of a rich centre of the Corinthian order, with a cupola rising from the roof, flanked by two large wings, the east of which was finished according to the original plan, while the west has been erected by Sir James Robinson, with little regard to the character of the rest of the building. The south, or garden front, is also magnificent, and though perhaps questionable in point of taste, is undeniably very striking. The surrounding park is an excellent specimen of an English demesne, and the view over it from the terrace is most charming. Within the house, the rooms are spacious to an unusual degree, and abound in all the luxuries of modern refinement. Choice pictures (among other treasures, "The Three Marys," Vandyke's "Snyders," and "The Adoration of the Kings"), rare pieces of antiquity, and costly furniture, meet the eye on all sides; and yet there is more magic in the simple name of Howard, associated as it is with the romantic features and the heroic achievements of English history, than in all these accumulated splendours.

While the sun seems still to linger on the wolds and hills of Yorkshire, we must notice one or two places more: HORNBY CASTLE, in the North Riding, a noble, but irregular pile, even now retains a portion of its baronial grandeur: it encloses an inner court or quadrangle, like the old colleges at Cambridge, though the general line of the building does not exceed two stories. Two embattled towers, the one, round in the centre of the east front, and the other, square at the end of the same side, are carried to a greater height, thus breaking what would else be a uniform and monotonous line; while on three of the sides—south, east, and north—is a separate entrance. The whole stands upon an eminence sloping gently to the river that winds around its base, and commands an extensive view of mountain and moorland, of fertile plain and valley. From its extent and massiveness it impresses the mind strongly with the rude greatness of former times, when man seemed, with a noble, but mistaken daring, to stamp "*esto perpetuum!*" upon all his works.

Previous to the reign of Henry IV., this castle belonged to the family of St. Quintin, till the male line becoming extinct, and the young heiress, Margaret St. Quintin, marrying Sir John Conyers, it of course passed into the possession of her husband. This family increased in wealth and rank for many years, when a daughter again succeeded to the inheritance, who married Thomas Lord D'Arcy, and thus transferred it to a new line. The same thing happened a third time in 1778, when Robert, Earl of Holderness, the lineal descendant of the Conyers, died, leaving an only daughter to inherit. This lady gave her hand to Francis-Godolphin, Marquess of Carmarthen, the eldest son of the Duke of Leeds, and in the Leeds family Hornby Castle still remains.

BOLTON CASTLE, in Wensleydale, at one time the prison of Mary Stuart, was for three centuries the stately residence of another illustrious northern family, the Baronial House of Scrope. It is situated on a high, bleak and barren hill, approachable by a toilsome ascent, and over the bed of a rapid torrent, and we cannot easily imagine why a great family, who had at their command all the luxuriant, fertile plain beneath, chose to take up their abode, generation after generation, exposed to storms and tempests without, and to darkness and discomfort within. Compared to Bolton Hall—the mansion of Lord Bolton, the present noble possessor of the demesne—its frowning predecessor forms a striking contrast : the one, the emblem of modern, polished life ; the other, the type and gloomy relique of feudal manners.

From "time immemorial" we trace the Scropes as resident in the lovely vale of Wensleydale—the most romantic and picturesque of the northern valleys—and, in the whole range of our nobility, we can scarcely point to a family more illustrious. An unbroken male descent from the Conquest, if not from the time of Edward the Confessor, their alliances, their achievements, and their possessions, sufficiently attest their antiquity and importance; whilst the mere enumeration of the dignities they attained, between the reigns of Edward II. and Charles I., proves the high rank they enjoyed. In this interval of three hundred years, the house of Scrope produced two Earls and twenty Barons, one Chancellor, four Treasurers, and two Chief Justices of England, one Archbishop and two Bishops, five Knights of the Garter, and numerous Bannerets, the most distinguished soldiers in the days of chivalry.

But to enumerate all that deserves record in Yorkshire, would prolong our ramble beyond any reasonable limit.

" ———— O famous York !
What county hath this isle, that can compare with thee ?"

Are there not Wentworth House, Thrybergh, Wortley, Harewood, Castle Howard, Allerton Park, Swillington, Kirklees, Gledstone, Aldwark, Nostell, Bolton Abbey,

Gilling Castle, Walton Hall, Heslington, Cannon Hall, Escrick, Brougton, Tong, Wentworth Castle, Rievaulx Abbey, Bretton, Bramham, Everingham, Chevet Hall, Byrom, Denton Park, Ganton, Gisburne Park, Howsham, Burton Agnes, Hornby Castle, Aske, Easby Abbey, Bolton Hall, Gunthwaite, Hovingham, Duncombe Park, Swinton, Hackness, Kirkleatham, Marske, Rokeby, Burton Constable, Studley Priory, Fountains Abbey, Bransby, Jerveaux Abbey, Norton Conyers, and Wombwell? One halt more only before quitting this magnificent county, which is so replete with historical associations, while in extent it is unrivalled by any two of the largest shires in England. The very name of TEMPLE NEWSAM brings us back to the age of the warrior-monks, who once set their mailed foot upon the necks of kings, and had well-nigh been an over-match for the Pope himself. Where the present spacious and noble mansion stands, there was formerly a preceptory of the order of the Templars, and from that circumstance is derived the first half of the modern appellation. Upon the suppression of these ambitious soldiers, the estate was granted by Edward III. to Sir John D'Arcy, with whose descendants it remained till Thomas Lord D'Arcy got himself embroiled with Henry the Eighth, who at all times administered justice in a summary way of his own, cutting off heads with as little pretence to reason as any Schah of Persia. In his day the Yorkshiremen raised a rebellion under the name of the "Pilgrimage of Grace," and Lord D'Arcy was suspected of treachery in having delivered up to them Pontefract Castle, whereupon the bluff monarch caused him to be hung upon Tower-hill. It is indeed far from certain whether the unlucky nobleman had really betrayed his trust to these *gracious pilgrims,* but Henry's suspicions were generally fatal to the object of them; and having thus removed his former favourite, he bestowed the property upon Matthew, Earl of Lennox, whose son, the celebrated Darnley, was born here. James the First granted it to the then Duke of Lennox, and from him it was purchased by Sir Anthony Ingram, who built the present splendid mansion. It stands upon the banks of the Aire, about four miles from Leeds, and nearly fourteen from York, in the midst of a beautiful and fertile tract, which is watered by one of the largest rivers in Yorkshire.

The legends which used to attach to the ruined Castles and decayed Abbeys of England, have, with few exceptions, passed out of men's memories; that such legends must have existed at one period cannot, we should think, be a matter of question; it seems but fair to presume that the bold barons who built or inherited these castles before they went to ruin must have done many a deed in their time that ought not to be forgotten; yet we must confess that small care has been taken to preserve our legendary lore; here and there, the antiquarian explorer meets with an oasis where the leaf is green, and the fountain is flowing, but generally speaking, he plods on for days, gleaning little by the wayside. Some chance, and not quite forgotten tradition, some family tale that still lingers in an old Baronial Hall, is all that rewards his toil—the more prized from its very rareness. One of these scarce legends is associated with HAIGH HALL, in Lancashire, and afforded Sir Walter Scott material for his story of "the Betrothed." In simple words we will endeavour to narrate it. An old MS. pedigree, which we have seen, describes Sir William Bradshaigh—the hero of our tale—as "a great trauveller and souldger," and records that, stimulated by his roving disposition and martial ardour, he set out for the Holy Land. There, we may safely infer that he was neither the least nor the lowest of the brave champions who fought for the Cross. Ten years elapsed, and according to rumour and general belief, the good knight had perished. Now, whether Mabel, his wife, was over-persuaded by her friends, or led away by her own fancy, does not appear, but she at length married again, and the object of her second choice was a Welsh knight. Shortly after, Sir William Bradshaigh, having safely returned to England, paid a visit, in the disguise of a palmer, to his own castle, and took his place amongst the recipients of the Lady Mabel's bounty. The moment, however, Mabel saw the palmer, she was struck by his resemblance to her first husband, and her astonishment was heightened when he presented her with a ring which he said Sir William had, in dying, entrusted him to bear to Haigh Hall. Old times came back on her memory, old thoughts were awakened, and she burst into tears; yet still without suspecting her former lord in the poor palmer. The Welsh Knight, jealous as is his countrymen's wont, "grew," says the old record, "exceedingly wroth," and, in his fury, struck the lady. The blow, and the lady's evidence of feeling, so much moved Sir William, that he threw off his concealment, made himself known to his tenants and retainers, and hastened to take revenge on the unchivalrous

Welshman. It seems, though, that the offender had somehow got notice of these hostile designs, and preferring the chance of flight to the chance of battle, rode off at full speed, without staying further question. But he was not destined to escape; Sir William overtook him near Newton Park, and slew him with his own hand; for which offence he was outlawed for a year and a day. As for Mabel, "she was enjoined by her confessor to doe penance by going onest every week, barefoot and barelegged, to a crosse ner Wigan from the Haghe wilest she lived." This cross is called Mabel's Cross even to our day; and the monument of Sir William Bradshaigh and Dame Mabel, his wife, reposing side by side, is still pointed out in Wigan Church. The son of the worthy pair succeeded to the fair inheritance of "the Haighe," and there, in a stately and splendid structure erected in modern times, now dwelleth the Bradshaighs' descendant, Lindsay, Earl of Crawford and Balcarres.

It is cheering to have a tradition of this romantic character, associated with the busy, manufacturing, money-making county of Lancaster; and it is yet more gratifying to know that that wondrous district, whose moors were once as barren as now they are teeming with life, has many still remaining of its ancient time-honoured seats: Bolton Hall, where Henry VI., defeated and fugitive, found an asylum with the Pudseys; Lathom House, memorable for the heroic defence of the Countess of Derby—Charlotte de la Tremouille—

> "'Twas there they raised, 'mid sap and siege,
> The banners of their rightful liege

> At their she-captain's call,
> Who, miracle of womankind,
> Lent mettle to the meanest hind
> That mann'd her Castle wall."

Knowsley, the home of the Stanleys; Trafford, the residence of the great Catholic house whose name it bears; and Lytham, and Croxteth, and Hale, and Foxholes, and Hulton, and many a one besides. Towneley still keeps house at Towneley, Hesketh at Rufford, and Hoghton at Hoghton Tower.

We are constantly being reminded, while travelling among the old English mansions, of how much that was once great and glorious has long since passed away. Sometimes the admonition comes in the shape of an antique fragment, which is yet allowed to form a portion of a modern wall; but more frequently it comes from our learning that the building we admire stands on the site of a demolished castle, or of an abbey that has been swept away by the hands of the desolator. Often, too, the appellation of abbey will yet remain clinging to the modern edifice, as we shall find in CIRENCESTER ABBEY, Gloucestershire, founded in 1117 by Henry the First, for canons regular of the Augustine order. The hand of Bluff King Hal—and it was never a light one—fell here with even more than its usual weight. On granting this part of his church spoil to Roger Basigne, he commanded that all the buildings within the abbey precincts should be pulled down and carried away; and so punctually was this Gothic mandate obeyed, that nothing now remains of the abbey or its adjuncts except the almonry gate, the spital gate, and a large barn. In course of time it reverted to the crown, and Queen Elizabeth finally sold it to Richard Master, her physician of the chamber, who erected a mansion upon the site of the abbey. This also was pulled down in 1772, when a new house was built, which is inhabited by Miss Master, a direct descendant of Elizabeth's physician.

SUDELEY CASTLE, also in Gloucestershire, built about the year 1442, by Sir Ralph Boteler, Lord Treasurer of England, derives historic interest from its association with the Seymours, and more especially with Queen Catherine Parr, who died here of a broken heart, or, as some suspect, of having been poisoned by her last husband, Lord Seymour of Sudeley, the ambitious Lord High Admiral.* Many a long year after, in 1782, some ladies who happened to be at Sudeley Castle, were induced to examine the ruined chapel, and observing a large alabaster block fixed in the north wall, they imagined it might be the back of some mural monument that had formerly been placed there. Acting upon this hint, they had the ground dug up not far from the wall, when they found, a little more than a foot below the surface, a leaden envelope, and having opened it in two places, the face and breast, they saw a human form, in every feature as perfect as one embalmed in a Theban sarcophagus—as perfect as life itself! but, alarmed at the sight, they ordered the earth to be thrown in at once, without stopping to replace either the

---

* Sergeant Atkinson devotes the first chapter of his delightful "Worthies of Westmorland" to Kateryn Parr. He asserts that the Queen died in childbirth of her daughter, and not of a broken heart or poison.

cloth or the lead. Still, enough had been seen of the inscription to prove that the body was that of Queen Catherine. In four years after, in 1786, the Rev. Dr. Nash reopened the grave, but found that the action of the air, and the damp, had destroyed the face. He discovered, however, in the lead which covered the breast, this inscription :—

"K. P. Here lyethe quene Kateryn wife to Kyng Henry the VIII. and last the wife of Thomas Lord of Sudely highe Admyrall of England and vncle to King Edward the VI. dyed 5 September MCCCCCXLVIII."

Eighty years before this, a yet more curious discovery of a somewhat similar nature had been made at Minster Lovel in Oxfordshire. It is related in the following letter from William Cowper, Esq., Clerk of the Parliament in 1737 :—

"Hertingfordbury Park, Aug. 7, 1737.

"Sir,—I met t'other day with a memorandum I had made some years ago, perhaps not unworthy of your notice. You may remember that Lord Bacon, in his History of Henry VII., giving an account of the battle of Stoke, says of the Lord Lovel, who was among the rebels, 'that he fled and swame over the Trent on horseback, but could not recover the further side, by reason of the steepnesse of the banke, and so was drowned in the river. But another report leaves him not there, but that he lived long after in a cave or vault.

"Apropos to this :—On the 6th May, 1728, the present Duke of Rutland related in my hearing that about twenty years before, viz. in 1708, upon occasion of new laying a chimney at Minster Luvel, there was discovered a large vault, or room under ground, in which was the entire skeleton of a man, as having been sitting at a table, which was before him, with a book, paper, pen, &c. In another part of the room lay a cap, all much mouldered and decayed, which the family and others judged to be this Lord Luvel, whose exit has hitherto been so uncertain.

"W. Cowper."

Hence it may reasonably be inferred that it was the fate of Lord Lovel (then only about thirty-two) to have fled to his house in Oxfordshire after the battle, and there to have intrusted himself to some servant, by whom he was immured, and afterwards deserted, either through treachery, fear, or some accident which befel that person—a melancholy period to the life and fortunes of one of the greatest and most active noblemen of the era in which he lived.

From Gloucestershire to Devon, although a tolerably long route in the maps, is a short flight for the imagination, which, like the electric telegraph, would almost seem to annihilate both space and time. Let us, then, fancy ourselves in the manor of Kenton, before the walls of POWDERHAM CASTLE, erected during the feudal ages for protecting the adjacent lands and vassals from the incursions of rival Barons. Upon the death of John de Powderham, in the time of the first Edward, it fell, by escheat or otherwise, to Humphrey de Bohun, Earl of Hereford, who gave it, with his daughter Margaret in marriage, to Hugh, Earl of Devon; and he again bestowed it, about the close of the fourteenth century, upon his fifth son,

Sir Philip Courtenay, a gallant soldier, who, together with his brothers, Hugh and Peter, received the honour of knighthood from Edward the Black Prince, the day before the battle of Navaret; and was constituted in 1383 Lord Lieutenant of Ireland for ten years. Ever since the time of this Sir Philip, Powderham Castle has remained uninterruptedly with his descendants, and is now possessed by their worthy representative, William Reginald Courtenay, Earl of Devon.

This castle is beautifully situated on the banks of the Exe, not more than three miles from its confluence with the British Channel. At high water the river in this part is full a mile and a half broad, the castle windows commanding a magnificent view of the ocean to the west, and of the shipping as it comes up to Topsham. The grounds, moreover, are unusually extensive. They embrace a circumference of nearly ten miles, in which is comprised a large park well stocked with deer, besides plantations, shrubberies, lawns, and pleasure-grounds. Nature, in fact, has done everything to render this one of the most enchanting spots in England, but the antiquary can hardly be expected to sympathize with the taste which has suggested the modern improvements upon the old edifice. Up to the year 1752 it still retained a portion of its original castellated form; but since then the machicolated gateway, with its formidable portcullis, has disappeared, the high turrets and massive embattlements have given way to what is called classic architecture, and many additions have been made to the north wing, adding much, no doubt, to the convenience of the inmates, but greatly to the discomfort of those who, like ourselves, are especial admirers of ancient Gothicism.

Devonshire has been at all times distinguished for its many eminent families; and it can still boast of some of the most illustrious houses in the kingdom, including those of Courtenay, Edgecombe, Seymour, Fortescue, Cary, Chichester, Walrond, Carew, Fulford, Clinton, Basset, and Strode. Many names that were once conspicuous in the county records, are now no more. Pomeroy, Holland, Redvers, Rolle, Martin, Mohun, Chudleigh, Arscott, Crewys, and Coplestone:

> "Croker, Crewys, and Coplestone,
> When the Conqueror came, were at home."

The pride of SUSSEX is ARUNDEL CASTLE: originally built by Alfred the Great, the Keep alone of all that remains could have existed at the time of the Conquest. From the period when the Castle fell into Norman hands, each possessor seems to have done something towards strengthening or extending it. ROGER DE MONTGOMERY, who received it from the Conqueror in 1070, erected the great Gatehouse, and the Barbican, known as Bevis's Tower, and successive Lords have at various epochs enlarged or restored the venerable edifice. Its tenure is popularly believed to confer the title of Earl:

> "Since William rose, and Harold fell,
> There have been Counts of Arundel.
> And Earls old Arundel shall have,
> While rivers flow, and forests wave."

Arundel Castle has been often forfeited; a dozen of its owners have lost their heads, the religion they professed has been proscribed, their Earl Marshalship has been taken from them; yet, somehow or other, proud Arundel still owns for Lord the heir of Queen Adeliza; the representative of Thomas of Brotherton is still Earl Marshal, and the chief of the noble Howards is still our premier Duke.

This permanence of English society is attributable as well to the national character as to the national law of primogeniture. A short time since, in one of the admirable leaders of "the Times," this subject was most ably discussed.

"It matters not," says the journalist, " how or where we got our patriarchal traditions, but they are deep in the blood, and centuries would not wear them out. The whole of a family conspire to create a head. Temporary inconvenience may betray itself in murmurs, but all naturally fall into the hereditary arrangement. The childless leave the property generally to the one who can best keep up the family. They feel it safest and most profitable to invest what they leave in the eldest son of the eldest. Experience amply confirms the wisdom of this course. The eldest son keeps up the place, makes his house the general rendezvous, sustains the social consideration of the family, links it with other families equal or higher in the social scale,—in a word, fights the life battle of his race. He is the chief. His one name has more influence than twenty smaller ones. If the juniors of his race have less than their deserts, their deserts are measured by his position, and their inferiority to him is their strong, though silent, claim to a share in the prizes of life. When it is objected that the estate is settled on the elder, and the youngers are thrown upon the public institutions of the country, that expresses a universal fact; but the fact is, the youngers get what they do get by the aid of the elder, and by the effect of his position. Instead of the estate being frittered away in subdivisions, its concentration makes it the nucleus of increase. The vitality of the seed is uninjured; it germinates, and bears fruit. Thus small families become great. Were it once the custom to divide landed property as soon as it had been got together, it would never be collected. Nobody would buy out every smaller man about him at an extravagant price to make a property for the mere pleasure of dividing it neatly in his will, or leaving his son to do so. Yet that great estates are better than small ones, both for agriculture, for social improvement, and for the political balance of the country, will hardly be questioned by any one who gives one candid thought to the subject. If churches, schools, roads, farm-buildings, cottages, and drainage, are to be done, it is of little use to look to small proprietors, still less to those who are obliged to live just on a fourth or a tenth of the income enjoyed by their fathers."

The name of NOTTINGHAMSHIRE will probably suggest few romantic or poetical fancies to the minds of most of our readers, except it be in connection with Sherwood Forest, and the celebrated outlaw, Robin Hood. This indifference has proceeded, we imagine, from the county having found but one historian, Thoroton, and he the dryest of the dry; his work, in three quarto volumes, is little better than a dusty record of names, for the most part without note and without interest, and never brightened by a single ray of imagination. Yet there is many a spot in this neglected county upon which a man of the least fancy would have dwelt with delight, and many a popular tradition that he might have caught up from the peasants, and leavened with it his heavy mass, till it became lighter and more palatable.

Let us pause awhile before WELBECK ABBEY, an interesting relique of ancient times, originally founded in Henry the Second's reign, for Præmonstratensian canons. Like all other institutions of the same kind, it affords a striking instance of the vicissitudes of the lives—if we may be allowed so questionable a phrase—of houses as well as men; it passed into several hands at the dissolution, and in 1604 it was converted into a private residence, by Sir Charles Cavendish, a younger brother to William, the first Earl of Devonshire. Upon his decease it was inherited by his son, the Duke of Newcastle, no less famous for his loyalty than for his horsemanship. Eventually it devolved by marriage to the Earl of Oxford, from whom it passed to the Bentincks,* his sole surviving daughter

* Kniephausen is the name of the principal territory of the family of Bentinck. It is situated on the shores of the German Ocean, and holds a very singular position as regards the German confederation. It is, in some measure, still an independent state, though of very limited extent; its circuit being one square mile (equal to five square English miles), with three thousand inhabitants. Count Bentinck, Lord of Kniephausen, can scarcely be said to belong either to the class of reigning or of mediatized princes. He was a reigning Count, and he has not been thoroughly mediatized. It has been jestingly said, that he was so small that he was forgotten when the other petty sovereigns were mediatized, and thus he still exists.

having wedded with one of that family. Some remains of the Abbey may still be traced in the cellar arches; an old chapel also was doubtless part of the original edifice; and it is said the sepulchral monuments have not been destroyed, but are only hid from sight in some of the chambers by hangings and wainscot panels.

Welbeck possesses the perfection of English woodland beauty, just as the grand demesne of Farnham, in Cavan, has all the best features of Irish scenery. It is the finest specimen of a magnificent park in the centre of England. Nothing can be more thoroughly sylvan, spreading out as it does to an immense extent, with undulating slopes, covered with thick woods, and adorned with gigantic trees. It is the most striking of the four "Dukeries," as they are called; far surpassing Thoresby, Clumber, or Worksop. Welbeck Abbey is situated on the margin of a large lake, which is surrounded by an extensive wood, containing some of the finest forest trees in England. The park is eight miles in circumference, and contains many oaks of extraordinary age and dimensions. The largest of these is the "Greendale oak," which is of incalculable antiquity. It measures in circumference thirty-three feet, and its branches are said to have covered a space not less than seven hundred square yards; but it has been, during many years, in a state of decay, retaining now only one branch, while the venerable trunk is clasped with iron, capped with lead, and supported on props. In 1724, a carriage way, ten feet high, and six feet three inches wide, was arched out in the stem of this immense tree. The tree called the "Duke's walking-stick" is another of these sylvan curiosities — 111 feet

6 inches high, and containing 440 solid [feet of timber. The two "Porters" stand at one of the park entrances, and are each one hundred feet high. From the remarkable tree called the "Seven Sisters," spring seven stems ninety feet high.

And we must not forget one spot in this fine county—now become classic ground—the old Augustine monastery of NEWSTEAD—the home of the poet Byron. On his first arrival at this ancient seat, in 1798, he planted an oak in the garden, and nourished the idea, that as the tree prospered or otherwise, so would it be with himself. On revisiting the Abbey during Lord Grey de Ruthven's residence there, he found the oak choked up by weeds and almost destroyed, which circumstance gave rise to his poem—

"Young oak, when I planted thee deep in the ground."

Soon after Colonel Wildman took possession of the estate, he one day noticed this tree, and said to the servant who was with him, "Here is a fine young oak; but it must be cut down, as it grows in an improper place." "I hope not," replied the man; "for it's the one my lord was so fond of, because he set it himself." The Colonel, of course, since that time, took every possible care of the tree. Strangers, already, when they visit Newstead, begin to enquire after *Byron's Oak;* so that it promises, one day, to share the celebrity of Shakespeare's *Mulberry.*

We now pass into SOMERSETSHIRE. This county is not unknown in story, and, till within late years, the remoteness of its geographical position caused both the country and its inhabitants to retain much of what was primitive in scenery, in dialect, and in manners. In this county the glorious banner of the Cross was first planted, and the piety of holier times is here attested by many beautiful and interesting ruins, such as Glastonbury, the Palace at Wells, and the Abbey of Cleve. Passing by, however, these decaying memorials, and the many striking historical events connected with Somersetshire, from the concealment of ALFRED in the Isle of Athelney, to the battle of Sedgemoor, we will confine ourselves (forgetful, for the moment, of Ashley Combe, Fairfield, Hinton St. George, Dunster Castle, Leigh Court, Halsewell, Newton, St. Looe, Ashton Court, Nettlecombe, Ammerdown, Mells Park, Brockley, Redlynch, Sandhill Park, Bagborough, Clevedon, Somerton Erleigh, and Nynehead), to one object amidst so many worthy of notice, and select MONTACUTE HOUSE, or rather take it as being the first that presents itself to memory. This estate has for several centuries belonged to the Phelips', who, like so many others of our old families, came over with William the Conqueror, and obtained large grants of land from that able soldier but unprincipled politician, for the assistance they afforded him in subjugating the country. The original settlement of the Phelips' was in Wales, but in the fourteenth century they migrated into Somersetshire, when they lived for many years at Barrington. Montacute House, which is built entirely of a brown stone found on the estate, was commenced in 1550, and as building did not proceed in those days with the steam-like rapidity that characterises modern times, it was not completed until 1601 : but its substantialness when done, and the richness of the ornaments, made it a splendid specimen of Elizabethan architecture. Its outlines present the form of the Roman letter E, in compliment no doubt to Elizabeth, for Sir Edward Phelips, by whom it was raised, had the good fortune to be a Queen's serjeant, a position which of course did not diminish his loyalty to his maiden mistress. The eastern or principal front of this immense pile is one hundred and seventy feet long, the wings are twenty-eight feet in width, and the whole is as rich as human art could make it with mullions, battlements, and all the multiplied creations of the Gothic fancy, or rather of the eastern, for there can, we suspect, be little doubt now-a-days of the Persian origin of the so-called Gothic architecture. But if the Serjeant loved show, he also exercised hospitality upon a scale of no less magnificence, and various inscriptions in different parts of the building give ample testimony to this feeling. Over the principal door we read,

"Through this wide opening gate
None come too early, none return too late."

Over the north porch the weary traveller is met by this pithy and significant invitation—

"And yours, my friend."

And on one of the lodges he will find himself greeted by an old saw, no less expressive of the owner's hospitable spirit—

"Welcome the coming,
Speed the parting guest.'"

We shall next pause in NORTHAMPTONSHIRE, famed for "spires and squires," adorned with a hundred churches, and full as many county seats, and so plentifully stored with gentry that Norden styles it "the Herald's garden." The grandest places are Burghley, to which we shall presently refer; Althorp, with its noble library, so rich in early printed works: Milton, where is still shown the tree under which Wolsey sat; Lilford, that charming specimen of an old English manor-house; Fawsley, "with its shield of 334 quarterings;" Drayton, the home of the de Veres, the Mordaunts, the Germaines, and the Stopfords; Apethorpe, where King James first met the youthful George Villiers; Boughton, one of the various seats of his Grace of Buccleuch; Castle Ashby; Dean; Easton Neston; Rushton;* and "the delightful bowers" round Rocking-

* "Rushton was the residence of the Viscount Cullen. There is a familiar legend connected with the marriage-feast of the second viscount. He had been betrothed, at the age of sixteen, to Elizabeth Trentham, a great heiress, but had, while travelling abroad, formed an attachment to an Italian lady of rank, whom he afterwards deserted for his first betrothed. While the wedding-party were feasting in the great Hall at Rushton, a strange carriage, drawn by six horses, drew up, and forth stepped a dark lady, who, entering the Hall, and seizing a goblet, 'to punish his falsehood and pride,' drank perdition to the bridegroom, and having uttered a curse upon his bride, in stronger language than we care to chronicle, to the effect that she would live in wretchedness and die in want, disappeared, to be traced no further. The curse was in a great measure fulfilled. She became a beauty of Charles II.'s Court, was painted with less than his usual allowance of drapery by Sir Peter Lely, twice gave an asylum to Monmouth in the room at Rushton, still called 'the Duke's room,' and, as might be inferred, living unhappily with her husband, died, notwithstanding her enormous fortune, in comparative penury at Kettering, at a great age, as late as 1713."—*Quarterly Review.*

ham castle. Then there are in addition the many good old mansions and picturesque residences of the well-descended gentlemen of Northamptonshire—such as Aynho, Thenford, Brockhall, Acton, De la Pré, Canons Ashby, Lamport, Blatherwyke, Eydon, Thorpe Malsor, Finedon, Bulwick, Fineshade, Sulby, Cosgrove, Glendon Hall, Norton, and Great Oakley.

An admirable Essay on this interesting county, full of fancy and thought, anecdote and local lore, appeared in the "Quarterly Review" for January, 1857; it extends to little more than fifty pages, and yet the amount of amusing information supplied is quite a marvel.

BURGHLEY HOUSE is about a mile from Stamford. It was built by the celebrated Lord Burghley, on the site of a minster called Burghe, and is a brilliant specimen of the Elizabethan style of architecture, in which the general plan was after the Gothic school as it prevailed in the reign of Henry the Eighth, while the ornamental parts were borrowed from Italy, according to a taste which had then newly arisen. So far as magnitude in the whole mass, and a profuse minuteness in the decorations can make any place worthy of notice, Burghley House in the highest degree deserves attention. The principal front, which looks to the north, is nearly two hundred feet in extent; at each corner are turrets surmounted by octangular cupolas, and terminated by vanes; a parapet goes round the whole building in a series of open-work, consisting of arches supported by balustrade with obelisks, interspersed with the armorial ensigns of the family; and the ascent to the porch, which opens to the hall, is by nine semicircular steps. The court measures one hundred and ten feet by seventy feet, crossed by paved walks, that divide it into four grass-plats. To the genuine antiquary, however, the most interesting parts are the glimpses of the old minster, which show themselves in divers fragments in the hall, chapel, and kitchen, upon the eastern side of the edifice.

The interior is "incredibly rich in Venetian furniture, royal beds, oriental china, Gibbon's carving, and historical heirlooms, from the Lord Treasurer's cup, given him by Elizabeth, to the candelabra of the Duke of Wellington's funeral." In the picture gallery, there is one portrait by Lawrence which is popular with all visitors, high and low. It is "The Cottager's Daughter," a faithful likeness of the village maiden who won the heart and hand of the late Earl of Exeter. Her simple tale, sung by Moore and Tennyson, is the prettiest episode of peerage annals. " I never wish," said Hazlitt, " to be a lord, but when I think of this story, which beats the 'Arabian Nights.' " Though Burghley still stands in all its pristine beauty, other Northamptonshire houses of historic note are sadly changed. Not one stone remains of Fotheringay Castle, to mark the spot where the tragedy of the 8th of February, 1587, was enacted; and Kirby, with its long gallery, down which

> "My grave Lord Keeper led the brawls,
> The seals and maces danced before him—"

is crumbling away, utterly desolate and neglected.

The course of our narrative, or, we should rather say, the caprice of fancy—now leads us to the county of DURHAM, of which RABY CASTLE forms so important a feature.

Some parts of this edifice manifestly belong to the Anglo-Saxon times, but the chief portion was built by John de Neville, 1379, he having obtained a licence for that purpose from the then Bishop of Durham. It occupies a rising ground, its foundation being upon a rock, and is surrounded by an embattled wall, which contains within its circumference about two acres. There is an entrance on the north, through a gateway defended by two square towers; a second on the west, the arch of which is groined, and has a gate with portcullis at each end; and a third has been made in a more modern style, leading to the hall. At irregular intervals are strong bulwarks, which have been named, after their respective founders, the Clifford and Bulmer Towers. The kitchen, from its ample size and curious arrangements, shews that the stout barons took no less heed to their stomachs than to their defences, and had as much relish for the good things of life as any modern citizen. Another of the most spacious apartments of the castle is the Banqueting Hall, ninety feet in length, thirty-six in height, and thirty-four in breadth. Here the ancient Baronial festivals were celebrated; and here seven hundred knights, who held of the Nevilles, are recorded to have been entertained at one time. The grounds correspond in extent and beauty with the fine old castle, the whole being worthy of the powerful Nevilles, to whom it belonged till forfeited by Charles, the sixth Earl of Westmoreland, for joining the northern rebellion against Elizabeth. Her successor, King James, consigned the estate to certain London citizens for sale, and from them it was bought by Sir Henry Vane, whose descendant, in the reign of George the Second, was created Viscount Barnard and Earl of Darlington by letters patent. In his lordship's representative, HENRY, DUKE OF CLEVELAND, K.G., Raby Castle now vests.

LUMLEY CASTLE, though with fewer historical recollections cleaving to it, is yet too picturesque, from its situation, not to arrest the attention of the passing traveller. Towards the east it hangs on the brow of a hill, overlooking a deep, well-wooded valley, and being separated from the steep descent only by a curtain between the castle walls and the edge of the precipice, below which runs the little river Beck, on its way to the Wear. Above this defence the edifice rises to the height of three stories, having mullioned windows strongly barred with iron. The centre is here formed by a stately entrance tower, with machicolated gallery, flanked by turrets. But indeed the whole of this front has undergone little, if any alteration from the time when it was first raised in Edward the First's reign, by Sir Robert Lumley, or perhaps when it was enlarged by his son, Sir Marmaduke. On the west side, at the base of the eminence, flows the Wear, and continues its course towards the south, where the front presents a more modern aspect. There also—on the west, that is —the principal gateway is seen, the entrance to which is by a double flight of steps, leading to a platform, that fills the entire space between the towers. The prospect from this side is eminently beautiful. King James I. rested a night at Lumley Castle, on his progress to London to assume the English crown. On that occasion, a remark made by his Majesty, on seeing the famous Lumley pedigree, which deduces the line of ancestry from ADAM, though well known, deserves repetition: "I never before," observed the King, "kenned the surname of Adam, but now I find it was Adam Lumley."

LAMBTON CASTLE, the Earl of Durham's fine seat, stands on the banks of the Wear, and about two miles from the old Hall, with which is associated a strange and striking legend. The story, which delighted Sir Walter Scott, has been told by many writers, and very pleasantly by Surtees, who, with all his antiquarian propensities, had a highly poetical imagination. Deriving our information from the great historian of Durham, and from "The Gatherings" of an esteemed and accomplished friend, Mr. Hylton Longstaffe, we will endeavour to give a correct edition of a tale current for generations, and still implicitly believed in.

The Lambtons, at the period the legend refers to, "were so brave, that they feared neither man nor God," wherefore this judgment befel them. The wicked heir of Lambton was fishing one Sunday, according to his profane custom, in the Wear, and after toiling in vain for some time, vented his dissatisfaction in curses loud and deep, to the great scandal of all who heard him, on their way to Holy Mass. At length he felt an extraordinary tugging at his line, and in the hope of catching a large fish, he drew it up with the utmost care; yet it required all his strength to bring the expected fish to land. It proved to be only a worm of most unseemly appearance, which he hastily tore from his hook, and threw, in a passion, into a well, hard by. He again cast in his line, when a venerable-looking stranger passing by, asked him "what sport?" He replied, "Why, truly I think I've caught the Devil," and directed the enquirer to look into the well, which he did, and remarked that he had never seen "the like of it" before—that it was like an eft, but that it had *nine* holes on each side of its mouth, and "tokened no good."

The Worm, neglected in the well, soon grew so large that it became necessary to seek another abode. It usually lay in the day-time coiled round a rock in the middle of the river, and at night frequented a neighbouring hill, twining itself around the base, and increased until it could *lap* itself *nine* times round this green mound, leaving on it vermicular traces, which remained within man's memory.

The Worm was now the terror of the neighbourhood, devouring lambs, *sucking* the cows' milk, and committing every injury on the cattle of the affrighted peasantry. The north side of the river soon afforded no further support, so it crossed the stream towards Lambton Hall, where the old Lord was then living in grief and sorrow; his son, the profane fisherman, having repented of his wickedness, had *gone to the wars in a far distant land,* or as some express it, *to wage war against the Infidels.* The terrified household assembled, and it was proposed by the steward, *far advanced in years, and of great experience,* that the large trough which stood in the court-yard should be filled with milk. The monster approached, eagerly drank the milk, and returned, without further ravage, to repose around his favourite hill. It came again next morning at the same hour, and the milk to be provided was found to be the produce of *nine kye;* and if any portion was neglected, the worm lashed its tail round the trees in the park, and tore them up by the roots in its rage. "The Worm was a terrible hugeous cretur" (said a woman to William Howitt), "it drank every day nine cows' milk; and even if th' family took a little sup out for their tea (!) it wor fain to rive a' doon!" Many a gallant knight had in vain sought to slay this terror of the whole country side, but always suffered loss of life or limb; for though the Worm had been frequently cut asunder, yet the several parts had immediately re-united, and it reigned undisturbed on its hill.

At length, after seven long years, young Lambton, the Knight of the Cross, returned, and found the broad lands of his ancestors desolate. He heard the wailings of the people, and hastened to his father's Hall, and received the embrace of the old man, who was worn out with sorrow and grief, both for the knight's supposed death, and the dreadful waste of the Worm. Young Lambton took no rest till he had crossed the river to examine the Worm as it lay coiled round the base of the hill, and hearing the fate of all who had fallen in the deadly strife, he consulted a witch or wise woman on the best means to be pursued. He was told that he himself had been the cause of all the misery which had been brought upon the country, which increased his grief and strengthened his resolution; that he must have his best suit of mail studded with razor blades, and taking his stand on the island craig, commend himself to Providence and to the might of his sword, first making a solemn vow, if successful, to slay the first living thing he met, or if he failed to do so, *the Lords of Lambton for nine generations would never die in their beds.* He made the solemn vow, and devoted himself to the Holy Ghost and the Virgin, in the chapel of his forefathers, and had his coat studded with the blades of the sharpest razors.

The hero directed his father, that as soon as he heard him sound three blasts on his bugle as a note of victory, he should release his favourite greyhound, which would immediately fly to the sound, and become the sacrifice. He then took his stand on the island rock, and unsheathing his trusty sword, commended himself to the will of Providence. At its wonted hour the Worm uncoiled its folds, and bent its usual course towards Lambton Hall, approaching the rock where it sometimes reposed. The Knight, nothing dismayed thereat, struck the monster on the head with all his might and main, but without producing any other visible effect than by irritating and *vexing* the Worm, which closing on the Knight, clasped its frightful coils around him, and endeavoured to strangle him in its poisonous embrace.

The more closely the Knight was pressed by the Worm the more deadly were the wounds inflicted by the coat of razor blades, until the river ran with a crimson gore of blood, the Worm's strength diminishing as its efforts increased to destroy its antagonist. At length, Lambton, seizing a favourable opportunity, made such good use of his sword that he cut the monster in two:—the severed part was immediately carried away by the force of the current, and the Worm being thus unable to reunite itself, was, after a long and desperate conflict, finally destroyed.

The afflicted household were devoutly engaged in prayer during the combat; but on the fortunate issue, the Knight, according to promise, blew a blast on his bugle to assure his father that he was safe, and that he might let loose his favourite hound, destined for sacrifice. But the Lord of Lambton forgot everything save his paternal feelings, and rushed forward to embrace his son. The Knight on the meeting was overwhelmed with grief; he could not be a parricide, yet hoping that his vow might be accomplished, and the curse averted by destroying the next living thing he met, he blew another blast on his bugle; his favourite hound broke loose, and bounded to receive his caresses; when the gallant Knight, with grief and reluctance, once more drew his sword, still reeking with the gore of the monster, and plunged it into the heart of his faithful companion. But in vain—the prediction was fulfilled, and the Sibyl's curse pressed heavily on the house of Lambton *for nine generations*. Some say that this was not part of the original declaration of the Sibyl, and that the heir of Lambton had again to resort to the witch, or wise woman, who pronounced the alternative, which, after all, had probably nothing very terrible to a martial spirit.

The legend is certainly one 'of the most finished romances, in all its parts, that England boasts of, for its posthumous history is most extraordinary. Nine ascending generations from Henry Lambton, the elder brother of the late general, in whom the curse was generally believed by the populace to expire, would exactly reach to that in which Robert Lambton, Esq., died without issue in 1442, leaving the Lambton honours to his brother Thomas, and bequeathing by his will to his " brother John Lambton, *Knight of Rhodes,* 100 marks." The hero of the legend will instantly suggest himself, and a curious entry in an old MS. pedigree, lately in possession of the Myddletons of Offerton, says, "*John Lambeton, that slewe the worme, was Knight of Rhoodes*, and Lorde of Lambeton, and Wod Apilton efter the dethe of fower brothers, sans csshewe masle. His son Robert Lambton was drowned at Newebrig." The *Inquisitio post mortem* of the Knight's father occurs in 1432-3, and his mother makes her will in 1439, naming "her son John Lambton, Knight." The curse commenced in her grandchildren; the hero's son was drowned near the chapel where his father offered up his unkept vow, and tradition fills up every generation of the main line with a *bedless* death. Sir William, a royalist, was slain at Marston Moor, and his son William (who, however, was not his heir) received his death at Wakefield in 1643. In the same year, John Lambton, of the Tribley branch, was killed at Bradford in the royal service. Great curiosity prevailed in the life-time of Henry, to know if the curse would "hold good to the end." He died in his chariot, crossing the New Bridge, in 1761, thus giving the last connecting link to the chain of circumstantial evidence connected with the history of the Worm of Lambton. His succeeding brother, the General, who lived to a great age, fearing that the prophecy might be possibly fulfilled by his servants, under the idea that he could not die in his bed, kept a horsewhip beside him in his last illness, and thus eluded the prediction. Yet though the spell is said to be broken, yet neither his son nor his grandson have been longer lived, nor have they died at home; and this to the squires of ancient time, would have been sorer punishment than dying in the battle field, for they loved to sleep in their own country, and with their fathers.

The pleasure which the traveller derives from our next county, STAFFORDSHIRE, will arise less from these remains so delightful to the antiquarian, than from modern elegance and modern associations. With all our love for the olden times, we are not so bigotted as to suppose that genius or desert are like the shield of Martin Scriblerus, that degenerated into a mere pot-lid, when the ancient ærugo was scoured off it, but can pause with as much pleasure before the walls of TRENTHAM HALL, however modern, as before some greyheaded castle, that dates from the time of the Conqueror. As a building, it borrows nothing from the times gone by, having been erected little more than a century, and even since then it has undergone considerable changes and improvements by its recent noble possessors. The estate takes its name from the beautiful river which winds through the park, and has so often been celebrated both in song and story.

It is not often that the old ruin and the more recent mansion remain, like the great grandfather of some family and his infant descendant in the third degree, to mark the contrast between the past and present. Generally speaking, the new building occupies the complete site of the old one that has been swept away, or at best it retains a few fragments mixed up—awkwardly enough—with its modern lightness. ALTON TOWERS is one of the exceptions to this remark. The ruins of the castle still remain standing upon an almost perpendicular rock, the walls being of prodigious thickness and extent. At the foot of this precipice, in a lovely valley, flows the little river Churnet, and adds not a little to the beauty of the scene as it winds its quiet way through the green herbage. The precise time when the castle was first built can no longer be ascertained, but it is supposed to have been soon after the Conquest, the presumed date of so many similar erections. In succession it has belonged to the Verdons, the Furnivals, then to the illustrious Sir John Talbot, the victor in forty battles, and who was most worthily created Earl of Shrewsbury. His death, too, was as glorious as his life, for he was killed by a cannon ball at Chastillon sur Dordon, in 1453. And what better end could a soldier wish for? surely to live into a drivelling dotage, like the great Marlborough, or even to pass away by lingering disease, going out like the snuff of a wasted candle, is a sorry catastrophe for a hero; the very bathos of life's tragedy, when its previous scenes have possessed the noblest and deepest interest.

The modern mansion, which has inherited the ancient name, is a splendid building, though somewhat irregular in form, and is placed amidst grounds of considerable extent and beauty in themselves, rendered yet more interesting by the surrounding landscape. In architectural beauty and grandeur of design, Alton Towers is a worthy memorial of the taste and princely munificence of John, Earl of Shrewsbury, and of the brilliant genius of Pugin.

Besides Trentham and Alton Towers, Staffordshire has many a stately English home; Beaudesert, Ingestre, Blithfield, Pateshul, Sandon, Chillington, Shugborough,

Hilton, Tixal, Ilam, Teddesley, King's Bromley, Wrottesley, Perry Hall, Chartley, and Great Barr.

KENT is another county remarkable for its beautiful seats; here are Knole Park, the Wilderness, Chilham Castle, Chevening, Hadlow Castle, Montreal, Waldershare, Surrenden Dering, Godinton, Holfield, Leyburn Grange, Preston Hall, Mersham Hatch, Sandling, Cale Hill, Lullingstone Castle, Charlton House, Leeds Castle, Cobham Hall, Eastwell, Godmersham, Knowlton, Lee Priory, Barham Court, Chipsted Place, and Belvidere.

Kent has been called, and with much reason, the garden of England: but this applies only to its picturesque hop-grounds, its fertile corn-fields, and its abundant orchards, for in comparison with some other counties, it can hardly be termed the garden of antiquaries. Still it has one shrine, at which the poetic pilgrim pays the warmest adoration; PENSHURST, where Sir Philip Sydney, "the President of Nobleness and Chivalrie," was born. Until within the last twenty or thirty years, Penshurst, though crumbling under the hand of time, which spares not the brightest associations, still preserved the form and the appropriate adornment of bygone ages. The fine old timber roof was then entire, and the side walls throughout were covered with pikes, lances, and matchlocks, while at the end of the hall, stood erect, in frowning dignity, whole rows of men-shaped suits of armour—one recorded to have been worn by the "incomparable knight himself." The creaking of the rusty gates, the desolate echo, and the noiseless calm, spoke of other days, and we unconsciously held communion with those mighty spirits, whose memory imparts undying interest to the scene. All the glory of Penshurst is of the past, and modern improvement and modern innovation tend but to dissolve the charm which encircles the Hall of the Sydneys. Of the dry antiquarian fruit which Kent produces, we have culled three specimens —KNOLE PARK, LEEDS CASTLE, and MEREWORTH, each of them in a greater or less degree deserving notice.

KNOLE itself stands in a beautiful park, a short distance from Seven Oaks, and from the time of the Conquest has been set down among the remarkable places in England, partly from its natural beauties, but still more from the associations belonging to it. After having been possessed by many illustrious families in succession, it was purchased by Thomas Bourchier, Archbishop of Canterbury, who re-built the house, enclosed the Park, and at his death, in 1486, left it to his late see for ever—for ever! a phrase that is constantly recurring in testament after testament, as if it were possible for a few mouldering bones to dictate from the grave an eternal pathway to the feet that are trampling on them. Surely the little real influence that any individual exercises, even in life, upon the great mass, might convince men how small a chance they stand of ruling the world when they are dead. And so it turned out in the present instance. When Cranmer succeeded to the Archbishopric, he resigned Knole to the crown, in whose possession it remained till Edward the Sixth granted it to John Dudley, Earl of Warwick, afterwards created Duke of Northumberland. Every one must recollect how this unfortunate nobleman supported the claims of Lady Jane Grey to the throne in opposition to Queen

Mary, and, being defeated, lost both estate and life. It thus, upon his attainder, devolved to the Queen, who gave it to Cardinal Pole; but when the latter died, it once more reverted to the crown. Elizabeth having succeeded to the throne, made a grant of this estate to Sir Robert Dudley, afterwards Earl of Leicester, in which character, with little to recommend him, he has obtained a conspicuous place in English history. In a few years, however, he rendered it up to her again, whereupon she gave it to Thomas Sackville, Esq., who was subsequently created Earl of Dorset.

In all probability he owed this especial grace to his having intermarried with the Boleyns, and thus becoming related to the royal family, though for the most part the maiden Queen was no great friend to the matrimonial ceremony amongst her courtiers; she seemed in general to look upon it as a sort of treason committed against her sovereign beauty, and if the law provided no sufficient punishment for the offence, she was often well disposed to supply such deficiency by an ample exercise of the royal prerogative.

Many detached fragments of the olden times may be found in this mansion, illustrative of the manners and habits of our forefathers. In the chimney of the great hall is a very curious pair of ancient dogs, a rude sort of grate, made of two cross bars of irons, such as even now may be seen in some very old farm-houses, except that in this case the dogs are remarkable for their elaborate workmanship. In the same part of the building, a dais, or raised floor, for the host and his superior guests, is still to be seen, as also the long tables originally constructed for the game of shuffleboard. The windows, too, of this hall yet retain their old stained glass, adding not a little to the general effect.

Knole at present belongs to Mary, Countess Amherst, oldest daughter and co-heiress of the third Duke of Dorset.

LEEDS CASTLE is a place, in some respects, of yet deeper interest. It is about five miles from Maidstone, and is bounded by a moat covering nearly three acres of ground, while within its walls is as much more. As opposed to the military skill of the feudal age, it must have been well nigh impregnable. Three causeways afford a narrow and defensible access from the north, south-west, and south-east, leading to the outworks of a gateway, which, judging from what remains, was fortified with unusual skill. These outworks were most probably erected by Edward the First, and contain within their round the castle mill. So late only as 1822, there existed two square towers on the right of the base court, the northernmost of which had at one time a communication with the moat, protected by a portcullis, but in that year they were pulled down. The whole fabric as it now stands, shows clearly enough, by its various styles, that it has been the work of different ages, even if we did not know that such were the fact, both from chronicle and tradition. The original castle was raised by Robert de Crevequer, who obtained the manor from William Rufus: but, after the usual fashion of those turbulent times, it was ere long forfeited and granted away, in what, from its frequent recurrence, may be called the regular order of things. Edward the First, who was an able soldier, soon perceived the strength of the fortress, and grew so jealous of it, that the possessor, William de Leyborne, considered it advisable to surrender his stronghold to the crown before it was taken from him, and perhaps with worse consequences. By Edward the Second this valuable possession was again alienated from the crown, he having given it to his favourite, Lord Badlesmere, who repaid this and other benefits by joining the Earl of Lancaster in his attempt to put down Piers Gaveston. If anything could have rendered rebellion yet more odious in the King's eyes it would have been such an object, for, as was earnestly understood, he valued this new favourite more, perhaps, than the crown itself. But other grounds of provocation were not long wanting, and these were afforded by Lady Badlesmere, who seems to have been filled with the same disloyal spirit as her husband. While the latter was absent with the other barons engaged against Hugh de Spenser, it so chanced that Queen Isabel coming that way, demanded hospitality at Leeds Castle for the night. The demand was not only refused, but several of the royal servants were killed in the attempt to force an entrance. Enraged at this affront offered to his consort, and reflectively to himself, Edward besieged the castle, and gaining possession of it after a severe struggle, he hanged the castellan, and committed Lady Badlesmere with her family to the Tower. The next year Lord Badlesmere shared the same fate as his castellan, but with some improvements; for after being hanged at Blean, near Canterbury, his head was cut off and fixed upon Burgate in that city.

The castle, which had sustained much damage from the siege, was repaired and considerably improved by William de Wykeham, who was constituted by Edward the Third chief warden and surveyor, with full powers for that purpose. In the reign of Henry the Fifth the castle attained yet greater notoriety, from being the place where that monarch imprisoned his mother-in-law, Joan of Navarre, for her traitorous attempt against his life. There, too, the Duchess of Gloucester underwent her trial for sorcery and witchcraft. At a later period, Edward the Sixth granted the fee simple of it to Sir Anthony St. Leger, and then, after having in the usual way with such mansions passed it from one family or another, it came at length, as a bequest from his uncle, Robert Lord Fairfax, to the Rev. Denny Martin, D.D., and is now possessed by CHARLES WYKEHAM MARTIN, Esq., M.P.

The oldest part of the castle as it appears at present, is the cellars, erected probably in the time of Henry the Third. At one period there was a Norman entrance to them, formed by a plain semicircular work of Caen stone, but which was covered up in 1822, when the southernmost of the two great divisions of the castle was pulled down and rebuilt. A draw-bridge originally supplied the means of communication between the old castle and this part of the building; but it was long ago replaced by timbers fixed and floored, which, at the time of the alterations just mentioned, were in their turn taken away, and a stone bridge of two arches substituted in their place. Some parts of the building date unquestionably from the reign of Edward the First, others from that of Edward the Third, and a very great portion was built by Sir H. Guldeford, in the reign of Henry the Eighth. Since 1822, many alterations have been made, which must be considered as allowable improvements, the old building having so materially lost its distinctive character that the changes have been rather wrought upon a modern than an ancient fabric. The whole presents an appearance both noble and imposing.

At Hadlow stands that singular and beautiful structure, HADLOW CASTLE, the seat of the late hospitable, eccentric, and amiable, Walter Barton May, Esq. Nigh to Hadlow Castle is MEREWORTH CASTLE, about seven miles from Maidstone, an elegant mansion erected by the seventh Earl of Westmoreland, after an Italian design—La Rotonda—built by Palladio in the vicinity of Vicenza. It occupies a gentle eminence, formerly the site of an ancient castle, which had belonged to the Lords Abergavenny. In the ground below, a little stream winds its course to join the Medway, amidst slopes and undulations that are highly cultivated on all sides.

At an early period Mereworth gave name to the family possessing it, for in Edward the Third's reign we find mention made of John de Mereworth, sheriff of Kent, and it remained in his line for two centuries, when it fell to Melmaines, and afterwards was the property of Brembre, Hermonstorpe, and Fitz Alan. From the Earls of Arundel the estate passed to the Lords Abergavenny and Le Despencer, and afterwards devolved with the title of Le Despencer on the first Earl of Westmoreland. Upon the death of John, 7th Earl, in 1762, without issue, he was succeeded in the estate by his nephew, Sir Francis Dashwood, Bart., in whose favour the abeyance of the Barony of Le Despencer was terminated in 1763; and that dignity is now the inheritance of Viscountess Falmouth, who, as Baroness Le Despencer, enjoys the Premier Barony of England.

It is seldom that the antiquarian traveller allows his course to be arrested by modern buildings, any more than the epicure would pause in a well-filled wine-cellar upon a pipe of new wine, when so many others of older vintage were demanding his attention. A few lines must consequently suffice for BEDFORDSHIRE, which is not rich in historic remains. It had few available military positions, and no fortresses of note. Bedford Castle, built by the Beauchamps, and esteemed in early times a garrison of such importance, that, as Camden observes, "there was scarcely a storm of civil fury that did not burst on it," was dismantled by Henry III., and after its fall no stronghold remained in the county.

Consequently during the wars of the Roses, and in the great civil contest in the reign of Charles I., Bedfordshire occurs but rarely, and thus was preserved from the desolation of battles and sieges.

Its monastic foundations were Elstow, Woburn, Walden, Dunstable, Bushmead, Caldwell, Rowenham, Harold, and Cricksand. In Fuller's time, Toddington, Houghton, and Woburn, stood foremost amongst the mansions of the nobility. Of these, Toddington, long the seat of the Cheneys and Wentworths, has altogether disappeared, and Houghton is in ruins; Woburn alone remains, still the princely home of the illustrious family of Russell. The other county seats deserving of notice in Bedfordshire, are WREST PARK (the Earl de Grey's), MELCHBOURN (Lord St. John's), SOUTHILL (Mr. Whitbread's), ODELL CASTLE (Mr. Alston's) ICKWELLBURY (Mr. Harvey's), TURVEY (Mr. Higgins'), and HINWICK (Mr. Orlebar's). Bletsoe, the old "historic land," from which the St. Johns derive the designation of their title, is now a farm-house. Here is said to have been born MARGARET TUDOR, mother of King Henry VII. Ampthill Castle, "builded," says Leland, "by Sir John Cornwall, of such spoils as he won in France," served as a retreat for Catherine of Arragon during the progress of her divorce—

> "In days of yore here Ampthill's towers were seen,
> The mournful refuge of an injured queen ;
> Here flowed her pure but unavailing tears,
> Here blended zeal sustain'd her sinking years ;
> Yet Freedom hence her radiant banner waved,
> And love avenged a realm by priests enslaved."

The castles of Windsor, Wallingford, and Reading, "the haunted towers of Cumnor Hall," and the field of Newbury—the fatal spot where the gallant Falkland fell—combine to invest BERKSHIRE with no inconsiderable share of historic notice. Its chief monasteries were Abingdon and Reading, each under the jurisdiction of a mitred Abbot; Sandleford Priory, Hurley, Bisham, and Farringdon. Old Fuller records that there were in his time "many neat houses and pleasant seats in this county, both on the Kennet and the Thames;" and most appositely may the remark be applied to our own days. There are WYTHAM ABBEY (the Earl of Abingdon's), ASH-

Down Park (Earl Craven's), Coleshill (the Earl of Radnor's), East Hampstead Park (the Marquess of Downshire's), Englefield (Mr. de Beauvoir's), Aldermaston (Mr. Higford Burr's), Holme Park (Mr. Palmer's), Bearwood (Mr. Walter's), Calcot (Colonel Blagrove's), Pusey, (Mr. Pusey's), Buscot Park (Mr. Pryse's), Shottesbrooke (Mr. Vansittart's), Greenham Lodge (Mr. Croft's), East Hendred (Mr. Eyston's), Wasing (Mr. Mount's), and Bessell's Leigh (Mr. Lenthall's). None of these seats are, however, of very ancient date; and it may be remarked as a singular fact, that there is not one family now resident in Berkshire which can shew a male descent from any of those mentioned in the list of gentry returned in the twelfth year of Henry VI. "Sure I am," we again quote Fuller, "that ancient gentry in this country sown thick in former, come up thin in our age."

> "Of names which were in days of yore,
> Few remain here of great store."

Of the ancient castles which at one period reared their stately structures at Wallingford, Newbury, Donnington, Reading, and Brightwell, scarcely a fragment can be traced; but one, the oldest and most celebrated of all, the regal residence of Windsor, remains still the palace of our sovereign, as it was of her royal predecessor, Henry Beauclerk, at the opening of the twelfth century—

> "Thy forest Windsor, and thy green retreats,
> At once the monarchs' and the muses' seats."

Buckinghamshire, the birthplace of John Hampden,

was one of the first counties that joined in an association for mutual defence on the side of the Parliament, and it continued to distinguish itself throughout the civil war by its hostility to the King's cause. Borstall House, however, situated about nine miles from Thame, held out gallantly as a royal garrison until 1646, having previously sustained successfully two severe sieges—one conducted by Skipton, the other by Fairfax; and Greenland House, also garrisoned by King Charles, was famous for its resistance to the Parliamentary General Browne.

Snellshall, Bradwell, Ankerwyke, and Little Marlow, were Benedictine monasteries in Buckinghamshire. The Cistercian monks had abbeys at Biddlesden and Medmenham, and the Austin Canons were gathered together at Messendel, Nutley, Chetwode, and Ravenston.

After the Conquest, and at the date of the Domesday survey, the great landed proprietor was Walter Giffard, Earl of Buckingham; and in the twelfth century the Grenvilles first appear as holding under the Giffards; thenceforward they progressed rapidly in local influence, and at length, by intermarriages with richly-portioned heiresses, attained the first position and highest title the county could bestow.

Contemporaneous with the Norman Giffards were the Hampdens, illustrious as the parent stem of John Hampden the patriot; and they flourished as Lords of Hampden in lineal male descent for twenty-four generations. There is a tradition that King Edward III. and the Black Prince once honoured Hampden with a visit, and that whilst the Prince and his host were exercising themselves in feats of chivalry, a quarrel arose, in which the Prince received a blow on his face; an indignity which occasioned him and his royal father to quit the place in great wrath, and to seize on some valuable manors belonging to his host. The story gave rise to the following rhymes:—

> "Tring, Wing, and Ivinghoe,
> Hampden did forgoe,
> For striking of a blow,
> And glad he did escape so."

Could any title of the peerage add to the nobility of the Hampden, upon whose sarcophagus is inscribed—

"*John Hampden, twenty-fourth hereditary Lord of Great Hampden.*"

The literary pilgrim has to visit in Bucks, Gayhurst, the birthplace of Sir Kenelm Digby, Stoke Pogis, the tomb of Gray, and Olney and Beaconsfield—the former, for a time, the abode of the poet Cowper, and the latter the cherished home of Waller and Burke.

One princely residence in this county we will stop to admire—Ashridge; "the hill set with Ash trees," originally the College of the Bonhommes, and now the magnificent heritage of the Earl of Brownlow. Of late years the succession to this great property gave rise to one of the most curious of our Causes Célèbres, Under the singular will of the seventh Earl of Bridgewater, the late Lord Alford succeeded to the hereditary estates of the Egertons, upon condition of his obtaining a higher grade in the peerage than that of Earl within five years; failing which, the property was to go to his brother, the Hon.

Charles Henry Cust, subject to the like term. But Lord Alford died within little more than one year, and then came the question, "was his brother or his son entitled to the estate?" On the one side it was urged that the late possessor being dead, without having obtained the stipulated grade, his descendants had thereby incurred the penalty of forfeiture. To this it was replied, that only one year having expired, the matter must as yet be considered doubtful. Both parties appealed to law, and law in its court of highest appeal—the House of Lords—has decided that the condition, being contrary to the principles of the English constitution, and one which the devisee had no legitimate means of controlling, should be passed over, and the will read without it. This judgment has confirmed the youthful Earl of Brownlow (Lord Alford's son) in this magnificent estate. What a curious volume might be compiled from the wills in Doctors' Commons of human weakness, bigotry, and singularity!

About two miles from Banbury, in OXFORDSHIRE, we come upon BROUGHTON CASTLE (Lord Saye and Sele's), which in its wholeness affords a striking example of the almost regal magnificence of the feudal barons. An old tower forms the entrance to the court, and the outer gate is still perfect, but there are no traces of the portcullis. There would appear also from the remaining staples to have been two other gates. The most ancient part of the building is the eastern side, at the south-east angle of which is a small tower with loopholes for the discharge of arrows. The hall is of large dimensions, the passages are curiously arched, and the present dining-room has likewise a roof of arched stone. Beyond is a staircase of the same material, leading to what was once the chapel, with very ancient arms upon the window, but it is now used for a dressing-room. The eastern side is supposed to have been built by the Broughtons, in the reign of one of the early Edwards: the north front was erected by the Fiennes' in the year 1544. A broad and deep moat, which is crossed by a stone bridge of two arches, surrounds the whole.

In gazing on Broughton, with its grey walls, its lofty battlements, its numerous gables, and its ivy-covered towers, the spectator cannot but perceive how much more picturesque it is than any building of Greek or Roman architecture. That the Gothic style has this advantage over its classic rivals is indisputable, as any one must admit who recollects how much deeper was the impression made upon himself when standing in the aisles of Westminster Abbey, than when placed under the mighty cupola of St. Paul's.

A short step in our present mode of travelling will bring us to HELMINGHAM HALL, in SUFFOLK, the splendid seat of John Tollemache, Esq., M.P. The building, which is wholly of brick, bears undeniable marks of belonging to the time of Henry the Eighth, when the embattled mansion had succeeded to the baronial castle. It is a quadrangle with a terrace and moat surrounding it, and stands in the midst of a park of about four hundred acres in extent, well stocked with deer, many of them remarkable for their size, and abounding with noble oaks which have long been celebrated as the finest in the county. To the credit of its successive owners, very few innovations have been made upon the old mansion; by an unusual stretch of forbearance, or by a kindly regard for other times, it has been allowed to retain the greater part of its ancient characteristics—its large bay windows, its embattled parapets, its gables terminated with richly wrought finials, and its chimneys ornamented with reticulated and indented mouldings. Once indeed some unlucky friend of improvement, who was no doubt shocked at the appearance of vulgar brick, covered the building with composition in order to make it look like stone; but this sin against good taste was afterwards removed by the better judgment of one of his successors. Things were once again restored to their pristine state, and we are told that even now the draw-bridges on the east and south fronts continue to be raised every night as they used to be in the olden time. Much care has been taken to attract the wild fowls to the place so peculiarly fitted to their habits, and, as they are never disturbed, the moat as well as a small lake in the park is always crowded with them.

From its earliest erection this Hall belonged to the Tollemaches, who long before the Norman Conquest possessed lands at Bentley in the same county, where, till very lately, this inscription might be seen in the old manor-house:

"When William the Conqueror reign'd with great fame,
Bentley was my seat, and Tollemache was my name."

Right pious folks too were these gallant Tollemaches, and so held when such a repute was not to be got by prayers and fastings alone, but must be purchased by devout largesses of land and gold to the church, which, it must be confessed, for the most part turned the popular bounty to excellent uses. Many a fair acre of glebe and pasture did the Tollemaches bestow on convent and monastery, whose inmates in requital prayed for their benefactors, and fed the poor from their superabundance, till Henry the Eighth appropriated to himself all the church property in the kingdom. The family, however, had the less reason to complain of this royal intermission with their charities, as they themselves must soon afterwards have embraced the new faith, for we find Sir Lionel, the then head of the house, in high favour with Elizabeth, who was not likely to have shewn any particular grace to a Catholic. On one occasion, in 1561, the maiden Queen honoured him with a visit for five days, during which time she stood godmother to his son, and gave his mother a lute, still preserved as an heir-loom among the family reliques and curiosities. A descendant of this fortunate gentleman married the heiress of the first Earl of Dysart, a title derived from the royal borough of that name in Fifeshire. Upon the decease of the last Earl without a child, the title devolved upon his sister, Lady Louisa Manners, the widow of John Manners, who in process of time was created Lord Huntingtower.

Another of the SUFFOLK seats—highly interesting to the antiquarian or architectural tourist—is HENGRAVE, successively the inheritance of the Hengraves, the Greys, the Kytsons, the D'Arcys, and the Gages. At the time when this mansion—still one of the chief ornaments of the county—was built, between the years 1525 and 1538, the old form of the Castle had yielded to the more convenient and less gloomy embattled manor-houses, distinguished in a particular degree by their richly-decorated portals, turrets, bay-windows and oriels. "The gateway of Hengrave," says Gough, "is of such singular beauty and in such high preservation, that perhaps a more elegant specimen of the architecture of the age in which it was erected cannot be seen."

Of the Lady Penelope D'Arcy, the heiress of Hengrave, the following quaint anecdote has been often told : "Sir George Trenchard, Sir John Gage, and Sir William Hervey, each solicited Lady Penelope in marriage, when, to keep peace among the rivals, she threatened the first aggressor with her perpetual displeasure, humorously telling them, that if they would wait, she would have them all in their turns ; a promise which was actually performed. The gentleman first favoured by her was Sir George Trenchard, of Wolverton, in Dorsetshire, who dying shortly after the marriage, without issue, she wedded Sir John Gage, of Firle, whose descendants have continued owners of Hengrave to the present day. Her last husband was Sir William Hervey, of Ickworth, but by him she had no child."

The ducal seat of Suffolk is EUSTON. Robert Bloomfield, the rustic bard of SUFFOLK, was born in its vicinity, and his muse loved to commemorate the beauties of "Grafton's rich domain," those favoured scenes, wherein his mind first became stored with that abundance of rural imagery, which, feeding his natural passion for the country, was one day to give an irresistible charm to the simple language of the untaught peasant. Magical is the power of genius! The humble "Shepherd's boy, he sought no better name," has imparted a poetic association to the princely home of Euston, more attractive than any other connected with its history.

The village of Euston is situated a mile from Fakenham, but the park extends nearly to that place. It was formerly the lordship of a family bearing the local name, and afterwards descended to SIR HENRY BENNET, who, by King Charles II., was made Secretary of State, and created Viscount Thetford, and Earl of Arlington. He enjoyed the estate for many years, and built the mansion of Euston Hall. In reference to this, we find the following remarks of John Evelyn:—

"A stranger preached at Euston church, and fell into a handsome panegyric on my lord's new building the church, which indeed for its elegance and cheerfulness is one of the prettiest country churches in England. My lord told me his heart smote him that after he had bestowed so much on his magnificent palace there, he should see God's house in the ruin it lay. He has also rebuilt the parsonage house all of stone, very neat and ample."

One more memory of SUFFOLK: in Lord Stradbroke's Park there still remains, or did remain a short while ago, in the last stage of decay, the famous Henham Oak, in the trunk of which, that valiant soldier Sir John Rous, Bart., concealed himself from the Roundheads after their victory at Worcester. In aftertimes, when the stout cavalier slept with his ancestors, and the Stuarts were driven into exile, it would seem that Sir John had bequeathed not only his estate but his devoted spirit of loyalty to his descendants. In the bosom of this same oak, where he had hidden himself, Sir Robert Rous held his Jacobitical symposia with two or three select friends, drinking deep potations, on bended knees, "to the King over the water."

Inclination would carry us to the lovely land of Hereford, rich in antiquities and historic families, but space deters us from entering on so prolific a field—Hampton Court, Wigmore, Erdisley, Bodenham, Stoke Edith, Treago, Goodrich Castle, all rise on our memory. There is, however, an old Manor House in the neighbouring shire of WORCESTER, which we must not pass altogether by—HAGLEY, the classic ground of poetry and wit, the theme of Thomson, and the home of the Lytteltons. Associated with the second Lord Lyttelton is a memorable ghost story, which has been often told, with frequent exaggeration and much false colouring: the true narrative we will endeavour to relate:

Thomas, Lord Lyttelton, born in 1744, was the son of George, Lord Lyttelton, the distinguished poet and historian, who built Hagley as it now stands. After a course of dissipation and profligacy, his Lordship's health became gradually impaired, and his constitution much weakened by frequent attacks of suffocating fits. Such was the state of things up to Wednesday, the 24th November, 1779; his Lordship was then resident at Pitt Place, near Epsom. On the evening of that day he was evidently worse, and went to bed at an earlier hour than usual. His servant having given him his customary medicine, retired for the night, but he had not been gone long before Lord Lyttelton was disturbed by a gentle fluttering of wings about the chamber. While he yet listened, he was still more struck by the sound of footsteps in the direction towards his bed. Astonished at these noises in the stillness of night, he raised himself up to learn what all meant, and beheld a lovely female, dressed in white, with a small bird perched, falcon-like, upon her wrist. Lord Lyttelton struggled to speak, but before he could articulate a word, the spectre warned him to prepare himself, for his death was nigh. "But three days more," said the vision, "but three days more, and at the hour of twelve you will die!" —words too distinctly uttered and too deeply impressed on the memory of the suffering patient to be easily forgotten. When he awoke in the morning, the apparition of the lady with the bird still haunted him, and the ominous prophecy pressed upon his mind—so much so, indeed, that he could not help relieving himself of what he felt to be a burthen by relating the circumstance at the breakfast-table. It was obvious that he wished to convince his hearers as well as himself, that there was nothing in the apparition more than a dream; and for so much of it as referred to the bird, he accounted for it by saying that, when he was in the greenhouse a few days before, he had taken some pains to catch a robin which had been shut in, to set it free. Still, the imagination, when once fairly excited, is not so easily to be set at rest again. So much did these gloomy apprehensions grow upon him, even while he seemed most to laugh at them as mere chimeras, that he was fain to call his friends about him, and fill the house with guests and revelry. . . . The third day had now come. Never was the gay and witty Lyttelton so animated. Admiral Wolseley and others who were staying with him, and were present at this death banquet, asserted, that never did his sprightly humour and convivial qualities shine out to greater advantage. But as night came on, these joyous feelings gradually gave way to gloom, and though he endeavoured to rouse his spirits, the effort was vain. His friends, meanwhile, used every precaution to counteract the influence of the apparition. By the help of his valet, they put on considerably his own watch as it lay upon his dressing-table, and the steward, at their request, did the same with all the other clocks and watches in the house. Nothing, however, availed to free him from his " thick-coming fancies," and at half-past eleven, as he conceived it to be, though in reality it was no more than eleven, he complained of weariness, and retired to his room. Having gone to bed, he desired his valet to draw the curtains at the foot, and to remain in the room, at the same time frequently and anxiously consulting his watch. At length, when it was nearly half-past twelve by the altered time, he asked to see his servant's watch, and was visibly pleased on finding it pretty nearly corresponded with his own. He then put them, one after the other, to his ear, to be assured that they were both going, and exclaimed, with no little satisfaction, " This mysterious lady is not a true prophetess, I find. Give me my medicine: I'll wait no longer." In obedience to this order, the servant went into the adjoining dressing-room, to prepare the physic—by the right time it was now exactly midnight,—but had not been thus employed more than a minute or two, when he thought he heard his master breathing unusually hard. Alarmed by the sound, he ran to him, and found that the prophetic vision had been a true one: his lordship was in the agonies of death, and in a few moments breathed his last!

BRAMSHILL, in HAMPSHIRE, is not the largest, nor the finest, nor the shewiest, nor the best plenished, of our ancient mansions; but it is as it was, and as it was intended to be. It has no new wing built, "in a modern style of convenience," in the middle of last century, nor has it any *restorations* (?) by Wyatt or his followers, or improvements by Kent or Brown. No! There it stands, as it stood two hundred years ago; a little more weather-dyed, perhaps, but still the same; and its wild and picturesque park, in all its main features, as it was half a century after it was reclaimed from the heath around it. Bramshill— for let us draw near to it—stands nobly before us, " built," as old Fuller tells us, "in a bleak and barren place." Yes! there it stands, with its park, like a green and wooded island in the midst of the great heathy plain which occupies this part of Hampshire: but we have now entered the long straight avenue of old oaks that leads us in a direct arrow-like line up to the west front; and, as we have opened quaint old Fuller's book, we must agree in the epithet he applies to the house, even more cordially than in those he bestows on the country round; for he calls it "a stately structure," and so it is; we feel that the quaint old man has just got the right word—it does seem a stately structure, as it looks down on us with its multitude of windows, its airy parapets, its clustered chimneys, its long front, so beautifully broken into light and shade by its projecting wings and richly-ornamented centre. There is a long history connected with Bramshill, successively held by the Zouches, the Henleys, and the Copes; but we will chronicle only one fact, and that the most recent —the visit of Queen Victoria and Prince Albert, in 1845.

The other chief seats of Hampshire are Strathfieldsaye, Highclere, Dogmersfield, Hackwood, Amport, Manydown, Tangier, Avington, Stoneham, Cranbury, Cadland, Stratton, Elvetham, Hurstbourne, Wherwell, Roch Court, Brockenhurst, Cams Hall, Idsworth, Paultons, Hursley, and Northwood.

While lingering in Hampshire, let us turn a thought to Carisbrooke Castle, King Charles's prison, in Hampshire's lovely Isle of Wight. There is scarcely any historic ruin that has prouder recollections than this. It interests alike the historian, the antiquary, and the lover of the picturesque.

> "Time, by his gradual touch,
> Has moulder'd into beauty many a tower,
> Which, when it frown'd with all its battlements,
> Was only terrible."

Crowning the top of a hill, beneath which is a pretty rural village, and at the distance of a mile, or mile and a half, from the little metropolis of the Isle of Wight, the ruins of Carisbrooke Castle allure the inquiring tourist. Nor is he disappointed of the object in his pilgrimage. So fair are these ruins, so important the events that they have witnessed, and so romantic and sad, that the Muses of Painting, History, and Tragedy might contend who should mark them for her own.

The transition from Hampshire to Surrey would scarcely offend the nicest sticklers for the dramatic unities; the traveller may be in the one county before he has any notion that he has got out of the other; and when here, the first thing to attract his attention will be CLAREMONT PARK, to which events in our day, associated with fallen royalty, have lent so painful an interest. The history of this place is shortly told. Sir John Vanbrugh, the architect of Blenheim and Castle Howard, bought some land here, upon which he built a low brick house for his own residence, choosing for its site precisely such a spot as would have been selected by his Dutch ancestors, so notorious for planting their houses amidst dykes and marshes. Avoiding with the greatest care any of the near rising grounds, that would have tempted ordinary men, he pitched his tent upon a low flat area, whence it was impossible to get the slightest prospect. He soon, however, grew tired of his own work, which will probably to most people seem less strange than that he should have found a purchaser for so uninviting a retreat; yet so it was: Thomas Holles Pelham, then Earl of Clare, and who in 1715 was advanced to the dignity of Duke of Newcastle, took the estate off his hands. But the new owner had a singular passion for improving, and, like the famous *capability* Brown, as he was called, would seem to have been never so happy as when, by the magic of his own taste, he was creating beauty from deformity. Setting to work with a good will and courage that may be almost termed chivalrous, considering the very unpromising materials he had to deal with, he soon effected such changes as must have made the place scarcely recognizable by the dull spirit that had first planned it. The low brick house was built into a mansion; the grounds were extended by further purchases, and a large portion of the adjoining heath was enclosed and added to the estate. As time had left no fragments, no ruined castle nor mouldering abbey, the noble owner drew upon his own fancy and the modern trowel to supply the defect. On a mount in the park, he erected a building to resemble a castle, and as a castle would obviously be nothing without a name, he reversed the usual order of things, by which men take their titles from their estates, and christened the new fabric after himself, CLARE—mont. Upon his death it was bought by the celebrated Lord Clive, who found the whole affair much too small for the grand notions he had brought with him from India. It was Gulliver in Lilliput. So forthwith he called in architects and masons, bricklayers and carpenters, men with pickaxes to pull down, and men with trowels to build up, and raised such a dust in the neighbouroood as perfectly blinded the eyes and ears of the natives, who had never been used to see things upon so large a scale. But his builder was a man of some judgment; he had none of Sir John Vanbrugh's passion for flats and marshes, but, on the contrary, chose an excellent site for the new fabric, commanding as good a prospect as the country afforded. The liberality of the employer kept pace with the fancies of the architect; even the grounds were remodelled; and upon the whole, it is said that upwards of a hundred thousand pounds were expended in bringing these comprehensive labours to a conclusion. When Lord Clive died, the property was bought by Lord Galway, who sold it to the Earl of Tyrconnel, and he again parted with it to Charles Rose Ellis, Esq. From him it was finally bought by the government, as a residence for the lamented Princess Charlotte, upon her marriage with Prince Leopold, to whom—now King of the Belgians—it still belongs. Here the exiled royal family of France found an asylum, and here Louis Philippe closed his eventful life.

On the banks of the river Thames, about a mile from Richmond—that lovely sunny spot, so correctly named "Sheen," or "the beautiful," by our Saxon forefathers—stands HAM HOUSE, a fine and curious specimen of the domestic architecture of the time of JAMES I. It was built in 1610 as a residence for Henry Prince of Wales, but underwent considerable alterations in the time of Charles the Second, when it was completely furnished by the Duke and Duchess of Lauderdale. Here, too, was born their grandson, John, Duke of Argyll, equally celebrated as a soldier and a statesman. The stranger who has never visited this seat, will easily form an idea of its internal magnificence when he is told that even the bellows and brushes in some of the rooms are made of solid silver, or of solid filagree. The gardens, from all appearance, have been little altered since they were first formed, bearing all the marks of those times when the grand object was to supersede nature by art, or to make her look as little like herself as possible. Terrace above terrace slopes down to the river, enclosed by walls that are ornamented with a series of busts, continued to the principal façade; in front is a colossal statue of Father Thames, and all the walks are distinguished by a perfect symmetry, that it must be owned is tame and monotonous. Sir Walter Scott, in an Essay on Landscape Gardening, has defended this artificial style with an eloquence and glow of fancy that may convince any one so long as he is under the influence of this arch-magician, who had the wonderful power of imparting his own brilliance to the least imaginative theme; but once you close the book, the spell is broken: formal walks, fraternal clumps of trees, and alleys made to match each other, will no longer be preferred to the simple and the natural, which characterise modern gardening, even though we should at times run a little wild in the pursuit of nature. Long avenues of majestic elms and groves of dark firs give a peculiar character to Ham House: from almost every distant point of view the mansion seems embosomed in foliage, and on a close inspection has an air of solemn, venerable grandeur. The building is constructed of red brick, and has two fronts; interiorly the apartments are very handsome, some lined with tapestry, and remaining well nigh as they were left by the Countess of Dysart (afterwards Duchess of Lauderdale), *temp.* Charles II. But the most attractive portion of this fine mansion is the curious old library, termed by Dibdin "a wonderful book-paradise," superlatively rich in Caxton's and other early black-letter productions of the English press, as well as in private documents and original letters of the period of Charles and James.

FARNHAM CASTLE, also in SURREY, occupies an eminence on the north side of Farnham, and is supposed to have been erected in 1129, by Henry de Blois, brother of King Stephen. During the rebellion of the barons against Henry the Third, it was seized by their ally the French Dauphin, and in the course of these civil broils got demolished by the royal party, but was soon rebuilt with a deep moat and donjon, with the other usual appurtenances of a castellated building. In the great civil war it had the singular fate of being governed at intervals by two poets; for zealous partizanship in those days, like the fear of invasion by republican France in our own times, made all men soldiers. Sir John Denham having secured it for the king's party in 1642, was appointed governor of the place, in requital for his good service. Then came Sir William Waller, the parliamentarian general, who blew up the defences and took the fortress, when the command of it was given by the parliament to George Withers, another poet, of a more quaint and original genius than the royalist bard. A few years afterwards, the Committee of Derby House ordered it to be rendered incapable of defence, imposing upon the county the expense of demolition. The castle, in consequence, was nearly pulled to pieces, the glass, iron, lead, and timbers, that had gone to its construction, being taken by the men and officers in part payment of the arrears due to them. Next came the restoration of Charles: the Cavaliers obtained once again the ascendancy, the church resumed her rights, and, in this general return to the old state of things, Farnham Castle was given back to the see of Winchester. It was, however, in too dilapidated a condition to serve, as it then was, for an episcopal residence, and Bishop Morley, it is said, expended full eight thousand pounds upon these ruins, so that in a short time they again rose, phœnix-like, stronger and more brilliant from their ashes. A considerable fragment of the oldest part of the castle still remains, and the entrance gateway deserves to be particularly pointed out, as retaining its ancient character. The fosse has been either drained or allowed to become dry, and is planted with oaks. Internally the principal apartments underwent considerable alterations so far back as the time of Charles the Second, the contrast between the styles of the different periods being too obvious to require any comment. The present bishop, who makes it his residence, has been at much expense in improving both the mansion and the grounds belonging to it; but with great taste and judgment, while laying out new roads and walks in the park, he has left untouched a noble avenue of elms nearly three quarters of a mile long, which has not only in itself an imposing effect, but has a peculiar interest as a living specimen of times gone, or a link as it were between us and the past. It may indeed be questioned whether the gnarled old oak, the growth of many ages, with decay at his heart, while putting forth his green leaves, is not a more vivid remembrance of those that are gone than abbey or castle ruin.

Formerly, there were two parks attached to this estate; the one called the Old, or Great Park, the other the New, or Little Park. The first of these, containing about one thousand acres, was disforested in the reign of Charles the Second. The Little Park, consisting of about three hundred acres, and adjoining the castle on the east side, still continues to be a woodland, which is rendered yet more picturesque by the Lodden running through it, from its well-head in the neighbouring county.

Two miles from Guildford is Loseley Hall, the last place that we shall mention in Surrey. It is a venerable pile, and large as it now is, bears undeniable marks of having been at one time considerably larger. In the reign of Henry the Eighth it was purchased by Christopher More, Esq., and remained in his family till 1689, when he died, leaving no nearer kin to claim the estate than three sisters. Of these, the two eldest died unmarried, and the youngest, Margaret, gave her hand, and with it the property of Loseley House, to Sir Thomas Molyneux, of the Sefton family.

It would be useless, as well as tedious, to record the various hands though which the mansion has passed since that time, or how one owner pulled down a turret, and another built up a chimney, according as whim or necessity might dictate; but we cannot help remarking upon the very great passion of the family for moral maxims, which they inscribed over window and portal, inside and outside, for the benefit of those who visited the place. Over the vestibule, for instance, now the butler's pantry, were placed three stone figures, from whose contradictory mottoes the sagacious wayfarer was no doubt expected to draw an edifying conclusion. To the left was Fortune treading upon a globe and holding a wheel, on which was written *Fortuna omnia;* to the right was *Fate,* grasping a celestial sphere, with the inscription, *Non Fors, sed Fatum;* and in the middle was a figure with one foot on a wheel, and the other on a globe, pointing to the page of an open volume wherein was written, *Non Fors, nec Fatum.* In addition to this learned conundrum, the traveller reads over the porch the following distich, explanatory of who would, and who would not be welcome:

" Invide, tangendi tibi limina nulla facultas ;
At tibi, amice, patent janua, mensa, domus."

Within the vestibule, above the hall door, the same idea repeated in a clumsy hexameter :—" Invidiæ claudor, pateo sed semper amico."

Over the kitchen door—a very appropriate place for such a motto—was an admonition to the visitor not to play the glutton :—" Fami, non gulæ."

Over the buttery was a similar caution against excess in the matter of the wine cup :—" Siti, non ebrietati."

Over the parlour door was a significant hint, that the open sesame to the lock was a good character:—" Probis non pravis."

And in the cornice of the great drawing-room was a mulberry tree, having inscribed on one side—" Morus tarde moriens." But on the other,—" Morum cito moriturum," which we need hardly say is a pun, and not a very clever one, upon the family name of More.

The estate is now possessed by James More Molyneux, Esq.

Had we space, DERBYSHIRE, styled by Kinder "the amphitheatre of renowned persons," would tempt our wanderings—Derbyshire, with its ancient Castles of Castleton and Codnor, with its time-honoured Halls of Haddon, Hardwick, South Winfield, Kedleston, Radborne, and Elvaston, and its stately edifices of Wingerworth, Willersley, Aston, Markeaton, and Calke Abbey. Derbyshire has more than its share of the picturesque, and its full share of the romantic. It abounds in ruins of feudal grandeur, but is poor in those of monastic institutions. There is, however, one relic of the latter kind of extreme interest and beauty, which is situated in so secluded and inaccessible a part of the county as to be little known and rarely visited. This is the Abbey of Depedale, more generally called "Dale Abbey." Those who would see our lovely land in all its fascination must be satisfied to quit the great roads, and even the byeways, for the nooks and corners of the country. Just such a spot is the low, sheltered valley where stands all that remains of Dale Abbey— one solitary Gothic arch of very large span and exquisite proportions.

But CHATSWORTH is, beyond all question, the pride of Derbyshire,—Chatsworth, the palace of the Peak, rising like a gem in the midst of a wild and somewhat rugged landscape. The hamlet of Chatsworth, long the residence of the Leches, passed by sale into the possession of Sir William Cavendish, the faithful friend of Cardinal Wolsey, and has since remained the chief seat of his descendants, the Dukes of Devonshire. The old Manor House of the Leches was demolished by Sir William, and the mansion, which he commenced, was completed by his widow, the celebrated "Bess of Hardwick," the notable dabbler in architecture, intrigue, and moneycraft, to whom Hardwick also owes its existence. Her Ladyship took for her last husband George, Earl of Shrewsbury; and Chatsworth, in consequence, (his Lordship being entrusted with the custody of Mary, Queen of Scots,) gained a more than common interest, as one of the prisons of that ill-fated Princess. There is no place, indeed, with which the remembrance of Mary's captivity is more intimately associated than Chatsworth. There we are in imagination carried back to the time when the ill-fated Queen looked from its turrets with vain hope. Little, however, is actually left of Mary at Chatsworth except her picture, and a romantic and curious raised plat of architectural garden in the park, called "Mary's Bower," where she is said often to have sat, pondering upon her eventful past and her uncertain future. The relics of Mary, which are exhibited at Hardwick Hall, were brought thither from Chatsworth, and formed the furniture of the apartment where the captive was confined. Bess of Hardwick survived the Earl of Shrewsbury many years, living to the verge of ninety, and even to the last hour indulging in her pride and worldly magnificence. Her passion was for building, and it is hard to say how many more noble monuments of her taste she might have left behind her, if a hard frost in 1607 had not compelled her workmen to stop suddenly, when engaged in improving the Norman keep of Bolsover. The magic spell was broken—the charm was ended—the witches' prophecy was fulfilled. Bess of Hardwick ceased to build, and accordingly died!

The present magnificent pile of Chatsworth originated in the taste and spirit of the first Duke of Devonshire, and the grand designs of his Grace have been more than realized by his successors. Dr. Kennet relates of Marshal

Tallard, who was taken at the battle of Blenheim, and remained seven years a prisoner in this country, that having been invited by the Duke of Devonshire to Chatsworth, and nobly entertained for several days, he was said to have parted with his host in these words:—" My Lord, when I come hereafter to compute the time of my captivity in England, I shall leave out the days of my enjoyment at Chatsworth."

From Derbyshire to Cumberland is a long distance, yet between the two there is sometimes a similarity of scenery. Watered by the silvery stream from which the name is derived, and embosomed in richly wooded groves, peculiarly our country's own, Edenhall, "aula ad rivum Eden," is one of those lovely spots so abundantly scattered over this favoured locality of our island.

The mansion of EDENHALL is a handsome stone structure, built by the late Sir Philip Musgrave on the site of the old house. It is said to be one of the best arranged and most comfortable residences in England, and throughout the grounds the most picturesque scenery opens on the view. Among the family treasures the most carefully preserved relic is the famous cup called the "Luck of Edenhall." The letters "I.H.S." on the leather case indicate its once sacred use. A legendary tale records that it was seized from a company of fairies, who were sporting near a well in the garden, called St. Cuthbert's Well, and who, after an ineffectual struggle to regain the pilfered cup, vanished into air, singing—

"If e'er this cup should break or fall,
Farewell the luck of Edenhall."

This fairy cup of rare device and shape may yet be seen at Edenhall. On rare occasions it is brought from its sanctuary with all the honours due to so ancient a relic, and being filled to the brim with the choicest wine, is presented to each guest in succession, It is yet safe and sound, and "the luck of Edenhall," exemplified in the prosperity of the right worthy family of Musgrave, still endures. Esto perpetua!

Many and many another home of unrivalled England comes back on our memory, and many a county, too, such as Essex, with its fine old halls of Audley End, Thorndon, and Belhus; Northumberland, adorned by Alnwick Castle, Howick, Chillingham, Hesleyside, and Wallington; and Cornwall, which has the grand ancestral seats of Caerhays, Port Eliot, Tregothnan, Penrose, Trefusis, and Menabilly; but we must end our wanderings.

With one or two more of "the stately homes of England," our random recollections are exhausted.

Bayons Manor, a castellated manor-house, in Lincolnshire, the seat of Right Hon. Charles Tennyson d'Eyncourt, suggests feudal associations, and recalls the expansive and dignified hospitality of the olden time. We shall not easily forget our first impression of this splendid specimen of the middle ages, its lofty but ruined donjon, the entrance over the moat by a drawbridge, through a barbacan, and three succeeding gates of powerful architecture, with two portcullises, its towers, posterns, machicolations and ivy-mantled walls, of which the outer line contains five or six acres.

It is impossible for anything to have presented a more

beautiful picture than did this fine castle, seen under the influence of an autumnal afternoon. The dark grey walls were deeply tinted, and the park abounding with deer, and broken by every variety of hill, dale, wood, and water, was shadowed over by the declining sun. Bayons is chiefly indebted to the existing proprietor, Mr. D'Eyncourt, and his late father, for its present aspect and condition, and the extensive additions made by the former are well adapted to the progressive history of the manor. The architecture is accordingly of different periods in the middle ages: the keep is Anglo-Saxon, or early Norman; the Eastern towers, the curtain, the large central flag tower, and two of the gates seem to bear a date prior to Edward III. The great hall and its oak fittings are in the style of Richard II., and the more decorated portion towards the west, represents for the most part the period between Henry V. and Henry VII. We will not attempt to describe the internal magnificence. When a guest at Bayons Manor, in 1848, Sir Edward Bulwer Lytton wrote his charming romance, "Harold," in the curious old tapestry chamber of the mansion, and most appropriately dedicated the book to Mr. D'Eyncourt. " What marvel (we quote Sir Edward's own words), what marvel that I lived in the times of which I wrote, Saxon with the Saxon, Norman with the Norman,—that I entered into no gossip less venerable than that current at the Court of the Confessor, or startled my fellow guests (when I deigned to meet them) with the last news which Harold's spies had brought over from the camp at St. Valery ? With all those disturbed spectres rampant in this chamber, all the armour rusting in the galleries, all those mutilated statues of early English Kings (including St. Edward himself), niched into the grey, ivied walls—say, in thy conscience, O host, shall I ever return to the nineteenth century again ?"

The Manor of STOWE, in Buckinghamshire, two miles and a half from the county capital, was originally possessed by the abbot and convent of Oseney. On the dissolution of the monasteries, the prudent abbot who then presided over Stowe managed to obtain a gift of it from Henry, and became the first bishop of Oxford. In 1590 he resigned it to the crown, when it was granted to Thomas Compton and another person, who immediately conveyed it, no doubt for a consideration, to John Temple, Esq., of a family that originally belonged to Sheepey, in Leicestershire, and afterwards to Burton Basset, in Warwickshire. From that time the family continued to increase in honours, rising rapidly from one step to another in the peerage, till the head of the house attained the dignity of Duke of Buckingham.

The old house, erected by Peter Temple in the time of Elizabeth, was pulled down and rebuilt by Sir Richard Temple, who died in 1697; but to this structure his son, Lord Cobham, added wings. Since then it has undergone yet further improvements, and been brought to the state of magnificence in which it remained until recently, by the successive alterations of Earl Temple, who died in 1779, and the first Marquess of Buckingham. As it now stands, the centre of the front presents a line of four hundred and fifty-four feet, and with the wings included, extends to nine hundred and sixteen. The gardens occupy four hundred acres, offering at a distance the appearance of an immense grove, with towers, columns and obelisks, glittering out from the deep mass of foliage. Nor does a nearer view of these celebrated grounds at all disappoint the expectations that may have been raised by the remoter glimpses of it. All that art could do to embellish nature, has here been done with much taste, and no regard to cost; grottoes, lakes, caverns, temples, and sculptures of all kinds, find a place in this fairy domain which Walpole, no mean judge of such matters, describes as "sometimes recalling Albano's landscapes to our mind; and oftener to our fancy, the idolatrous and luxurious vales of Daphne and Tempe."

We have spoken of Stowe in the present tense, as if it still existed in its ancient glory, being willing to keep up the pleasing illusion of memory as long as possible. But alas! the proud mansion of Stowe, like its rival Canons, has been despoiled, and its contents scattered through a thousand different channels.

LEICESTERSHIRE has been so long famous for fox-hunting, that people are apt to forget that it is famous for ought else. Yet has it ancient Forests, ancient Castles, and ancient Halls, abounding in materials of rich romantic incident and deep historic interest. It has Preceptories and Commanderies of the Templars and Hospitallers; and many a time-worn Leicestershire church still bears proof that those religious knights were no mean architects and no niggardly builders. One object in Leicestershire has a world-wide fame, and, next to Windsor Castle, is, perhaps, the noblest baronial residence in England—justly the glory of the Midlands. We refer to Belvoir Castle. To Leicestershire, Lincolnshire, and Notts, it presents the grandest sight in the distant prospect, and is well called "Belvoir," were it only for the view it has of a beautiful valley at the foot of the eminence on which it stands. In part, it has great claims to antiquity, its foundations having been built by Robert de Todeni, a noble Norman, who was standard-bearer to William the Conqueror. After having continued among his descendants for many years, the Castle passed by marriage, in Henry the Third's reign, into the possession of Robert de Roos. From him again it devolved to the noble family of Manners, with whom it has remained ever since.

In the wars of the white and red roses, this building was demolished by William, Lord Hastings, and continued in ruins till rebuilt by Thomas Manners, Lord Ros, whom Henry the Eighth created Earl of Rutland. The great civil war between Charles and his Parliament was scarcely less fatal to Belvoir than the earlier conflicts. Occasionally the Castle was garrisoned by either party, and, as a natural result, from both it suffered very considerable damage. With the return of quiet times upon the Restoration, it was once more repaired; and here the first Duke of Rutland maintained old English hospitality, residing altogether in the country, and, for many years before his death, never once journeying to London.

Various improvements were made upon this magnificent pile by the late Duke, at an expense, it is said, of at least two hundred thousand pounds; but the great work was scarcely completed, when, on the 26th October, 1816, a fire broke out, which reduced the vast structure to a blackened ruin. The Duke, however, nothing daunted, resolved that the Castle should rise again with more than its former splendour; and in a few years the towers of Belvoir re-appeared, phœnix-like, from their ashes. On one occasion, when his Grace entertained here the Prince Regent, the ancient and well-nigh forgotten ceremony of presenting the keys of Staunton Tower was revived, to do honour to the royal visitant. The custom may be thus explained. Staunton Tower is an outwork, which in troubled times was the chief defence of Belvoir, and its command was entrusted to the Staunton family by *tenure of castle-guard*, a tenure imposing upon them the duty of its defence in case of danger, or when summoned thereto by the lord of the castle. Hence, in the olden time, the tendering of the keys was an expressive act of homage, acknowledging the authority of the lord paramount; but in modern days, losing its original import, it has ceased to be anything more than a mere holiday pageant, which, like the giants of Guildhall, excites an indefinite idea of something venerable, from the simple fact of its being out of harmony with modern observances.

But we begin, at length, to find ourselves in the condition of a traveller, who has loitered so often and so long upon a pleasant road, that he is overtaken by night before he reaches his appointed limits. Nothing then is left for him but to speed over the way which remains, regardless of much that when he first set out in the morning he had fully expected to enjoy. In like manner we must now hurry our wanderings to an end, concluding with the appropriate tribute rendered to the gentlemen of England by the Chevalier Lawrence:—

"The late King of Wurtemburg (these are the Chevalier's own words) used to say that he could form no idea of an English gentleman till he had visited several at their family seats, and seen their manner of living in the country. The books (continues the writer we are quoting) to form an opinion by, of the dignity of an old English gentleman, are the County Histories; and these seldom come into the hands of foreigners. The Englishman's baronial castle, or his no less sumptuous mansion of a more modern date, is there depicted. A stately avenue conducts to his residence, and a coach-and-six, escorted by a troop of outriders, the usual appendages of his quality, is seen driving into his gates; and when, at length, his numerous tenantry have accompanied the heraldic pomp of his funeral to the neighbouring cathedral, the next print represents him there, sleeping in dull, cold marble, but blazoned with all the escutcheons of his house. Such are the Halls that embellish Whitaker's History of Richmond; such, in Nash's History of Worcestershire, are the Monuments of the Sheldons, of the Vernons, and of the Talbots, whose numerous quarterings would not have disparaged an Elector of Mayence or a Prince Bishop of Wurtzbourg."

HERALDRY.

"Every man of the children of Israel shall pitch by his own standard, with *the ensign* of their father's house."—*Numbers*, Chap. II.

This brief essay is addressed to the uninitiated only, in the hope that it may serve to popularize Heraldry, and to give the general reader a slight insight into the history and laws of a science which Glover, Guillim, Nisbet, Camden, Vincent, Segar, and Nicolas did not deem too insignificant to study and elucidate. The heraldic enquirer, who desires a deeper knowledge, can refer to the writings of those distinguished men, and to the other ancient and modern authorities, and examine the stores of information on the subject in the Harleian, Lansdowne, and other MSS. in the British Museum. My present aim will be accomplished if this little treatise tend to create or augment, in ever so trivial a degree, a taste for my favourite pursuit.

Although the age of chivalry is gone, the feelings which gave it birth still glow with the same warmth as ever, and will endure so long as "trouthe, and honour, freedom, and curtesie," are held in men's estimation. "It was chivalry," says Edmund Burke, "which, without confounding ranks, produced a noble equality, and handed it down through all the gradations of social life. It was chivalry which mitigated kings into companions, and raised private men to be fellows with kings. Without force or opposition, it subdued the fierceness of pride and power; it obliged sovereigns to submit to the soft collar of social esteem; compelled stern authority to submit to elegance, and gave a dominating vanquisher of laws to be subdued by manners." Many of the institutions of this famous order have long since passed away, but HERALDRY still remains a venerable and cherished relic, associated with all the achievements and romance of history, with the pious warrior of the Crusades, and the steel-clad baron of Agincourt. Memory loves to dwell on the stirring times of the Plantagenets, to recall the gorgeous tournament and the feudal fortress, when,

> In rough magnificence array'd,
> Our ancient chivalry display'd
> The pomp of her heroic games,
> And crested chiefs and tissued dames
> Assembled at the clarion's call,
> In some proud castle's high-arch'd hall.

Yet how much of the brilliancy of these pastimes, how much of the gratification with which the mind reverts to them, may be traced to the pride and pomp of Heraldry! This, however, is but one of the reasons why "the gentle science of armourie" should be encouraged and studied. Among the sources of genealogical information, arms and quarterings have long been the unerring guides to the elucidation of family history, and frequently, when all other channels fail, the genealogist owes to heraldry the indications which lead him to the object of his research. Thus, in the great peerage case of Huntingdon, one of the principal links in the chain of evidence—the marriage of Henry Hastings, fifth Earl of Huntingdon, with the daughter of Ferdinando Stanley, Earl of Derby—was established by the production of a very old armorial shield, exhibiting the ensigns of Hastings impaled with those of Stanley. Bigland asserts that he knew three families who acquired estates by virtue of preserving the arms and escutcheons of their ancestors; and Burton, the author of the History of Leicestershire, a lawyer of repute, was so sensible of the value of coats of arms, that in order to make them still more useful to posterity, he collected copies of these ancient memorials from stained glass windows, monuments, and churches, for the avowed purpose that they might " rectify genealogies, and give such testimony and proof as might put an end to many differences." In Wales, descent can be more easily traced by arms than names; and even in England there are many descendants of ancient houses that can only now be classed in their proper places in the family pedigree by an inspection of the ensigns they bore on their seals.

HERALDRY may be defined, " The art of Blazoning and assigning Coat Armour;" or more particularly, " The art of arranging and explaining in proper terms all that appertains to the bearing of arms, badges, and other hereditary marks of honour." The marshalling of processions and the conducting of public solemnities come also within the province of a herald's duties. The origin of badges and emblems may certainly be traced to the earliest times, and the enthusiasm of some of the primitive writers on the subject has led them to gravely assert that even Noah and Japhet had distinctive armorial bearings! But while it may be admitted that in the ancient world warlike nations bore on their shields and standards distinguishing devices, it is not clear that our Heraldry can in strictness be traced to a more remote period than the twelfth, or, at furthest, the eleventh century.* Numerous

* The Grimaldi family, of Italy, consider their arms, *lozengy, argent and gules,* to have been borne by them hereditarily from a period antecedent to the Norman Conquest. A branch sprang from the parent stock of this family about fifty years prior to the invasion of England, and settled in Normandy, in consequence of their kindred to the Duke of that country. Three individuals of this branch, who accompanied their cousin to England, on his invasion, are named as Tenants in Capite in Domesday. The Earl Fitzwilliam is the descendant of one of these tenants in capite. The Earl's charters have seals with the arms—lozengy, argent and gules—from the year 1117. These arms have been borne by the Fitzwilliam family to the present time. (See *Collins' Peerage*—all editions. Title "Fitzwilliam.") The Grimaldis of Italy have used these same arms, lozengy, argent and gules, from the earliest time to which their records ascend. The evidence of their seals does not ascend to a more remote date than the thirteenth century; but the genealogy of that family, published in folio at Paris in 1647, offers evidence of their use of these arms in 1087, from sculpture on their castle then erected by them.

It seems difficult to deny that the foregoing statement affords evidence of the usage of these arms by a common ancestor of the Italian and English families; and if so, that they have been hereditary from a period antecedent to the Norman Conquest.

tombs exist of persons of noble blood, who died before the year 1000, yet there is not an instance known of one with an heraldic bearing. The Père Menestrier made a minute and extensive search through France, Italy, Germany, and Flanders, and the most ancient Coat of Arms he was able to discover was that upon the monumental effigy of a Count of Wasserburg, in the church of St. Emeran, at Ratisbon: the ensigns were " Per fesse arg. and sa. a lion rampant counterchanged;" and the date 1010. Yet even here "there is good reason to believe," says the learned Frenchman, "that this tomb was restored some time after the Count's death by the Monks of the abbey he had endowed."

Sir John Ferne is of opinion that the science was borrowed from the Egyptians. Sir George Mackenzie ascribes it to the age of Charlemagne, and says that it began and grew with the feudal laws, but took its origin, perhaps, in the time of Jacob, who, blessing his sons, gave them marks of distinction, which the twelve tribes afterwards bore on their ensigns: but our old reliable friend, Guillim, will have it that Heraldry—as a science in England—cannot go back to an earlier epoch than about the year 1200. For my own part, I consider that the registry of its birth may be found among the archives of the Holy Wars, that its cradle was rocked by the soldiers of the Cross, and that its maturity was attained in the chivalrous age of Feudalism.

The word *Heraldry* is derived from the German Heer, a host, an army—and Held, a champion; and the term *blazon,* by which the science is denoted in French, English, Italian, and German, has most probably its origin in the German word Blazen, "to blow the horn." For whenever a new knight appeared at a Tournament, the herald sounded the trumpet, and as the competitors attended with closed vizors, it was his duty to explain the bearing of the shield or coat-armour belonging to each. Thus, the knowledge of the various devices and symbols was called *Heraldry*, and as the announcement was accompanied with sound of trumpet, it was termed "blazoning the arms." The Germans transmitting it to the French, it reached us after the Norman Conquest.

At first, armorial bearings were probably like surnames, assumed by each warrior at his free will and pleasure; and as his object would be to distinguish himself and his followers from others, his cognizance would be respected by the rest, either out of an innate courtesy or a feeling of natural justice, disposing men to recognize the right of first occupation, or really from a positive sense of the inconvenience of being identified or confounded with those to whom no common tie united them; where, however, remoteness of stations kept soldiers aloof, and extensive boundaries, and different classes of enemies from without, subdivided the force of a kingdom into many distinct bands and armies, opportunities of comparing and ascertaining what ensigns had been already appropriated would be lost, and it well might happen, even in the same country, that various families might be found unconsciously using the same arms.

Is has long been a matter of doubt when the bearing of coats of arms first became hereditary. The Norman tiles engraved in Mr. Henniker's letter to the Antiquarian Society, were supposed to have fixed the date at the period of the Norman Conquest, but Mr. Montague very ably argues that it is not at all clear that these tiles were of the same antiquity as "the Abbaye aux Hommes at Caen," in which they were found; indeed he seems to prove quite the contrary. Certain it is that it was not until the Crusades that Heraldry came into general use. In the History of Battell Abbey, Richard Lucy, Chief Justice *temp.* Henry II., is reported to have blamed a mean subject for carrying a private seal, when that pertained, as he said, to the King and nobility alone. Under Edward I., seals of some sort were so general, that the Statute of Exon ordained the coroner's jury to certify with their respective signets, and in the following reign they became very common, so that not only such as bore arms used to seal, but others fashioned signets, taking the letters of their own names, flowers, knots, birds, beasts, &c. It was afterwards *enacted by statute*, that every freeholder should have his proper seal of arms; and he was either to appear at the head court of the shire, or send his attorney with the said seal, and they who omitted this duty were amerced or fined.

The earliest Heraldic document that has been handed down to us, is a ROLL OF ARMS, made between the years 1240 and 1245. It contains the names and arms of the barons and knights of the reign of Henry III., and presents incontrovertible evidence of the fact that Heraldry was at that time reduced to a science. It is curious, too, as indicating the changes that have taken place between a period approximating so nearly to its origin and the present; and invaluable, as offering contemporary testimony of the exact bearings of the ancestors of some of our most distinguished families. This important manuscript (as well as three other similar collections, "The Siege of Carlaverock," "A Roll of Arms, *temp.* Edward II.," and "A Roll of Arms, *temp.* Edward III.") were published by the late Sir Harris Nicolas, accompanied by prefatory remarks and occasional notes, evincing the profound knowledge and the conclusive reasoning of that able and learned writer.

"THE SIEGE OF CARLAVEROCK" is a poem descriptive of the banners of the peers and knights of the English army who were present at the siege of Carlaverock Castle in Scotland, in February, 1301. The ROLL OF ARMS of the time of Edward II., made between the years 1308 and 1314, is divided into counties, and comprises the names and arms of about eleven hundred and sixty persons. It still remains in the Cottonian Library, British Museum, (Calig. A. xviii.) The FOURTH ROLL, to which we have referred, appears to have been compiled between the years 1337 and 1350. Its plan was most comprehensive, embracing the arms of all the peers and knights in England, arranged in the following order:—

I. The King, the Earls and the Barons.

II. The Knights under their respective counties.

III. The great personages who lived in earlier times.

In addition to these Rolls, for the publication of which we are indebted to the genealogical zeal of Sir Harris Nicolas, other collections of arms have been published, adding much to our information on the subject. In these ancient rolls Heraldry first assumes the appearance of a science, and it would seem that the rules by which it is governed then existed.

The earliest writer on the subject, whose work has descended to us, is Nicholas Upton. His treatise was composed in the reign of Henry V., and translated in that of his successor, in the work well known to all admirers of the art as "The Boke of St. Albans." With the decline of chivalry the study of heraldry was neglected, and the exaggerated dignity to which Ferne, Mackenzie, and other enthusiasts endeavoured to raise it, only gained for it contempt: but a taste for the study of antiquities generally has gradually revived; and the use of heraldry as a key to history and biography is becoming every day more and more acknowledged, not only in England, but throughout Europe.

Much curious traditional and historical information is associated with the origin and assumption of armorial bearings. The singular cognizances used as crests, the peculiar charges on the shield, and the pointed allusive mottoes, recall, in many instances, the achievements of some renowned ancestor, and perpetuate in others some remarkable event or illustrious alliance. The cross, the crescent, and the escallop, are the symbols of the Crusaders; the red and the white roses commemorate the wars of York and Lancaster: and the crown and the oak tree indicate the loyalty of those to whom King Charles II. owed his preservation. I will instance a few of the arms, crests, and mottoes, the derivation of which may be traced to some interesting exploit or well-founded tradition:—

In the reign of Kenneth III., about the year 980, the

Danes, having invaded Scotland, were encountered by that prince near Longcarty, in Perthshire; the Scots at first gave way, and fled through a narrow pass, where they were stopped by a countryman and his two sons, men of great strength and courage, with no other weapon than the yokes of their ploughs: upbraiding the fugitives for their cowardice, they succeeded in rallying them; the battle was renewed, and the Danes totally discomfited. It is said that after the victory was achieved, the old man lying on the ground, wounded and fatigued, cried " HAY! HAY!" which word became the surname of his posterity. Tradition further relates, that the King, as a reward of the signal service rendered, gave the aged husbandman as much land in the Carse of Gowrie as a falcon should fly over before it settled; and that the bird being accordingly let off, passed over an extent of ground six miles in length, afterwards called ERROL, finally alighting on a stone still named Falkinstone. The same authority also asserts that Kenneth assigned three shields or escutcheons for the arms of the family, to intimate that the father and his two sons had been the three fortunate shields of Scotland. For ever after, even unto the present day, the great northern house of Hay, ennobled under the titles of ERROLL, TWEEDDALE, and KINNOUL, bears for *Arms*, " Arg. three escutcheons gu.;" for *Crest*, "a falcon rising ppr.;" and for *Motto*, " Serva jugum."

The CHENEYS possess the following traditional account of the origin of their crest :—Sir John Cheney, of Sherland, an eminent soldier under the banner of the Earl of Richmond, at Bosworth, personally encountering King Richard, was felled to the ground by the monarch, had his crest struck off, and his head laid bare: for some time, it is said, he remained stunned, but recovering after a while, he cut the skull and horns off the hide of an ox which chanced to be near, and fixed them upon his head, to supply the loss of the upper part of his helmet; he then returned to the field of battle, and did such signal service, that Henry, on being proclaimed king, assigned Cheney for crest the "bull's cap," which his descendants still bear. Whatever may be the credence given to this story, certain it is that Sir John Cheney was most instrumental in the successful issue of Richmond's cause, and was created by the Tudor monarch Baron Cheney, and made a Knight of the Garter.

The WALLER crest has a very honourable origin. Sir Richard Waller, of Groombridge, in Kent, a gallant participator in the glory of Azincourt, took prisoner, on that memorable occasion, Charles, Duke of Orleans, whom he brought to England, and held in "honourable restraint," at his mansion of Groombridge, during the lengthened period of twenty-four years, and until the prince was ransomed for 400,000 crowns. In accordance with the chivalric notions of the time, the captor and the captive lived together on terms of the strictest friendship; and so great was the regard entertained for the English knight by his royal prisoner, that the latter rebuilt, at his own expense, the seat of the Wallers, and was a munificent benefactor to the parish church of Speldhurst, where his arms remain in stone-work over the porch. In memory of this episode in the life of Sir Richard Waller, the family crest, "a walnut-tree fructed ppr.," received the addition of "a shield appended to one of the lower boughs, and charged with the arms of France, viz.: az. three fleurs-de-lis, or, differenced with a label of three points."

An old tradition in the family of BAIRD, records that William the Lion, while hunting in one of the south-west counties, happening to wander from his attendants, was alarmed at the approach of a wild boar, and called out for assistance, whereupon a gentleman of the name of Baird, who had followed the king, came up, and had the good fortune to slay the object of the monarch's alarm. For this signal service William conferred upon his deliverer large grants of land, and assigned him for armorial bearing, "a boar passant," with the motto "Dominus fecit;" which arms are to be seen upon an ancient monument of the Bairds of Auchmedden, in the churchyard of Banff.

The DUDLEYS, of Clapton, in Northamptonshire, who descended from the marriage of Dudley of Clapton with Agnes Hotot, bore for crest, "on a ducal coronet, or, a woman's head with a helmet thereon, hair dishevelled, and throat latch loose, ppr.;" and the occasion of its first adoption is thus recorded in a manuscript written in 1390, by a monk, who was Parson of Clapton:—"The father of Agnes Hotot, the great heiress who married Dudley, having a dispute with one Ringsdale, about the title to a piece of land, the competitors agreed to meet on the debateable ground, and decide the affair by combat. Hotot, on the day appointed, was laid up with the gout; but his daughter Agnes, rather than the land should be lost, armed herself cap-a-pee, and mounting her father's steed, went and encountered Ringsdale, whom, after a stubborn contest, she unhorsed; and when he was on the ground, she loosed her throat latch, lifted up her helmet, and let down her hair about her shoulders, thus discovering her sex." In commemoration of this exploit, the crest of the female head was ever afterwards used.

The Desmond FITZGERALDS derived their crest of a "monkey" from the following tradition :—Thomas Fitz-Maurice was only nine months old when his father and grandfather fell at the battle of Callan. He was then residing with his nurse at Tralee, and his attendants, rushing out at the first astonishment excited by the intelligence, left the child alone in its cradle, when a baboon, kept in the family, took him up and carried him to the top of the steeple of the neighbouring abbey; whence, after onveying him round the battlements, and exhibiting him to the appalled spectators, he brought the infant safely back to its cradle. Singularly enough, a similar tradition is handed down in the family of Fitz-Gerald of Offaly, and is made to refer to John Fitz-Thomas Fitz-Gerald, Lord Offaly, afterwards first Earl of Kildare. I give the Offaly version in a subsequent page in my sketch of the Geraldines.

The MULLET or STAR, of five points, borne in the first quarter of the unsullied shield of DE VERE, has a pious and poetic origin. "In the year of our Lord 1098" (we quote from Leland), "Corborant, Admiral to the Soudan of Percea, was fought with at Antioch, and discomfited by the Christians. The night cumming on yn the chace of this bataile, and waxing dark, the Christianes being four miles from Antioche, God willing, the saufté of their army, showed a white star or molette of five points on the Christen host; which to every mannes sighte did lighte and arrest upon the standard of Albry de Vere, there shyning excessively." The Knight, thus distinguished by Divine favour, in the latter end of his days, assumed the cowl and died a monk. He was ancestor of the De Veres, Earls of Oxford, whose last male descendant, Aubrey de Vere, 20th Earl, died in 1702.

Fuller styles the PILKINGTONS "a right ancient family," and relates that they were gentlemen of repute in the shire of Lancaster before the Conquest, at which period the chief of the house, being sought after by the Norman soldiery, was fain to disguise himself as a thresher in a barn; from this circumstance, partly alluding to the head of the flail falling sometimes on the one, and sometimes on the other side, and occasionally on himself, he took for motto " Now thus! now thus!" and his descendants have since carried as their crest " A husbandman ppr."

The arms which were granted *temp.* Queen Elizabeth to the great sea Captain, SIR FRANCIS DRAKE, and are still borne by his representative, Sir Trayton Drake, Bart., of Nutwell Court, co. Devon, are "sa. a fess wavy between the two Pole stars arg." The *Crest* also refers to the maritime services of the famous circumnavigator. It is "a ship under reef, drawn round a terrestrial globe by a hand out of the clouds, with an escroll inscribed 'Auxilio divino.'" "Such was the worth (says Guillim) of this most generous and renowned knight, Sir Francis Drake, as that his merits do require that his coat-armour should be expressed in that selected manner of blazoning that is fitting to noble personages, in respect of his noble courage and high attempts atchieved, whereby he merited to be reckoned the honour of our nation and of the naval profession." The most important achievement of Drake's eventful career was his celebrated voyage round the world, accomplished within three years, and to this the blazonry of the armorial bearings alludes. On Drake's return, in 1581, Queen Elizabeth went on board his ship, the Golden Hind, and conferred upon the gallant and enterprising seaman the honour of knighthood, ordering, at the same time, the preservation of the vessel, that it might remain a monument of Sir Francis and his country's glory. It is observed by Camden, that on the occasion of her Majesty's visit, there was such a concourse of people, that the wooden bridge over which they passed broke, and upwards of one hundred persons fell into the river: by which accident, however, nobody was hurt; as if, he adds, the ship had been built under some lucky constellation. The application of the heraldic ensigns is well explained in the verses, made at the period of the royal visit, by the scholars of Winchester College, and nailed to the mainmast of the ship:—

> "Plus ultra Herculeis, inscribas, Drace, Columnis,
> Et magno, dicas, Hercule major ero.
> Drace, pererrati quem novit terminus orbis,
> Quemque simul mundi vidit uterque Polus;
> Si taceant homines, facient te sidera notum.
> Sol nescit comitis non memor esse sui."

Drake's ship remained for many years an object of public

admiration at Deptford, but her timbers falling at length into decay, it was found necessary to break her up, when a chair, made out of her planks, was presented by John Davies, Esq., to the University of Oxford, upon which the poet Cowley wrote the following lines:—

> "To this great ship which round the world has run,
> And match'd in race the chariot of the sun;
> The Pythagorean ship (for it may claim,
> Without presumption, so deserved a name);
> By knowledge once, and transformation now,
> In her new shape, this sacred port allow.
> Drake and his ship could not have wish'd from Fate
> A happier station or more blest estate.
> For lo! a seat of endless rest is given
> To her in Oxford, and to him in heaven."

After the death of King Robert the Bruce, in 1329, Sir Simon Locard of Lee accompanied James Lord Douglas to the Holy Land, with the heart of the deceased monarch for interment. From this circumstance, the DOUGLASES bear in their arms a crowned heart, and Sir Simon changed his name to LOCKHEART (as it was until lately spelt), and for part of his arms got a heart within a lock, with the motto, "Corda serrata pando." In the possession of the Lockhart family is that singular piece of antiquity called the "Lee penny," upon which is founded Sir Walter Scott's romance of "The Talisman." The account given of it is, that Simon Locard, during his stay in the Holy Land, took prisoner a Saracen chief, whose wife came to ransom him, and on the counting out of the money or jewels, this (which is a stone or composition of a dark red colour and triangular shape, set on a silver coin) fell; she hastily snatched it up, which Simon observing, insisted upon having it, and procured it before giving up his prisoner. More of this singular relic, and its alleged properties and virtues, may be found in Sir Walter Scott's preface to "The Talisman."

The HAMILTONS are said to be descended from Sir William de Hamelden, one of the younger sons of Robert de Bellomont, 3rd Earl of Leicester, which Sir William de Hameldon's son, Sir Gilbert Hamilton, having expressed himself at the court of Edward II. in admiration of King Robert Bruce, received a blow from John de Spencer, which led the following day to a rencounter, wherein Spencer fell: subsequently Hamilton fled into Scotland, but, being closely pursued, he and his servant changed clothes with two woodcutters, and taking their saws, were in the act of cutting through an oak tree when his pursuers passed by. Perceiving his servant notice them, Sir Gilbert hastily cried out to him, "*Through*," which word, with the oak and saw through it, he took for his crest, in commemoration of his deliverance. This detail is, however, liable to many objections. Sir William Dugdale, in his account of the Earls of Leicester, is totally silent as to the descent of the Hamiltons from Robert, 3rd Earl Leicester.

Sir JOHN PELHAM, ancestor of the Earls of Chichester, the Dukes of Newcastle, and the Earls of Yarborough, shared in the glory of Poictiers, and had the honour of participating personally in the capture of the French King, JOHN; for which exploit he had, as a badge of distinction, the BUCKLE of a belt, which was sometimes used by his descendants as a seal manual, and at others, on each side of a cage, being an emblem of the captivity of the French monarch. Collins thus refers to the story: "Froissart gives an account that with the king were taken, beside his son Philip, the Earl of Tankerville, Sir James of Bourbon, the Earls of Ponthieu and Eu, with divers other noblemen, who being chased to Poictiers, the town shut their gates against them, not suffering any to enter; so that divers were slain, and every Englishman had four, five, or six prisoners; and the press being great to take the king, such as knew him cry'd '*Sir*, yield, or you are dead:' whereupon, as the chronicle relates, he yielded himself to Sir Dennis Morbeck, a knight of Artois, in the English service, and being afterwards forc'd from him, more than ten knights and esquires challeng'd the taking of the king. Among these, Sir Roger de Warr, and the before-mentioned John de Pelham, were most concerned; and in the memory of so signal an action, and the King surrendering his sword to them, Sir Roger la Warr, Lord la Warr, had the crampet or chape of his sword for a badge of that honour; and John de Pelham (afterwards knighted) had the buckle of a belt as a mark of the same honour, which was sometimes used by his descendants as a seal manual, and at others, the said buckle on each side a cage, being an emblem of the captivity of the said King of France, and was therefore borne for a crest, as in those times was customary. The buckles, &c. were likewise used by his descendants in their great seals, as is evident from several of them appendant to old deeds."

The crest of "the eagle feeding an infant in its cradle," borne by the STANLEYS, Earls of Derby, is derived from the family of Lathom, of Lathom, in the county of Lancaster, the heiress of which, Isabel, daughter of Sir Thomas Lathom of Lathom, and Knowsley, married Sir John Stanley, K.G., Lord Deputy of Ireland. Tradition narrates that one of the Lathoms having abandoned and exposed an illegitimate son in the nest of an eagle, in the wood of Terlestowe, near his castle, afterwards discovered that the bird, instead of devouring the infant, had supplied it with food and preserved its life. This miraculous circumstance, continues the legend, so touched the father's feelings, that he repented of his cruel intention, and taking home the child made him his heir. Thus is popularly traced the origin of the singular crest of the house of Stanley; but the story is so improbable, that we can afford it slight credence. Mr. Ormerod, of Sedbury, the able historian of Cheshire, himself nearly connected with a branch of the Lathoms, has written an interesting paper on the " Stanley Legend," in the Collectanea Topogr. et Genealogica.

In memory of the royal alliance of their ancestor, Sir John Lyon, with Lady Jane Stewart, daughter of King Robert II., the EARLS OF STRATHMORE bear for crest, " a lady habited as a princess, and couped below the girdle, inclosed within an arch of laurel, and holding in her right hand the royal thistle, all ppr. ;" and ever since the marriage of Lady Jane Seymour with Henry VIII., the Dukes of Somerset have quartered with their paternal arms, " Or on a pile gu. between six fleurs az. three lions of England," a coat of augmentation originally granted by the bluff monarch.

The tenure of the lands of Pennycuick, in Midlothian, enjoins that the possessor attend once a year in the forest of Drumsleigh, near Edinburgh, to give a blast of a horn at the king's hunting; and from this custom the Clerkes of Pennycuick bear for *crest* a "demi huntsman habited vert, winding a horn, ppr.;" and for *motto*, the words "Free for a blast." The GROSVENOR crest of "the talbot" has reference to the ancient office—that of *Grosvenor* or great huntsman to the Dukes of Normandy, which was formerly held by the family: and "the sword erect" of the DYMOKES is the symbol of their dignified service as Champions to the sovereigns of England.

Of the honourable augmentations granted by Charles II. to the devoted partizans whose loyalty protected him after the fatal issue of the battle of Worcester, we may mention those of Lane, Carlos, and Penderell. The first-named family received the additional crest of a "demi-horse salient arg. spotted dark grey, bridled ppr., sustaining with his fore feet a regal crown or," allusive to the assistance rendered to the fallen monarch by Jane Lane, of Bentley, whose servant the King personated, by riding before her on horseback, in his flight to Somerset. To the Penderells, the humble but no less faithful protectors of the fugitive prince, tradition records that this coat of arms was assigned, viz. "Arg. on a mount, an oak tree ppr., over all a fesse sa. charged with three regal crowns ppr.;" but I have been unable to trace any such Grant. Identical bearings, differing in tincture only, were certainly given to Col. Carlos. The pension of 100 marks, granted at the same time to Richard Penderell, still continues to be paid to his representative; and several members of the family, in various conditions of life, have been connected for some generations with the county of Sussex. "One of them, (says Mr. Lower, in his admirable work, 'Curiosities of Heraldry'), a few years since, kept an inn at Lewes, bearing the sign of the *Royal Oak.*"

These few examples will shew the connection of the arms of many of our most distinguished families with the achievements and events of former times.

Right to bear Arms.

"Ensigns," says a learned writer, "were, in their first acceptation, taken up at any gentleman's pleasure, yet hath that liberty for many ages been deny'd, and they, by regal authority, made the rewards of merit or the gracious favours of princes."

In the reign of Henry V. a proclamation issued prohibiting the use of heraldic ensigns to all who could not show an original and valid right, except those " who had borne arms at Agincourt ;"* but, despite the royal ordinance, a multiplicity of abuses found their way into all matters touching descent and arms, which called aloud for reformation, and gave rise, in the earlier part of the sixteenth century, to the HERALDS' VISITATIONS, documents of high authority and value. The royal commissions under

* "Quod nullus cujuscunque, status, gradus seu conditionis fuerit, hujusmodi arma sive tunicas armorum in se sumat, nisi ipse jure antecessorio vel ex donatione alicujus ad hos sufficientem potestatem habentis, ea possideat aut possidere debeat, et quod ipse arma sive tunicas illas ex cujus dono obtinet, demonstrationis suæ personis ad hoc per nos assignatis manifeste demonstret, exceptis illis qui nobiscum apud bellum de Agincourt arma portabant, &c."—*Ordinance of Henry V.*

which the Visitations were held, empowered the kings of arms "to peruse and take knowledge of all manner of coat armour, cognizances, crests, and other like devices, with the notes of the descents, pedigrees, and marriages, of all the nobility and gentry therein; and also to reprove, control, and make infamous by proclamation, all such as unlawfully, and without just authority, usurped or took any name or title of honour or dignity." In these invaluable documents are set forth the principal hereditary achievements of the kingdom; and all who can deduce descent from an ancestor whose armorial ensigns have been acknowledged in any one of the Visitations, are entitled to carry those arms by right of inheritance. When, however, no such descent can be shown, the party must, if it be possible, prove his right as descending from some original grantee, or, in fault of that proof, must become a grantee himself.

These observations apply to the usage of arms in England. The custom in Ireland, Scotland, and Wales differs materially.

In England and Wales, which are under the Earl Marshal's control, arms are granted by "Garter;" in Scotland, by "the Lord Lyon;" and in Ireland, by "Ulster."

Marshalling Arms.

"Marshalling arms" is defined by Guillim and Mackenzie to be "the conjoining of divers coats in one shield," or, strictly speaking, the proper arrangement on an escutcheon, either by impaling or quartering, of various ensigns.

"IMPALING" applies to the method of using the wife's arms, and is usually practised by dividing the shield into two equal parts, and placing the husband's arms in the dexter, with the wife's in the sinister. When there happens to be a border round one or both of them, the portion is omitted where the two coats unite. There are, however, two rules to be attended to. No husband can impale his wife's arms with his own on a surcoat, ensign, or banner, nor can a Knight of the Garter, or of any other Order, when surrounding the shield with the motto of his knighthood, bear his wife's coat within it.

EDWARD III. appears to have been the first that quartered arms in England, when, in right of his mother, Isabella, daughter and heiress of Philip IV. of France, he assumed the *fleur-de-lis* on the national banner; and John Hastings, second Earl of Pembroke, was the first subject who imitated his royal master's example.

The intention of QUARTERING is to show the descent of one family from heiresses or co-heiresses* of other houses. Thus, the children of an heiress are entitled, at her death, to quarter with their paternal coat her arms, as well as all arms which she may have inherited. In marshalling quarterings, the *first*, after the paternal arms, is the shield of the *earliest heiress*, which the bearer's ancestor has married, and then succeed any quarterings her descent may bring in; with the second heiress the same

---

* An heiress or co-heiress in Heraldry is a lady, who is, by having no brother, or by her brother or brothers having died without issue, a representative in blood of her father. The term "heiress" in Heraldry does not apply to the succession to property.

rule is followed and so on, in chronological rotation, to the end of the chapter. When a daughter becomes heiress to her mother, also an heiress, and not to her father, which happens when the father has a son by another wife, she bears her mother's arms with the shield of her father on a canton, taking all the quartering to which her mother was by descent entitled. When married, she conveys the whole to be borne on an *escutcheon of pretence* by her husband, and transmits them at her death to be borne as quarterings by her descendants.

If a man marry a widow, he impales her maiden arms. A widower entering on a second marriage, marshals with his own the arms only of his second wife. He is not, according to the laws of heraldry, entitled to continue the usage of his deceased wife's ensigns. The colours of the liveries are governed by the colours and metals of the arms: thus, if the field be *azure*, and the first charge *argent*, the liveries should be blue and white.

The Shield of Arms.

According to the received authorities, there are ten classes of arms:—

1. ARMS OF DOMINION, those borne by Sovereigns and annexed to the territories they govern.

2. ARMS OF PRETENSION, used by Sovereigns who are not in possession of the dominions to which such arms belong, but who claim, or pretend a right to them. Thus, the arms of England from Edward III. to George III. quartered the arms of France.

3. ARMS OF COMMUNITY, those of bishopricks, universities, cities, and other corporate bodies.

4. ARMS OF ASSUMPTION, adopted without the grant of the Sovereign or of a King-at-Arms, and used as a proper right. For instance, if a prince or nobleman be taken prisoner in lawful war, the victor may bear the arms of the person so taken, and transmit them to his heirs.

5. ARMS OF PATRONAGE, borne in addition to their family arms by governors of provinces or lords of manors, as a token of their rights of jurisdiction.

6. ARMS OF SUCCESSION are used by those who inherit certain estates or manors, either by will, entail, or donation, and are incorporated with their own arms.

7. ARMS OF ALLIANCE: these are adopted by families or private persons, and are joined with their own heraldic bearings to denote the alliance which they have contracted by marriage. Arms of this description are impaled, or are borne in an escutcheon of pretence by those who have married heiresses. But the latter arrangement (that of the separate escutcheon) is not allowed until the death of the father of the lady.

8. ARMS OF ADOPTION are borne by a stranger in blood, and are specially granted by the Sovereign to empower the person applying for them to obtain certain moneys or estates bequeathed on the condition of his assuming the name and arms of the testator.

9. ARMS OF CONCESSION, augmentations granted by the Sovereign of part of his own ensigns or regalia, to such persons as he pleases so to honour.

10. Arms Paternal and Hereditary are those transmitted from the first possessor to his heirs; the son, being a gentleman of second coat armour; the grandson, a gentleman of blood; and the great grandson, a gentleman of ancestry.

The Shield admits of various forms, and is divided into nine integral parts to mark the position of the several *charges*, but I shall only here allude to the relative positions of the principal parts.

First, it is to be observed, that the side of the escutcheon opposite the *left* hand of the person looking at it, is the *dexter*, or right side, and that opposite to the right hand, the *sinister*, or left. The *centre* of the shield is called the less point; the top of the dexter side, the dexter chief; the top of the sinister side, the sinister chief. The *bottom* of the shield is called the *base*, and its respective sides are called the dexter and sinister *base*.

The Colours common to shields and their bearings are called *tinctures*, and are of seven different kinds; two metals and five colours, viz. *or*, gold; *argent*, silver; *azure*, blue; *gules*, red; *vert*, green; *purpure*, purple; and *sable*, black. Some writers on the science admit two additional, *tawney* or *tenné*, orange; and *sanguine*, blood colour; but they are rarely to be met with in British Arms.

When natural objects are introduced into heraldry, they are often represented in their ordinary colours, and this is expressed by the term *proper*.

A shield is said to be *quartered* when it is divided into four equal parts by horizontal and perpendicular lines crossing the centre; that at the top of the dexter side is called the first quarter; the top of the sinister side is called the second quarter; the third quarter is at the bottom of the dexter side, and the bottom of the sinister side is the fourth quarter. When the shield is divided into two equal parts by a perpendicular line, it is called IMPALING: the dexter being the man's side, the sinister the woman's. Dividing the shield into two equal parts by a horizontal line is called *per fess*.

CHARGES are the various figures depicted on shields, by which the bearers are distinguished from one another.

All *charges* of Arms are either proper or common; those charges are said to be *proper* which by a certain property do particularly belong to the Art of Heraldry, and are of *ordinary* use therein: hence they are styled "ORDINARIES:" the *common* charges are the representations of all the emblems which retain their own names in the blazon. The principal ORDINARIES are—the CHIEF, the PALE, the BEND, the FESS, the CROSS, the SALTIRE, and the CHEVRON. The SUB-ORDINARIES are—the BORDER, the ORLE, the INESCUTCHEON, the QUARTER, the CANTON, the PAILE or PALL, the GYRON, the PILE, the FLAUNCH, &c.

DIFFERENCES, or MARKS OF CADENCY, are the distinctions used to indicate the various branches or cadets of one family. The ELDEST SON (during the lifetime of his father) bears a LABEL; the SECOND, a CRESCENT;[*] the THIRD, a MULLET; the FOURTH, a MARTLET;[†] the FIFTH,

[*] "The Crescent" is the double blessing that gives hope of future increase.

[†] "The Martlet," a bird without legs, cannot alight on the land, and is consequently the mark of the younger brother, who has usually no land to light on.

an ANNULET; the SIXTH, a FLEUR-DE-LIS; the SEVENTH, a ROSE; the EIGHTH, a CROSS-MOLINE; the NINTH, a DOUBLE QUATREFOIL.

Blazonry.

In Blazoning a coat of arms, brevity is to be studied, and tautology avoided, care being still taken to give a minute description of every bearing, its position, place on the shield, tincture, &c. Though the same metal colour, or fur, may occur more than once, the repetition of its name should scrupulously be guarded against, by describing the charge, which happens to be of a tincture, already mentioned, as *of the first, second,* or *third,* according to the relative position that tincture may hold in the blazon; for example, the arms of Preston of Furness Abbey are, " Ar. two bars gu. on a canton *of the second,* a cinquefoil or." In this blazon the colour of the canton is described *of the second,* to obviate the repetition of the word "gu." The next general rule to be observed is to begin the blazon with the description of the field, its tincture or tinctures, name, then the partition lines, if any, wherewith it is divided, as *per fesse, per pale, per saltire, &c.* The principal ordinary, if any, should next be described, with its tincture, &c.; and then the charges around it generally, giving the surcharges upon such ordinary, after those between which it is borne; the chief, canton, or any charge placed in a particular point of the shield, with its surcharges, if any, being generally blazoned last.

If a coat consist of two colours only, it is blazoned, as in the arms of KYRLE of Herefordshire, viz.: "Vert, a chevron between three *fleurs-de-lis*, or," which indicates that both the chevron and *fleurs-de-lis* are of the tincture, *or;* when the last-mentioned charge, or bearing, is of the same tincture as that one named immediately before it, and yet cannot be included under one word, it is necessary to describe it as "*of the last:*" thus, in the arms of DAWSON of Sutterby, "Ar. two pales sa. and a chevron gu. on a canton *of the last,* a battle axe, or." *Of the last* is used to prevent a repetition of "gu."

If there be two sets of charges of equal number on any parts of the shield, or one set of charges on an ordinary between the same number of charges on the shield, the repetition of the number must be avoided, by describing the second set of charges by the words "*as many.*" Thus, in the arms of PARTRIDGE of Breakspeares, "gu. on a fess engrailed cotized, or between three partridges, rising, as many torteaux;" the words "*as many*" prevent the repetition of the number "three" in this example.

When charges are borne without the interposition of the ordinaries, the exact position they occupy on the shield —*fesseways,* or *in fesse,* if in line across the field; *paleways,* or *in pale,* if perpendicular, by one over the other; and *bendways,* or *in bend,* if placed diagonally from the dexter chief to the sinister base, must be described, as well as the attitude and tincture of such charges, *ex. gr.*

"HACKETT (Hackettstown, Ireland), Az. three hake fishes hauriant *in fess* ar., on a chief of the second three shamrocks ppr.," *in fess,* denoting that the fishes are to be borne in a horizontal line across the field. "MAULE-

VERER (Arncliffe, co. York). Sa. three greyhounds courant, *in pale,* ar. collared or :" *in pale* signifying that the greyhounds are borne perpendicularly one above the other.

When charges are three, whether with or without ordinaries, the usual way they are borne is two in chief and one in base, and this is understood without being mentioned; but if they be not so placed, or exceed the number three, their position must be specifically described, according to the preceding rule; or, if horizontal rows, of an equal or unequal number, their number, &c., must be stated. The last remark the arms of BROUNKER will tend to elucidate, viz.: "Arg. six pellets in pale, three, two, and one, a chief embattled sa." implying that the six pellets are borne in three rows, three in the uppermost, two in the second, and one in the lowest.

Attitudes or Positions of Animals.

When a lion or other beast of prey stands upright, with only one ear and one eye seen, he is termed *rampant;* when walking forward, with one eye and ear seen, *passant;* when sitting, *sejant;* when lying down, *couchant.* If in any one of these positions the animal look full face, so that both eyes and ears may be seen, the word *guardant* is annexed to passant, rampant, sejant, or couchant, as the case may be; and if he look back, the word *reguardant.* An animal is *salient* when leaping forwards bendways.

To griffins the term *segreant* is given, in place of *rampant.* Animals of the deer kind have their positions otherwise blazoned. Thus, when looking full-faced, they are said to be *at gaze*; when standing, *statant*; when walking, *tripping*; when leaping forward, *springing*; when running, *courant*; and when at rest on the ground, *lodged.*

A horse when running is blazoned *courant*, or *in full speed*; when leaping, *cabré, effray*, or *saliant*; when rearing, *forcené.*

Birds are blazoned, when standing with their wings down, *close*; when preparing to fly, *rising*; when flying, *volant*; when spread open, with both wings stretched out, and their breasts seen, *displayed*. The wings open and against each other are called *indorsed*. One wing is a *demivol.*

Fishes, when placed, horizontally, are *naiant*; when perpendicularly, *hauriant*; when drawn in an arched form like a dolphin, they are *embowed.*

When any living creature proceeds from the bottom of an ordinary, it is termed *Issuant*; where placed over two colours, *Jessant*; when coming from the middle of an ordinary or charge, so as to show but half the body and tip of the tail, *Naissant*. A serpent placed horizontally is said to be *gliding.*

𝕮𝖗𝖊𝖘𝖙𝖘, 𝕸𝖗𝖊𝖆𝖙𝖍𝖘, 𝖆𝖓𝖉 𝕭𝖆𝖉𝖌𝖊𝖘.

" Various in shape, device, and hue,
  Green, sanguine, purple, red and blue,
  Broad, narrow, swallow-tailed, and square,
  Scroll, pennon, pensil, bandrol, there
      O'er the pavilions flew.
  Highest and brightest was descried
  The ancient crest."—WALTER SCOTT.

The CREST yields in honour to none of the heraldic insignia. It was the emblem that served, when the banner was rent asunder, and the shield broken, as a rallying point for the knight's followers, and a distinguishing mark of his own prowess. How often did the bull's head of Neville indicate the irresistible course of the gallant Warwick!

   And who, in field, or foray slack,
   Saw the blanche lion e'er fall back?

The Crest, named by the French *Cimier*, from *Cime*, the top or apex, and by the Italians *Cimiero*, originated in the necessity of distinguishing one chief from another, and making him known in the battle-field and the tournament; consequently, no crest is ever allowed to a female. As early as the year 1101, a seal of Philip, Count of Flanders represents him with his crest; but at that period, and for a century and a half after, few of lesser degree than sovereigns and commanders in the wars ventured to carry this mark of distinction.* After the institution, however, of

---

* The first example of a crest upon the helmet among English sovereigns occurs in the second great seal of Richard Cœur

the Garter, the knights of that illustrious order adopted crests, and the practice soon became so general, that these emblems were assumed indiscriminately by all those who considered themselves legally entitled to a coat armour.*

At their first adoption, crests were usually assumed from some charge in the shield; and thus, in very many ancient houses, we find the crest a mere emanation of the arms. Little information remains to us of the crests borne by the early nobility, and the little we do possess we owe to monumental effigies and illuminated manuscripts. Froissart, in particular, affords many curious examples. Nisbet and some other writers contend that these heraldic ornaments might be changed according to the good pleasure of the bearer, but this has long been forbidden by the Kings of Arms. If crests be the distinguishing tokens by which families may be known (and this seems most assuredly to be the intention of the device), one might as well alter a coat of arms as an hereditary crest.

de Lion. The helmet has several vertical openings in front, and upon the top is placed a golden lion guardant. The seal, too, of Roger de Quincy, Earl of Winchester, one of the holy warriors of the reign of Henry III., exhibits on a cylindrical casque a dragon as a device.

* The monument of Sir Oliver de Ingham, in Ingham church, Norfolk, who lived *temp*. Edward III., " affords," says Meyrick, "one of the earliest specimens of the jousting helmet of his times, surmounted by its crest; and the sepulchral effigy of Sir John Harsick is a remarkable example of English armour towards the close of the reign of the second Richard. The knight is represented with his helmet on, over his coat of chained mail, so as to display the mode of wearing the crest and the mantle."

Still, however, circumstances may arise in which a change becomes desirable; but this should never be made on slight or unimportant grounds. In early times, Thomas Mowbray, Duke of Norfolk, Earl Marshal of England, was, by the special concession of Richard II., allowed to carry the crest of England—" the lion passant guardant or ;" and John Howard, in a subsequent reign, having married the daughter and heiress of Mowbray, substituted for the old crest of Howard, viz., " two wings, each charged with the family arms," the new but honourable cognizance of the golden lion. No one is entitled to more than one crest unless he bears two names, or has received the additional device by a specific grant. The Germans, indeed, have long been accustomed to display in a row over their shields of arms the crests of all the houses whose ensigns they quarter; but their heraldry is peculiar, differing from that of the other countries of Europe. In truth, the impropriety of the practice of carrying more than one crest is remarkably striking, if we consider for a moment the purpose for which these cognizances were first designed.

Originally crests were carved in light wood, or made of boiled leather passed into a mould, in the form of some animal real or fictitious, and were fastened to the helmet by the WREATH, which was formed of two pieces of silk, " twisted together by the lady who chose the bearer for her knight." The tinctures of the Wreath are always those of the principal metal and colour of the arms; and it is a rule in delineating the wreath (shewn edgewise above the shield) that the first coil shall be of the metal, and the last of the colour of which the achievement is constituted. Such are the wreaths in general use, but occasions have arisen when crowns and coronets supply their place.

Crests have sometimes, but very improperly, been confounded with "BADGES," altogether distinct devices, intended to distinguish the retainers of certain great noblemen, and wrought or sewn upon the liveries with which they were supplied by their lord. The badge appeared also emblazoned on the chief's standard or pennon, and was much esteemed until the reign of Elizabeth, when the last brilliant relics of the feudal system—the joust, the tournament, and all their accompanying paraphernalia—fell into disuse. Henry II. bore *an escarbuncle, or;* and also introduced the famous badge borne so constantly by his successors, of the broom sprig or Plante Genet (" Il portait ung Gennett entre deux Plantes de Geneste"); and his son, Richard I., on assuming the title of King of Jerusalem, hoisted the banner of the Holy City—the dormant lion of Judah—the badge of David and Solomon. Edward I. had a *rose, stalk green and petals gold.* Edward II. commemorated his Castilian descent by the badge of a gold tower. Edward III. bore " silver clouds with rays descending." Richard II. adopted the white hart,* the device of

* " Among the few friends who attended Richard II. after his capture by the Earl of Northumberland, was Jenico d'Artois, a Gascoigne, that still wore the cognizance or device of his master, King Richard, that is to say, *a white hart*, and would put it away from him neither by persuasion nor threats; by reason whereof, when the Duke of Lancaster understood it, he caused him to be committed to prison, within the Castle of Chester. This man was the last (as saith mine author) which wore that device, which showed well thereby his constant heart towards his master."—*Hollingshed.*

his mother, the Fair Maid of Kent, and used besides *a White Falcon:* and his successor, Henry IV., introduced the red rose of Lancaster, which became ever after the badge of the Lancastrians, as opposed to the white rose of York. He also had for cognizance the antelope: as well as the silver swan of the De Bohuns. When he entered the lists against Mowbray, Duke of Norfolk, his caparisons were embroidered with the antelope and swan. Henry of Agincourt carried a beacon and fleur-de-lis crowned. "The white rose," en soleil, denotes the fourth Edward, and "the white boar," the third Richard. Henry VI. had for badge a *Panther*, and also two ostrich feathers in saltire, one silver, the other gold. His Queen, Margaret of Anjou, adopted a "daisy," in allusion to her name:

"The daise a floure white and rede,
In French called la belle Margarete."

Henry VII. carried "the red dragon" of Wales, and also the portcullis as well as the red and white roses combined, emblematic of the union of the rival houses. "In the marriage procession of Henry Tudor and Elizabeth of York," says an agreeable writer, "each partizan of Lancaster gave his hand to a lady of the York party, holding a bouquet of two roses, red and white entwined; and at the birth of Prince Henry, the armorists composed a rose of two colours (the leaves alternating red and white), as an emblematical offspring of the marriage. Horticulturists, too, forced nature into an act of loyalty, and produced the party-coloured flower known to the present day as the rose of York and Lancaster."

The same cognizances were used by Henry VIII. and

Edward VI., the former of whom displayed sometimes a greyhound courant and collared; and at others, after the siege of Boulogne, a white swan, the arms of that city. Queen Mary, before her accession, adopted the red and white roses, but added a pomegranate, to show her descent from Spain; but, on assuming the sceptre, she took "Winged Time drawing Truth out of a pit," with " Veritas temporis filia" for motto. The badges of Queen ELIZABETH were the red and white roses, the fleur-de-lis, and the Irish harp, all ensigned by the royal crown, to which James I. added the Scottish Thistle. Many of the greater nobility followed the royal example; Beauchamp had "the bear and ragged staff;" FitzAlan, "the white horse of Arundel;" Vere, "the blue boar;" Percy, "the crescent and manacle;" Stafford and Bourchier, "the Knot."

The Motto.

The MOTTO is, according to Guillim, " a word, saying, or sentence which gentlemen carry in a scroll under the arms, and sometimes over the crest." It had its origin, most probably, in the " cri de guerre," or the watchword of the camp, and its use can be traced to a remote period. The learned Camden assigns the reign of Henry III. as the date of the oldest motto he ever met with, that of William de Ferrars, Earl of Derby, who encircled his shield with the legend, " Lege, lege;" and the same antiquary mentions the old seal of Sir Thomas Cavall, who bore for his arms a horse, and for his motto, " Thomæ credite, cum cernitis ejus equum." Other authorities, however, refer to several cases, that of Trafford of Trafford in particular, and carry up the adoption of mottoes to a much earlier epoch. Be this as it may, their general usage may be accurately dated, if not from an earlier period, certainly from the institution of the Order of the Garter; and after that celebrated event they became very general, and daily gained in public favour. During the wars of Henry V., Henry VI., and Henry VIII., innumerable mottoes graced the shields of the warriors of the time, and in the courtly days of Elizabeth devices were especially fashionable.

Mottoes may be taken, changed, or relinquished, when and as often as the bearer thinks fit, and may be exactly the same as those of other persons; still, however, the pride of ancestry will induce most men to retain, unaltered, the time-honoured sentiment which, adopted in the first instance as the memorial of some noble action, some memorable war-cry, or a record of some ancient family descent, has been handed down from sire to son through a long series of generations.

"Montjoye St. Denis" was the *cri de guerre* of the French kings, "St. Andrew" of the Scottish monarchs, and "St. George for merry England," of the English. "Dieu ayde au premier Chrétien" rallied the Montmorencys; and "A Douglas! a Douglas!" was not unfrequently heard on the English borders, in answer to the Percy "Esperance."

The same conceit, as in Heraldic Bearings, of accommodating the motto to the name, has prevailed occasionally either in Norman-French or Latin; thus we have "Mon Dieu est ma roche," for Roche, Lord Fermoy; "Let

Curzon holde what Curzon helde," for Curzon; "Strike, Dakyns, the devil's in the hempe," for Dakyns; "Cavendo tutus," for Cavendish; "Forte scutum salus ducum," for Fortescue; "Set on," for Seton, Earl of Winton; "Ne vile velis," for Neville; "Vero nihil verius," for Vere; and "Ver non semper viret," for Vernon; the last declaring, like the Parthian oracle, in the same line the permanence of the family, and warning them not to lose an opportunity. This motto is alluded to by Diana Vernon in "Rob Roy:" "Like the solemn vice, iniquity, we moralize two meanings in one word."

How admirably suited is "Pro magnâ chartâ" to the Premier Barony, Le Despencer; and how plaintive is the expressive motto adopted by the once regal Courtenayes of Powderham, after the loss of the Earldom of Devon, "Ubi lapsus! quid feci." The "Fuimus" of the Earl of Elgin tells that the Bruces were once Kings; and the "*Crom a boo*" of the Geraldines recalls the times when an Act of Parliament made it treason to repeat that famous war-cry.

Mottoes are also frequently allusive to the arms and crests, and very often commemorative of some deed of chivalry. With reference to "the Hedgehog," the crest of the Kyrles of Herefordshire, the family of "the Man of Ross," is the inscription "Nil moror ictus" (*I do not care for blows*); the Gores, whose ensigns comprise the cross crosslet, have "In hoc signo vinces." "Caen, Cressie, Calais," the motto of the Radclyffes, commemorates the services of Sir John Radclyffe, Kt., of Ordsall, at the sieges of Caen and Calais, and at the battle of Cressy; and "Boulogne et Cadiz," borne by the Heygate family, records the presence of their ancestor at those famous sieges.

"GRIP FAST," the device of the LESLIES, has remained unchanged since the time of Margaret, Queen of Scotland, by whom it was given to Bartholomew Leslie, the founder of the family, under the following circumstances:—In crossing a river, swollen by floods, the Queen was thrown from her horse, and in danger of being drowned, when the knight plunging into the stream, seized hold of the royal girdle, and as he brought her with difficulty towards the bank, she frequently exclaimed, "Grip fast," words which she desired her preserver to retain for his motto, in remembrance of this circumstance.

The traditionary origin of "Lamh derg eirin" (the Red Hand of Ireland), the motto of the O'NEILLS, is this:— In an ancient expedition of some adventurers to Ireland, their leader declared that whoever first touched the shore, should possess the territory which he reached. O'Neil, ancestor of the Princes of Ulster, bent upon obtaining the reward, and seeing another boat likely to land, cut his hand off and threw it upon the coast.

Many mottoes are allusive either to a portion of the heraldic bearings, or to the family surname. "Leoni non sagittis fido," *I trust to the lion not to the arrows*, is that of the EGERTONS, whose shield exhibits a lion between three pheons; and the MARTINS use these singular words: "He who looks at Martin's ape, Martin's ape shall look at him!" having reference to their crest, of "an ape observing himself in a looking-glass." The AITONS of Kippo, a branch of Aiton, of that Ilk, adopted for motto, "Et decerptæ dabunt odorem," an elegant allusion to their crest of " a rose bough ppr.," and of their being an offshoot of the parent stem.

The generality of mottoes, however, are expressive of sentiments of piety, hope, or determination.

Many of the most ancient houses in Scotland, Ireland, and Wales, adopted for their motto the war-cry of their race, which was sometimes derived from the name of the chieftain's feudal castle; thus Colquhoun of Luss bears " Cnockelachan;" Fitz-Gerald of Leinster, "Crom a boo;" and Hughes of Gwerclas, " Kymmer-yn Edeirnion." Mottoes not unfrequently indicate the antiquity and derivation of the families by whom they are borne. In "Loywl as thow fynds," we recognise the Saxon origin of the Tempests of Tong, and in "Touts jours prest," the Norman ancestry of the Talbots of Bashall: but this rule is far from being general: many families of Norman origin used English mottoes at a very early period, as Darell of Calehill, " Trow to you."

Crowns, Coronets, Chapeaux, Helmets, and Mantles.

CROWNS were not originally marks of sovereignty, but were bestowed on those who gained a prize at the Olympic games, and at first were only bands or fillets, but subsequently they assumed various forms according to the peculiar feat of valour the person to whom they were granted performed.

The Crown, as a distinctive badge of royalty, was anciently made open, but is now generally closed at the top with arches varying in number, and is usually called *the*

Imperial Crown. That used at the coronation of the Sovereigns of England is made in imitation of the Crown supposed to have been worn by Edward the Confessor. The present Imperial Crown has the rim adorned with four crosses, and as many fleurs-de-lis alternately. From each cross rises an arched diadem closed at the top under a mound supporting a cross. The cap within the Crown is of purple velvet (heraldically represented crimson), and turned up with ermine.

The CORONET of the PRINCE OF WALES is similar to the preceding, except that instead of four arches it has but two, rising from as many crosses, one arch only from the centre cross appearing in the representation. The Prince of Wales also bears as a badge a plume of three ostrich feathers, placed in the centre of a coronet adorned with crosses and fleurs-de-lis; the motto peculiar to this badge being "Ich dien."

The CORONET of the PRINCES of the *blood royal* is a circle of gold; on a circle, within which is a cap of crimson velvet bordered with ermine, with a tassel of gold, are raised four fleurs-de-lis and as many crosses.

The PRINCESSES bear a similar coronet, but instead of the four crosses and four fleurs-de-lis, it is adorned with three strawberry leaves alternately, with a similar number of fleurs-de-lis and crosses.

The Arms and Coronets of the Members of the Royal family are always assigned by the Sovereign to them individually.

The Coronet of a Duke is composed of a crimson velvet cap and gold tassel turned up with ermine, within a circlet of gold, having raised on it eight strawberry leaves, five of which are seen in representation. It is sometimes used as a charge in armorial bearings, or in the composition of crests, and then it is represented without the cap and tassel, or the ermine.

The Coronet of a MARQUESS is like the preceding, but is charged with four strawberry leaves and as many large pearls alternately; when represented, only two pearls and three leaves appear.

An EARL's Coronet has eight pyramidical points raised on the circlet, each of which supports a large pearl, the spaces between the points being filled up at the bottom with strawberry leaves, not rising as high as the pearls. Only five of the pearls appear when heraldically displayed.

A VISCOUNT bears on his Coronet a circle of gold supporting sixteen pearls, nine of which appear in the representation; and

The Coronet of a BARON has six pearls, four of which are seen in paintings.

The three last-named coronets have the crimson velvet cap with the tassel, and the edging of ermine, the same as those of a duke and marquess.

As the crown of the Sovereign of England is not exactly similar to those borne by other potentates, so most of the coronets of foreign noblemen are different from those of British peers.

The ARCHBISHOPS and Bishops of England and Ireland place a *mitre* over their coat of arms. It is a round cap, cleft at the top, from which hang two pendents fringed at the ends.

The HELMET, *helme, casque, morion,* has varied in shape in different ages and countries. The most ancient form is the simplest, composed of iron, of a shape fitted to the head, and flat upon the top, with an aperture for the light. This is styled the Norman helmet, and appears on very old seals, attached to the gorget, a separate piece of armour which covered the neck. In the twelfth century, a change was made, to mark the rank of the individual bearer.

The *helmet* assigned to *Kings and Princes of the Blood Royal* is full faced, composed of gold, with the beavoir divided by six projecting bars, and lined with crimson.

The *helmet* of the *nobility* is of steel, with five bars of gold; it is placed on the shield inclining to a profile.

The *helmets* of *knights* and *baronets* is the full-faced steel helmet, with the vizor thrown back, and without bars.

The *helmet* of *esquires,* always depicted in profile, is of steel, with the vizor closed.

Each of these helmets is placed immediately above the escutcheon, and supports the wreath on which is the crest.

The MANTLE, Guillim informs us, was named from the French word *"Manteau,"* and served as a protection (being spread over and pendent from the helmet) to repel the extremity of wet, cold, and heat, and withal to preserve the accoutrements from rust. Guillim thus continues: "Mantles, like other habits, have not escaped transformation, but have passed through the forge of fanatical conceit, in so much as (besides the bare name) there remaineth neither shape nor shadow of a mantle. But as they are used in achievements, whether you call them mantles or flourishings, they are evermore said in blazon to be doubled, that is, lined throughout with some one of the furs."

The mantling is sometimes termed a *Lambrequin* or *Lamequin*. The numerous strips and cuts into which it is usually divided, are supposed to indicate that it has been thus torn and hacked in the field of battle.

The CHAPEAU (cap of mainentance or dignity) is of crimson velvet, lined with ermine, turned up into points at the back. It was formerly a badge of high dignity, and is now borne under the crest of several eminent families, instead of the wreath.

Supporters.

SUPPORTERS date from the fourteenth century. Menestrier and other authorities ascribe their origin to a practice at the tournaments, and the ground on which they base their opinions seems tenable enough. In those chivalrous pastimes no one was suffered to participate but he who was of noble descent or warlike renown, and each champion, to prove his title to those qualifications, exhibited his armorial shield upon the barriers and pavilions within the lists. Pages and esquires attended to watch their masters' escutcheons, and to report the name and quality of any knight who thought proper to challenge to the encounter. The chroniclers further relate that on these occasions the armour bearers, who were thus employed, assumed the most grotesque, fantastic costume, enveloping themselves in the skins of lions or bears, and that hence arose the custom of using supporters. Of these masquerade characters, several curious specimens may be found in the illuminated manuscripts of Froissart in the British Museum.

The appropriation of supporters, as legitimate parts of armorial bearings, does not appear to have been recognized in England earlier than the reign of Edward III. An heraldic document, compiled by Cooke, Clarenceux, in 1572, indicates the various changes the royal supporters underwent: Edward III. adopted *dexter*, a lion rampant; and *sinister*, a raven, both crowned; Richard II. a lion and a stag; Henry IV. an antelope and a swan; Henry V. a lion and an antelope; Henry VI. an antelope and a leopard; Edward IV. a bull and a lion; Richard III. a lion and a boar; Henry VII. a dragon and a greyhound; Henry VIII. the same; Edward VI. a lion and a dragon; Queen Mary, an eagle and a dragon; and Elizabeth the same as her brother Edward. King James I., on ascending the English throne, introduced the unicorn of Scotland, and from that monarch's reign to our own times the lion and the unicorn have remained the royal supporters.

The position of these external ornaments of the shield is, in genuine and ancient heraldry, always erect; and surely nothing can be more at variance with true blazonry than the absurd attempt of some modern artists to display them in picturesque attitudes. Thus the characteristics of a rude and contemporary era are violently destroyed, and the vestiges of the graphic art confused or annihilated.

In England the right to bear supporters is confined to PEERS OF THE REALM, KNIGHTS OF THE GARTER, THE THISTLE, AND ST. PATRICK; KNIGHTS GRAND CROSS OF THE BATH (G.C.B.); KNIGHTS GRAND CROSS OF ST. MICHAEL AND ST. GEORGE (G.C. ST. M. ST. G.); and to those Baronets and others (of which the number is extremely

limited) who may have obtained them by special grant.
Further, in addition to these, supporters are assumed and
borne, but without any legal right, by the heirs apparent
of dukes, marquesses, and earls, and by all the children of
peers, to whom courtesy allows the prefix of "Lord" or
"Lady." In ancient times, too, many eminent though
unentitled families used these appurtenances to their
shields. Edmondson says, "It may be justly concluded
that those who used such additions to their shields, or on
their shields, banners, or monuments, or had them carved
in stone or wood, or depicted on the glass windows of their
mansion, and in the churches, chapels, and religious
houses of their foundation, as perspicuous evidences and
memorials of their having a possessory right to them, are
fully and absolutely well entitled to bear them, and that
no one of their descendants ever ought to alienate such
supporters, or bear their arms without them." Among the
distinguished houses that use supporters under these circumstances, we may mention those of Fulford of Great
Fulford, Devon, Trevanion of Cornwall, Savage of Cheshire, Luttrell of Somersetshire, and Tichborne of Hampshire. In Scotland, the chiefs of clans take and carry
supporters. "I crave liberty to assert," (these are the
words of Sir George Mackenzie, lord advocate), "that
all our chiefs of families, and old barons of Scotland, may
use supporters." In Ireland, the heads of the different
septs assert their claim to them; and in Wales, the barons
of Edeirnion in Merioneth and their descendants have
invariably adopted these heraldic appendages.

Banners and Standards.

> "With all their banners bravely spread,
> And all their armour flashing high;
> St. George might waken from the dead
> To see fair England's standards fly."

MUCH misconception exists on the subject of Banners and Standards; those ensigns under which the victories of Poictiers, Cressy, and Agincourt, were gained.

The BANNER is coeval with the introduction of Heraldry, and dates consequently from the 12th century. It was of nearly a square form, exhibiting the owner's arms, and it served as the rallying point of the several divisions of which the army was composed. To judge from the siege of Carlaverock, it would seem that early in the 14th century there was a Banner to every twenty-five or thirty men at arms, and that thus the battle array was marshalled. At that period the English forces comprised the tenants in capite of the crown, with their followers; and it appears that such tenants were entitled to lead their contingent under a Banner of their arms: but the precise number of men so furnished, which conferred this privilege, has not been ascertained. When the tenant in capite was unable to attend in person from illness or other cause, he nevertheless sent his quota of soldiers or archers which the tenure of his lands enjoined, and his banner was committed to the charge of a deputy of equal rank to his own. Thus, at Carlaverock, the Bishop of Durham sent one hundred and sixty of his men at arms, with his Banner entrusted to

John de Hastings; and "the good Edmund, Lord d'Eyncourt," who could not attend himself, "ses deux bons filz en son lieu mist," sent his two brave sons in his stead, and with them his banner of "Blue, billetée of gold with a dancetté over all."

The right to bear a banner was confined to bannerets and persons of higher rank. In 1361, Edward III. granted to Sir Guy de Bryan two hundred marks a year for having discreetly borne the king's banner at the siege of Calais in 1347; and Thomas Strickland, the esquire who so gallantly sustained Henry's banner at Agincourt, urged the service as worthy of remuneration from Henry VI. In France, so long as the chivalry of the old regime endured, and the observances derived from St. Louis, Francis I., and Louis XIV. were respected, the custody of the Oriflamme was hereditary; and still in Scotland the representative of the great house of Scrymgeour enjoys the honour of being banner-bearer to the Sovereign. Ireland claims a higher antiquity in the use of banners and standards than any other European nation — penetrating even beyond the Christian era. The office of standard-bearer was hereditary in families, as, for instance, the O'Hanlons were hereditary standard-bearers to the O'Neills, and the Macaffreys to the Maguires. "Three lions rampant" were borne on the banner of O'Brien, and "the red hand" was emblazoned on that of O'Neill. The different septs or clans rushed to battle with their banners borne aloft, and uttering war-cries. That of O'Neill was *Lamh derg aboo!* "Victory to the red hand," and of O'Brien, *Lamh laider aboo!* "Victory to the strong hand;" but after the Anglo-

Norman period these war-cries became Anglicised, as, for instance, "*O'Neill aboo!*" "*O'Donnell aboo!*" i. e. "Victory to O'Neill," "Victory to O'Donnell." The great Anglo-Norman families followed the example, by adopting similar war-cries. The Fitz-Geralds had "*Crom aboo!*" the Butlers of Ormond, "Butler aboo!" and the Burkes or De Burgos had "Clanrickard aboo!" and "MacWilliam aboo!"

The STANDARD was long and narrow, and split at the end. In the upper part of the English standard appeared the Cross of St. George, the remainder being charged with the motto, crest, or badge, but never with the arms. It is difficult to determine the qualifications which constituted a right to a standard, but there is reason to believe that no person under the rank of a knight could use one.

The length of the standards varied according to the rank of the bearer; the King's was from eight to nine yards in length; that of a Duke, seven yards; of a Marquess, six yards and a half; of an Earl, six yards; of a Viscount, five yards and a half; of a Baron, five yards; of a Banneret, four yards and a half; and of a Knight, four yards.

Two manuscripts in the British Museum, not older in date than the reign of Henry VIII., afford the most authentic information as to the size of banners, standards, and pennons; and extracts from them, affording all the necessary information, are printed at the end of an admirable article on banners, which appeared some years since in the Retrospective Review. That valuable work, "Excerpta Historica," has also many interesting details on the subject.

Hatchments.

"These, but the trappings and the suits of woe."
SHAKSPEARE.

How many are there who look on these heraldic decorations as mere general emblems of mortality, indicating nothing more than that a death has lately occurred. Yet we can, on making ourselves acquainted with the simple rules by which the arrangement of the several achievements is regulated, at once know what rank the deceased held when living. If the hatchment be that of a lady, whether she was unmarried, a wife, or widow; if that of a gentleman, whether he was a bachelor, a married man, or a widower.

To show how easily this information can be acquired, I will briefly state the several distinctions.

On the morning of interment, a hatchment is placed on the front of the house belonging to the deceased, and another over the vault or tomb after burial.

The funeral escutcheon of *a bachelor*, represents his paternal arms single, or quartered with those to which he may be entitled, and accompanied with the helmet, crest, and motto. The ground of the hatchment (the vacant canvas on each side of the shield) is black.

For *a maiden*, her paternal arms are placed in *a lozenge*, single or quartered as those of a bachelor, with no other ornament than a gold cord loosely knotted at the top of the lozenge. The ground outside the shield is, like the former hatchment, black.

When *a husband* dies, leaving his wife surviving, the

ground on the dexter side of the hatchment (that is, the side of the escutcheon opposite the left hand of the person looking at it) is black; and that on the sinister side (opposite the right hand of the spectator) is white. The arms in this case are impaled, that is, divided by a perpendicular line down the centre of the shield; those of the husband at the dexter side being black, to indicate his death. The crest is placed over the shield, and beneath it the family motto.

When *a wife* dies, leaving her husband surviving, the ground of the hatchment is black on the side opposite to the right hand of the person looking at it: at the opposite side, white. Their arms are displayed as in the preceding case, but without crest or motto, and the shield appears suspended by a ribbon in a bow, and ornamented with a cherub's head and wings.

The hatchments of ladies (except peeresses, who are entitled to a robe of estate) are invariably painted without mantle, helmet, crest, or family motto, although funeral words and sentences are sometimes introduced.

A *widower's* hatchment represents his arms with those of his wife in the same manner as when living; that is, impaled, or divided by a perpendicular line down the centre of the shield. His crest and motto are also emblazoned, and all the ground outside the escutcheon is black.

The hatchment of *a widow* represents her arms impaled with those of her husband, and enclosed in a lozenge, having a bow of ribbon at the top, and ornamented with a cherub's head and wings; all the ground outside the shield being black.

For *a man leaving his second wife*, the hatchment represents his arms (not impaled) on a black ground. On the dexter side, or that opposite the left hand of the spectator, is placed, apart from the shield of the husband, a small funeral escutcheon, on which his arms, with those of his first wife, are impaled; all the ground at this side of the hatchment being black, to indicate her decease. On the opposite side of the hatchment, that is, facing the right hand of the person looking at it, another small escutcheon similarly placed apart from the husband's shield, and on it are displayed his arms impaled with those of his second wife; the ground at the extreme sinister side of the shield being white, to show that she survives him.

If a widower or bachelor be *the last of his family*, a skull or death's head (heraldically termed a *mort*) is annexed to the escutcheon—the arms, crest, and motto being displayed in the manner already described; and the hatchment of a maid or widow, who is the last of her house, represents the arms in a lozenge, with a *mort* annexed.

The hatchments of peers and peeresses have their distinguishing coronets.

On the hatchments of baronets a front-faced, open helmet is placed over the shield, on some part of which is displayed the red hand.

The armorial bearings of knights are surrounded with the insignia of their respective orders, and surmounted with the front-faced open helmet, which is also assigned to knights bachelors.

The hatchments of archbishops and bishops represent their arms impaled with those of their diocese; the latter being placed on the dexter side, that is, opposite the left hand of the person who looks at it, consequently the opposite side is painted black, that under the arms of the see being white.

The hatchment of the wife of an archbishop or bishop represents two shields; that to the left of the spectator displays the arms of the diocese impaling the paternal coat, and surmounted by the mitre. The sinister shield (that to the spectator's right) is suspended by a knot, bearing the prelate's family arms impaled with those of his wife; the surface of the hatchment underneath the sinister shield being black, to denote the lady's death.

The same rule is observed with respect to the hatchments of the wives of knights of the different orders, while those of peeresses who have married commoners display the arms of their dignity at the sinister side (that is, the side opposite the spectator's right), apart from the heraldic bearings of their husbands.

Seize Quartiers.

If title be with us the test of position and precedence, the Seize Quartiers have been considered in Continental Europe as the test of blood, or what is strictly signified by the term "birth." It is the reverse of what is generally understood by "a family tree," for there, the stream commencing with the earliest known ancestor, flows down to the living generation; but in the "seize quartiers," beginning with the latter, the stream, dividing on the mother's and father's sides into two lines, thence continues to ascend, ramifying into the several sources whence it derives the vital current. Thus at a glance is displayed and analysed the heraldic componency of the warm blood circulating beneath each blazoned breast, betraying any alloying admixture that may exist, and may, as in the pedigree of a race-horse, (if I may venture to use the simile,) disentitle it to the character of " thorough-bred."

Increasing by a regular succession of reduplications in every generation, the range of that of the great great-grandfather displays a series of sixteen shields of arms, the "seize quartiers;" the generation beyond has thirty-two shields, that succeeding it, sixty-four, and so on till in the thirtieth generation the series of names for that generation alone would exceed the present estimated population of the whole globe; and when the number, diminishing by one half in each descending step, is added to the above, the total of individuals whose blood is transmitted into the living man is something prodigious; consequently the number ascending to the beginning of the world would be utterly uncountable. In this latter case it must be observed that the same individual must have figured several times in different positions of relationship, for otherwise in the generation contemporaneous with the creation of man, the broad array of progenitors would be totally incompatible with the solitary Adam and Eve, the fountain sources of all human blood.

The ancient chivalry of St. John of Jerusalem, which bore successively the titles of Knights of Rhodes and Knights of Malta, was variously exacting in its requirements of proof of noble birth from candidates seeking admission to its ranks. Vertot, the historian of the Order, tells us that the languages of Provence, Auvergne, and France were obliged to prove eight quarters, or coats of arms, that is the generation of great-grandfathers and great-grandmothers; Italy, only four quarters or shields; *i. e.* the grandfathers and grandmothers; but it was required that these four quarters should belong to families of a noblesse acknowledged for the preceding two hundred years. Four quarters was the number also required from the language of Arragon and Castile, including Portugal, but for German knights sixteen quarters were necessary, that being the number demanded by the Teutonic Order from its postulants. This is and was at all times considered a very rigorous ordeal, requiring often most laborious searches among archives and sources difficult of access, as well as condemning numbers to exclusion, for it is not alone in our days that ruined gentle blood sought to establish itself by union with merely plebeian gold: title availed nothing.

The mode of proceeding in drawing up a pedigree of "Seize Quartiers," is as follows, and the progression is very simple, though not generally understood: the very words being familiarly comprehended neither as to their verbal import, the rarity of the possession of such a pedigree, even among some of the most proudly titled families in the peerage, its intrinsic genealogical value abroad amid heraldic nations, or its being the real and actual test of the nobility of the blood of any individual.

First write down the name of the person, then above his name those of his father and mother, which form thus two quarters: the father's father and mother then follow, and the mother's father and mother fill up the line of generation, *i. e.* the grandfathers and grandmothers. Proceeding in the same way, we next mark down the father and mother of each grandfather and grandmother, which form the line of great-grandfathers and great-grandmothers, eight individuals, quarters or coats of arms; and the succeeding line of fathers and mothers of each great-grandfather and great-grandmother, constitute the series of the great-great-grandfathers and great-great-grandmothers, or sixteen quarters. This ramification, however, is best understood by a glance at the following diagram:

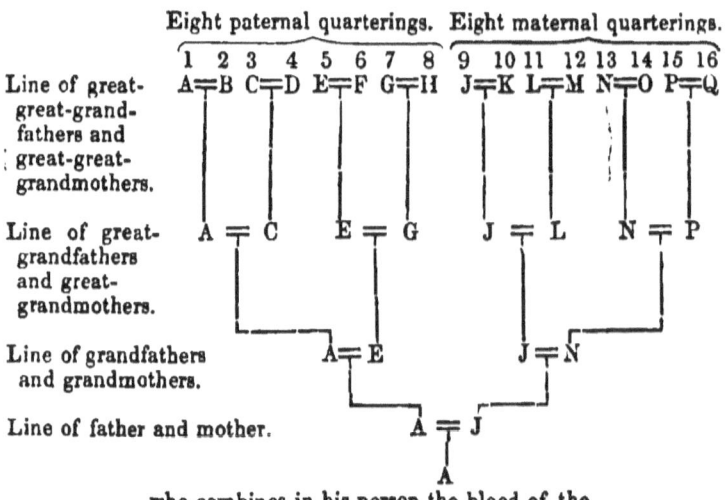

who combines in his person the blood of the sixteen families, arrayed in the uppermost line, and displays sixteen coats of arms in 'his shield, as a postulant in chivalry.

I have thus endeavoured to explain to the unlearned the exact meaning of the "Seize Quartiers." By the universal consent of continental Europe, the *sixteen quarters* have been considered the test of blood; they have at all times been *the Sesame* which has opened the door of every presence chamber of royalty, of every high place at foreign courts, and of every rich and noble Chapter. Nevertheless, according to our English notions, this test is rather, I think, one of curiosity than real value; for, compare the continental nobility, which very generally still possesses it, with the British nobility, which very rarely does, and mark the difference between them. Our own aristocracy yields to none other in high breeding, honour, noble daring, brilliancy of ancestry, talent, and simple unostentatious grandeur of character, and yet, comparatively speaking, few even among the elevated class can trace their descent up to sixteen families on both sides entitled to armorial bearings; or, at least, in cases where this is practicable, many of the progenitors are of a very secondary station, and belong to a gentry wholly without illustration. The proof of value is its result; and considering that the aristocracy of Britain may justly claim superiority over the more *exclusively* well-born aristocracy of the rest of Europe, I cannot bring myself to believe that the test of "the Seize Quartiers" enters, necessarily, into the composition of a first-rate English nobleman or gentleman. That which is truly ennobling is a long line of gentle ancestors, either from father to son, or through heiresses bringing the right of representation, combined with honourable and appropriate alliances. Who would venture to dispute the nobility of birth of the ducal representative of the Douglases and the Hamiltons, on the ground that an alliance with a Gunning or a Beckford might perchance interfere with the perfection of the German test of "the Seize Quartiers?"

Kings of Arms and Heralds.

"Heralds and pursuivants, by name
Bute, Islay, Marchmont, Rothsay, came
In painted tabards, proudly showing
Gules, argent, or, and azure glowing,
  Attendant on a King-of-arms,
Whose hand the armorial truncheon held,
That feudal strife had often quell'd,
  When wildest its alarms."—MARMION.

THE office of "King of Arms" is of feudal origin, and was one of the attributes of the pomp and splendour annexed to feudal sovereignty. There is no trace of such an institution anterior to the Norman invasion, which overturned the pre-existing system in England, formed as it had been by a fusion of the usages of the ancient Britons, Saxons, and Danes. Having so overturned it, the Normans introduced the military and chivalrous code of feuds, with its homage, and fealty, and services. Sir Henry Spelman is of opinion that the title of King of Arms was attributed to such heraldic officers in England as belonged immediately to the person of the king's majesty, while those who appertained to princes of the blood royal, or to the nobility, were styled simply Heralds. Another learned author states that the title of "King of Heralds (of later times called King of Arms) was given to that personage, who was the chief or principal officer presiding over the heralds of any kingdom, or of any particular province usually termed *the marches*, or of any order of knighthood."

The primary duty of the English Kings of Arms and

Heralds, at the time of their establishment, corresponded with that of the Heralds of foreign princes; they carried and delivered all messages of importance to allies, enemies, and rebels, gave solemn defiances and denunciations of war; summoned cities, castles, &c. to surrender; made propositions of peace, truce, and accommodation, and offered mercy and pardon to rebellious subjects and insurgents. They had also the cognizance, inspection, marshalling, and regulation of coats of armour, and the several marks of distinction connected with them; they received all foreign nobility and others coming to England to perform feats of arms, and gave safe conduct to them from their arrival to the time of their leaving the kingdom; assisted at tilts, tournaments, and feats of arms, and attended to the honour and reputation of military persons, and to the safety, welfare, and defence of the king and his realms. They had also the arrangement, order, and progress of legal combats; were likewise employed in marshalling and conducting coronations, marriages, baptisms, funerals, interviews, and other august assemblies, processions, pomps, and solemnities of the ancient monarchs, and took care that the orders, rites, and ceremonies established for those ceremonials were duly observed; and that the rules of precedency were strictly adhered to.

The pride and ambition of the nobility prompted them to imitate, and oftentimes to vie with, their monarchs in state and magnificence. Hence it is that we find the Heralds attending at the funeral rites and ceremonies of the nobility, as well as at the celebration of their marriages, christenings, and other festivities, and practising the same forms and grandeur as were observed at those of the royal family.

Noble and illustrious descent having also been held in high esteem, strict attention was paid to the observance of a just and exact distinction between the different ranks or classes of the people. The ignoble never presumed, in those ancient times, to arrogate a participation in the rights annexed to eminence of parentage, or to claim honours to which their superiors alone were entitled. And the nobility and gentry, cautiously jealous of their dignity, avoided mixing with the vulgar, and were sedulously careful for the preservation, on all public and solemn occasions, of that purity of rank and precedence which was due by the feudal system to their birth and station in life. Family arms being the general criterion which distinguished the gentleman from the peasant, no persons were suffered to enter the lists to tourney, or exercise any feats of arms, unless they could, to the satisfaction of the King of Arms, prove themselves to be gentlemen of "Coat Armour." And the ancient gentry took particular care to have their arms embroidered on their common-wearing over-coats, and would not suffer any person of the lower class, although become rich, to use such tokens of gentle birth and distinction; nay, so jealous were they of any infringement of the armorial rights to which they were entitled, that whenever the arms which they and their families had borne happened to be claimed by any other gentleman, they vindicated their rights in the military courts, and very often by a duel. Under those circumstances it became essential and was a necessary part of the duties of Heralds, to draw out, with accuracy and exactness, the authentic genealogies of noble families, and families of " gentle birth," to continue, and from time to time, to add to and preserve their pedigrees in direct and collateral lines; and to have a perfect knowledge of all hereditary arms, ensigns, badges of honour, and the external marks as well of personal as of family rank and distinction.

Some portion of the ancient duties of the Herald has become obsolete with the decay of the feudal system, but enough remains to render the office important and useful. That branch of his labours connected with genealogy is valuable in the highest degree. Genealogical tables and authentic pedigrees, regularly deduced, contain memorials of past transactions and events, and from them chronologers and historians have drawn very considerable assistance: they have operated to the detection of frauds, forgeries, and impostures; cleared up doubts and difficulties; established marriages; supported and defended legitimacy and purity of blood; ascertained family alliances; proved and maintained affinity and consanguinity; vindicated and corroborated the titles of lands to their possessors; and have been of essential use in settling claims and rights of inheritance without litigation, by furnishing effectual evidence. Such has been, and ever must be, the utility of genealogies, when they are framed with integrity and authenticated by evidence.

The HERALDIC AUTHORITY over England and Wales is delegated by the Crown to the EARL MARSHAL, and to three Kings of Arms, GARTER, CLARENCEUX, and NORROY, who form, together with the HERALDS and PURSUIVANTS, the College of Arms. Of these, the principal is "Garter King of Arms." In his Patent he is styled Principal King of English Arms, and Principal Officer of Arms of the most noble Order of the Garter. To him immediately belongs the adjustment of arms in England and Wales, and likewise the power of granting arms within his jurisdiction to persons qualified to bear them. "Clarenceux King of Arms," so named from the Dukedom of Clarence, has authority over the south-east and west parts of England; and "Norroy King of Arms," the most ancient of the heraldic sovereigns, possesses as his province, England north of the Trent He is the North King—"*Norroy.*" The English HERALDS bear the designation of "Chester," "Lancaster,"* "Richmond," "York," "Windsor," and "Somerset;" the PURSUIVANTS are known by the names of "Portcullis," "Rouge Dragon," "Bluemantle," and "Rouge Croix."

The Chief Officer of Arms in SCOTLAND is "THE LORD LYON:" and under him is a ·Lyon-Depute' and several Heralds.

In IRELAND, ULSTER KING OF ARMS has the sole heraldic jurisdiction: he is, *ex officio*, Knight Attendant on the most illustrious Order of St. Patrick.

The title of "Ulster King of Arms" was created in the

* My accomplished and learned friend, Albert Woods, Esq., is the present "Lancaster Herald;" and to his courtesy, kindness, and extensive information, I feel myself most deeply indebted.

reign of Edward the Sixth. But the office itself, under the designation of "Ireland King of Arms," had its origin in more remote times,—as early as the introduction of the feudal system into Ireland by the Anglo-Normans.

The first express mention of Ireland King of Arms is in the sixth year of King Richard the Second, 1482; Froissart, vol. ii., calls him "*Chaundos le Roy d'Irelande.*" A regular succession of officers by the title of "Ireland Kings of Arms," continued from that time to the reign of King Edward IV., who promoted Thomas Ashwell to that office.

This title of "Ireland," as Sir Henry Spelman and Sir James Ware say, was afterwards, by Edward VI., altered into that of *Ulster.* That King himself, in his journal, takes notice of it as follows—" Feb. There was a King of Arms made for Ireland, whose name was Ulster, and his province was all Ireland." The patent passed under the great seal of England with an ample preamble, in testimony of the necessity and dignity of the office, which was given to Bartholomew Butler, York Herald.

The general precedence of Ulster King of Arms was affirmed by his Majesty King William IV. by royal warrant, dated at St. James's, 17th day of May, 1835, which was issued for revising and making alterations in the statutes of the Order of St. Patrick. After reciting that, by the Act of Union, Ireland became part and parcel of the United Kingdom, and "our King of Arms of all Ireland has not had, *since that event,* any specific place or precedence assigned to him among our Kings of Arms by special ordinance or royal authority; We do hereby direct and command that in all ceremonials and assemblies Ulster King of Arms shall have place immediately after the Lord Lyon, King of Arms of Scotland." Hence, the general precedence of the Kings of Arms for Great Britain and Ireland stands arranged thus: 1st. Garter King of Arms of England; 2nd. The Lord Lyon King of Arms of Scotland; 3rd. Ulster King of Arms of all Ireland; 4th. Clarenceux King of Arms; and 5th. Norroy King of Arms.

The local precedence of Ulster King of Arms at the Irish Court was established at the institution of the office in Ireland, and the place assigned him the head of the officers of state, and next the person of the Viceroy. This order of precedence was afterwards confirmed by successive Lords Lieutenants and Lords Justices. In an ordinance of the Earls of Orrery and Montrath, Lords Justices, dated at Dublin Castle, 18th April, 1661, the programme of precedence of the officers of state at the Irish Court was set forth in detail, and stated therein to have been "what had formerly been used" by the "lords deputies or lords justices," and the place of the King of Arms was therein set forth as first in order, and next to the lords justices as representatives of the sovereign.

The Duke of Bolton, by an ordinance dated at Dublin Castle, 17th day of August, 1717, confirmed that order of precedence, and assigned the place of Ulster King of Arms to be next to the person of his Excellency; and after Ulster, the other official personages of the Court.

By another order, of Lord Carteret, dated from "his Majesty's Castle of Dublin, the 29th day of October, 1724," the same roll of precedence was affirmed and ordered.

The last order upon the subject of the precedence of the person holding the office, was the royal warrant of his Majesty King William IV., already mentioned.

Very considerable powers and duties, in addition to the due control and registration of arms and pedigrees, were from time to time conferred and imposed upon the Ulster King of Arms, in matters of official proceedings and courtly duties, which he regulates, whence the archives of his office present not only an interesting record of the various ceremonials observed from time to time at the Irish Court, but are also landmarks of Genealogy, and consist not merely of genealogical materials and references, but in a great measure of genealogies of families, full, ample, and complete.

THE GERALDINES.*

The Geraldines! the Geraldines! 'tis full a thousand years
Since, 'mid the Tuscan vineyards, bright flashed their battle
    spears;
When Capet seized the crown of France, their iron shields were
    known,
And their sabre-dint struck terror on the banks of the Garonne;
But never then, nor thence till now, has falsehood or disgrace
Been seen to soil Fitz-Gerald's plume, or mantle in his face.
                                            THOMAS DAVIS.

AN historical memoir of the illustrious house of Fitz-Gerald has been issued from the press by the accomplished descendant of the Geraldines, the Marquess of Kildare. The example thus set is deserving of all commendation; and most anxiously do we hope that it may lead to other equally valuable contributions to biographical literature.

His lordship's story of the Geraldines is simply and gracefully told; full of anecdote and historic lore—a worthy memorial of a time-honoured race. Is it not a subject of national reproach to England, that the Talbots, the Percys, the Nevilles, and the Stanleys, and to Ireland, that the Butlers, the Nugents, the De Courcys, the St.

* The Earls of Kildare and their Ancestors, from 1057 to 1773. Dublin: Hodges, Smith, and Co., 1857. This review appeared in the "Dublin University Magazine," of January, 1858.

Lawrences, the O'Briens, and the O'Neills, whose achievements form the brightest episodes of our annals, have no such printed histories, commemorative of the ancestors to whom they owe the wealth, station, and power they possess?

True it is, that the tree of Irish genealogy is ofttimes but a barren trunk; yet it is not always so. Many an old stem still flourishes, with the green leaves of tradition and ancestral renown hanging freshly around it; and foremost in this class are the Fitz-Geralds. "*Hibernis ipsis hiberniores,*" they stand the highest on the roll of our nobility—a nobility which, despite the pretensions of France, Germany, Spain, and even Venice, commands a very prominent place in European genealogy.

The utmost limit to which the Montmorencys, the Premier Barons Chrétien, the Tremouilles, the Rochefoucaults, the Richelieus, can go back, with any degree of certainty, is the eleventh century; none of the grandees of Spain, of whom it was arrogantly said, "*Principibus præstant et regibus æquiparantur,*" ascend higher than the tenth; and in Germany, the best descended and noblest families can very rarely establish so early an ancestry. In Italy, indeed, loftier pretences appear sustainable, especially those of the patricians of Venice, and the houses of Massimo, Falconieri, Ursini, Frangipani, and Colona, at Rome; but, after strict investigation and poising the facts fairly in the balance, few of the continental nobility will be found parallel in antiquity to the O'Briens, the O'Neills, and the O'Connors, of Ireland, whose progenitors were sovereign princes on the arrival of the English in the twelfth century.

Inferior only to these in regality of origin, their superiors in historic distinction, are the Fitz-Geralds; and it is most gratifying to see the noble heir of this renowned race, revisiting, as it were, the mausoleums of his fathers, and, in the double affiliation of a son of Ireland, and the Geraldines, passing along the line of their common illustration, with reverence and affection. And they were men of no common order, those Geraldines—on the battle field where they conquered, mid the ruined strongholds where they dwelt, in the sacred fanes which they founded or enriched, or wherein their ashes repose—unconquerable, like Gerald, "who should rule Ireland because all Ireland could not rule him;" brilliant, like "Silken Thomas;" lovely and beloved, like the fair Geraldine, whom Surrey sang; and amiable and interesting, even in error, like Lord Edward. Was not Ireland their glory, and they the glory of Ireland?

The Fitz-Geralds are descended from "Dominius OTHO," who is supposed to have been of the family of Gherardini of Florence;* and this notion is confirmed by the Latin

* Remote as was the kinship of the Fitz-Geralds to the Gherardini of Florence, it was a source of much pride and gratification to "the Great Earl," as appears from the following letter, found among the Gherardini papers, and reproduced in the Marquess's volume:—

"To be given to all the family of the Gherardini, noble in fame and virtue, dwelling in Florence, our beloved brethren in Florence. Gerald, Earl of Kildare, Lord Deputy of the Kingdom of Ireland, sends greeting to all the family of Gherardini dwelling in Florence.

"Most grateful to us have been your letters to us, most illustrious men From them we have learned to know the fervour of form of name, Geraldini, assumed by his descendants. This noble passed over into Normandy, and thence, in

the fraternal love that you bear to your own blood. But, in order to increase your joy still more, I will briefly inform you of the state of your relations in these parts. Know, then, that my predecessors and ancestors passed from France into England, and having remained there for some time, they, in the year 1140 (1170), arrived in this island of Ireland, and by their swords obtained great possessions and achieved great feats of arms; and up to the present day have increased and multiplied into many branches and families, insomuch that I, by the grace of God, possess, by hereditary right, the earldom, and am Earl of Kildare, holding divers castles and manors, and by the liberality of our most serene lord the King of England, I am now his deputy in the whole of Ireland, during the pleasure of his majesty; an honour frequently obtained, heretofore, by my father and my predecessors. There is also a relation of ours in these parts, called the Earl of Desmond, under whose lordship there are one hundred miles, in length, of country. Our house has increased beyond measure, in a multitude of barons, knights, and noble persons, holding many possessions, and having under their command many persons. We are most desirous to know the deeds of our ancestors; so that if you have in your possession any history, we request you to communicate it to us. We wish to know the origin of our house and their numbers, and the names of your ancestors; whether there are any of them settled in France; and who of our family inhabit the Roman territory. I also wish to know the transactions of the present time, for it gives me great joy always to hear news of our house. If there is anything that we can procure for you through our labour and industry, or anything that you have not got, such as hawks, falcons, horses, or dogs for the chase, I beg you will inform me of it, as I shall, in every possible way, endeavour to obey your wishes. God be with you, and do you love us in return. From our Castle of Castledermot, 27th day of May, 1507.—GERALD, Chief in Ireland of the family of the Geraldines, Earl of Kildare, Lord Deputy of the most serene King of England, in Ireland."

1057, into England, where he became so great a favourite with Edward the Confessor, that he excited the jealousy of the Saxon Thanes. However derived, his English possessions were enormous, and, at his death, they devolved on his son WALTER, who, it is somewhat remarkable, was treated after the Conquest as a fellow-countryman of the Normans. This fortunate heir put the cope-stone to his prosperity by a marriage with Gladys, the daughter of Rhiwallon ap Cynfyn, Prince of North Wales; and his son, GERALD FITZWALTER, though with little of the same good fortune, married Nesta, the daughter of Rhys ap Gruffyd, Prince of South Wales, a lady, like the Grecian Helen, more remarkable for her charms than her purity.

We will not pause to give the narrative of the beautiful Nesta's abduction by Owen ap Cadwgan, or of the revenge taken by her husband, Gerald Fitzwalter. The romantic story forms an interesting episode in Lord Kildare's volume.

Gerald and Nesta's son, MAURICE FITZGERALD, was the patriarch of the Irish Geraldines. In 1168, Dermot Mac Murrough, King of Leinster, driven from his territory by Roderick O'Connor, King of Ireland, sought assistance from the English, and succeeded in enlisting in his cause the renowned Richard de Clare, Earl of Pembroke, popularly known in Ireland by the name of Strongbow. Having reached St. David's, on his way back to Ireland, Dermot was hospitably received by David Fitz-Gerald, Bishop of the diocese; and at the prelate's persuasion, his younger brother, Maurice, and his half-brother, Robert Fitzstephen, engaged to assist Mac Murrough with their forces. Soon after, Maurice embarked for Ireland with two ships containing a small body of soldiers, and after having been invested with the lordship of Wexford, marched forward and took Dublin. But the Irish king was no idle or unconcerned spectator of this achievement. In 1171, he had gathered such an increase of strength, that though Morris was by this time joined by Strongbow, Roderick was able to invest Dublin with 30,000 men, while at sea he blockaded it with a fleet of thirty Manx vessels. The case of the English, with only six hundred troops, seemed well nigh desperate. In this emergency, by Maurice's advice and earnest and inspiriting exhortations, the beleaguered garrison, like Havelock at Lucknow, determined to trust to their superior warlike prowess and daring, and, regardless of the disparity of numbers, to encounter the foe. The bold exploit was crowned with success: the Irish were completely defeated; and the king, Roderick, with difficulty escaped. Maurice died at Wexford, in 1177, and was buried in the Abbey of Grey Friars, without the walls of Maynooth. "His death," says the old chronicler, "was not without much sorrow of all his friends, and much harm and loss to the English interest in Ireland. He was a man witty and manful; a truer man, not stedfaster, for constancy, fidelity, and love, left he none in Ireland." "In truth," continues Geraldus Cambrensis, "Maurice was an honourable and modest man, with a face sunburnt and well-looking, of middle height; a man well-modelled in mind and body; a man of innate goodness; desiring rather to be than to seem good; a man of few words, but full of weight, having more of the heart than of the mouth, more of reason than of volubility, more wisdom than eloquence; and yet, when it was required, earnest to the purpose. In military affairs valiant, and second to few in activity, neither impetuous nor rash, but circumspect in attack and resolute in defence; a sober, modest, and chaste man; constant, trusty, and faithful; a man not altogether without fault, yet not spotted with any notorious or great crime."

Notwithstanding the quaintness of this eulogy, its language is as energetic as it is simple, and reminds us much of some of Froissart's admirable descriptions. Nor, judging from all his actions, was Maurice unworthy of such a chronicler. Upon a wider field of action, and one of more general interest to the world at large, his life would have formed one of those brilliant pages of history upon which the memory loves to dwell, and which are read and re-read with unabated gratification. But mankind, partly from necessity, and in part from inclination, are so much wrapped up in the present, that they have little time to spare for the records of the past: and of that little the greater portion is, of course, devoted to the actors on the largest and most familiar stage. The son of this redoubtable warrior was GERALD FITZMAURICE, who received summons to Parliament, as BARON OFFALY, in 1205, and died the same year. MAURICE, the second baron, who bore the name of his grandfather, the gallant companion of Strongbow, was not unworthy of it. Piety, it is evident, formed a strong ingredient in his character; for, in 1216, he introduced into Ireland the Order of the Franciscans; in 1224, that of the Dominicans; and, in two years after, he built the Franciscan Abbey of Youghal. In connection with this event, Lord Kildare relates a story which strikingly illustrates his kindly disposition. As a statesman, the second Lord Offaly exhibited considerable ability in the office of Lord Justice of Ireland; and, as a soldier, he seems to have fallen little short of his gallant predecessor, Maurice Fitz-Gerald.

Like him, he marched from victory to victory, his career being as splendid as that of many a modern conqueror; and yet how little does it interest a reader of the present day to be told of his burning towns, storming castles, and subjugating provinces. History, in this case, touches the harp of the past in vain; the sound which it returns has little power over our feelings in the nineteenth century, when the very results of the hero's deeds have as much mouldered away as his own bones. Eventually, Lord Maurice, exchanging the casque for the cowl, retreated from the world's conflicts, and in the calm retreat of his own monastery of Youghal, ended his days in holiness and peace. Passing over a succession of names, all more or less illustrious, we stop for a moment at the sixth baron, to relate the curious traditions which explain how the monkey came to be the crest of the Geraldines of Offaly.

JOHN FITZ-THOMAS FITZGERALD, afterwards the first EARL OF KILDARE, then an infant, was in the Castle of Woodstock, near Athy, when there was an alarm of fire. In the confusion that ensued, the child was forgotten; and on the servants returning to search for him, the room in which he lay was found in ruins. Soon after, a strange voice was heard on one of the towers, and upon looking up, they saw an ape, which was usually kept chained, carefully holding the child in his arms. The earl afterwards, in gratitude for his preservation, adopted a monkey for his crest; and some of his descendants, in memory of it, took the additional motto, "*Non immemor beneficii.*"

But stories of this kind generally assume a multitude of changing hues and forms, according to the memory or imagination of the narrator. Another less romantic, and certainly less pleasing, tradition tells us, that "Thomas Fitzmaurice (of the Desmond line) was only nine months old when his father and grandfather were slain at the battle of Callan in 1261. The child was at Tralee; and on his attendants rushing out, alarmed at the intelligence, he was left alone in his cradle, when a tame baboon or ape took him up in his arms, and ran with him to the top of the tower of the neighbouring abbey. After carrying him round the battlements, and exhibiting him to the frightened spectators, he brought the infant back to its cradle in safety. Thomas was, in consequence, surnamed, in Irish, *An Appagh* (*Simiacus,* or the *ape*), and became ancestor to the Earls of Desmond."

The life of John Fitz-Thomas Fitzgerald, the child thus miraculously preserved, abounds in adventures that would form a fitting subject for romance. He was at variance with William de Vesci, Lord of Kildare, a baron much esteemed by the reigning monarch, Edward I.; their disputes arising from the contiguity of their estates. De Vesci, who was Lord Justice of Ireland, openly declared that John Fitz-Thomas was the cause of the existing disturbances, and that he was "in private quarrels as fierce as a lyon, but in public injuries as meeke as a lambe." This having been reported to Fitzgerald, he, in the presence of the lords of the council, replied, "You would gladly charge me with treason, that, by shedding my blood, and by catching my land into your clouches, that but so neere upon your lands of Kyldare, you might make your sonne a proper gentleman." "A gentleman!" quoth the Lord Justice. "Thou bold baron, I tell thee the Vescis were gentlemen before the Geraldines were barons of Offaly; yea, and before that Welsh bankrupt, thyne ancestaur, fethered his nist in Leinster;" and then accused him of being a "supporter of thieves, and upholder of traytours." "As for my ancestor," replied the baron, "whom you terme a bankrupt, how riche or how poore he was upon his repayre to Ireland, I purpose not at this time to debate; yet this much I may boldly say, that he came hither as a byer, not a beggar. He bought his enemies' land by spending his bloud: but you, lurking like a spider in his cobweb to entrappe flies, endeavour to beg subjects' living wrongfully by despoyling them of their lives. I, John Fitz-Thomas, Baron of Offaly, doe tell thee, William Vesci, that I am noe traytour, noe felon; but that thou art the only battress by which the king's enemies are supported."

Both parties being summoned to the royal presence, Fitz-Gerald maintained the same bold language, accusing the justiciary of corruption, and saying that, while the nobility were excluded from his presence, "an Irish cow could at all times have access to him. But," continued

Offaly, "so much as our mutual complaints stand upon, the one his yea, and the other his nay, and that you would be taken for a champion, and I am known to be no coward, let us, in God's name, leave lieing for varlets, bearding for ruffians, facing for crakers, chatting for twattlers, scolding for callets, booking for scriveners, pleading for lawyers; and let us try, with the dint of swords, as becomes martial men to do, our mutual quarrels. Therefore, to justify that I am a true subject, and that thou, Vesci, art an arch traitor to God and to my king, here, in the presence of his highness, and in the hearing of this honourable assembly, I challenge the combat."

De Vesci accepted the challenge, amidst the applauses of the assembly; but either he doubted the goodness of his cause, or feared to contend with so formidable an adversary. Before the appointed day he fled to France, whereupon the King declared Offaly innocent, adding, "Albeit, De Vesci conveyed his person into France, yet he left his lands behind him in Ireland;" and he granted them to the Baron of Offaly, who subsequently, in many a hard-fought day, showed himself no less true than valiant. For his good services the English monarch (Edward II.) created him EARL OF KILDARE, and assigned to him the town and castle of that name.

Again we pass over many illustrious chiefs of this house, to come to GERALD, the eighth Earl of Kildare; and here we cannot help remarking on a singular fact. While in the royal succession of England we never find a continuity of three distinguished monarchs—not often two—there does not appear to have been an Earl of Kildare who did not fully maintain the name and honour of his race. Not one of them but stands out prominently as an honourable landmark in the Irish annals.

Gerald, eighth Earl of Kildare, called by the Irish "Geroit More," or the Great, both in his character and the events of his life, presents us with all the brilliant colours of romance. He was constituted lord deputy; but his feuds with the Butlers, and the enmity of the Bishop of Meath, were the cause of the King's revoking the appointment, and sending over Lord Grey, of Codnor, to supersede him. To this mandate, sealed with the king's private seal, the undaunted Gerald paid no attention, but set the new deputy at defiance. The consequence was, that the king summoned both parties to appear before him, when the earl managed matters so adroitly, that he was re-appointed to the office of deputy to Richard Duke of Gloucester—a conclusive proof that he was no less politic than valiant. Confirmed Yorkist as the earl was, still the accession of the Lancastrian prince, Henry VII., did not prevent his continuance in office; till after a time, the king, suspecting he was engaged in a plot against him, commanded his attendance in England. This order Gerald dexterously evaded. He summoned a parliament, and induced the lords to send letters to the king, representing that, in the affairs about to be discussed, the lord deputy's presence was absolutely indispensable. But the king's suspicions were justified by the event. The earl joined in acknowledging Lambert Simnel as the veritable Edward, Earl of Warwick, son of George, Duke of Clarence, who, in that character, pretending to have escaped from the Tower, set up a claim to the English throne in opposition to the king *de facto*. The example of Kildare, in countenancing the impostor, was followed by nearly all the lords of the pale. Simnel was crowned, with much solemnity, in the cathedral of Christ Church, Dublin—a crown being placed upon his head that had been borrowed from a statue of the Blessed Virgin in St. Mary's Church, near Dame-gate. But Simnel, returning to England to try his fortunes, was met at Stoke, and utterly defeated; and the Earl of Kildare, like his companions, was fain to implore the king's pardon. This was at once granted by Henry, who limited the expression of his anger to a taunt upon their gullibility with reference to Simnel, observing, that "they would at last crown apes, should he be long absent." At the same time, well knowing the earl's influence with the lords of the pale, he sought yet further to confirm him in his allegiance, by continuing him in his office of chief governor of Ireland.

It would be a long and not very profitable task to follow the earl through his various feuds upon his return to his own country. In 1491 "a great war broke out between Con O'Neill and Hugh Roe O'Donnell; and they went to the lord justice, the Earl of Kildare, but they returned without peace." The origin of this feud has outlived the details of the feud itself, and is sufficiently characteristic to be recorded. "Send me tribute, or *else* ———," was the brief but threatening message of O'Neill. "I owe you no tribute; and *if*———," was the equally laconic reply of O'Donnell.

A new claimant to Henry's crown arising in the person

of Perkin Warbeck, the earl again became an object of suspicion with the English monarch, who, in consequence, removed him from the office of lord deputy. He had also contrived about this time to quarrel with the Bishop of Meath, against whom he was so bitterly exasperated, that he one day followed him into a church, whither he had fled for sanctuary. The earl bade him come out, and, upon his refusal, entering, sword in hand, the chancel, where the prelate was kneeling, swore, "by St. Bride," (his usual oath,) "were it not that I know my prince would be offended with me, I could find it in my heart to lay my sword upon thy shaven crown." But, though he spared the bishop's life, he kept him prisoner until the lord deputy demanded his release.

Receiving the promise of a pardon for these and other offences of the same kind, the earl ventured, in all good faith, to Dublin. The lord deputy, however, had him arrested in the evening; but, as timid as he was false, did not choose to pronounce judgment upon his prisoner, and sent him over to England in a barque which had been kept in readiness for that purpose. There he was detained for two years a prisoner in the Tower of London, when he was at last brought before the council. The outrage on the bishop stood foremost on the list of his offences, whereupon he said—" he was not sufficiently learned to make answer to such weighty matters. The bishop was a learned man, and so was not he, and therefore might easily outdo him in argument." The king then said, " he might choose a counsellor." The earl replied, "I doubt I shall not have that good fellow that I would choose." The king assured him that he should, and added, that "it concerned to get counsell that was very good, as he doubted his cause was very bad." The earl replied : "I will choose the best in England." "And who is that?" asked the king. "Marry, the king himself," quoth the earl, "and by St. Bride, I will choose no other." At this the king laughed, and turning to the council, said, "A wiser man might have chosen worse." The earl was then accused of having burnt the cathedral of Cashel, in consequence of a feud with the archbishop, and many witnesses were present to prove the fact; but, contrary to their expectation, he not only confessed it, but exclaimed, "By my troth I would never have done it, but I thought the bishop was in it." The archbishop being present, and one of the busiest of the accusers, the king laughed heartily, and was so favourably impressed by the bluntness and frankness of the earl, that on the Bishop of Meath exclaiming, "All Ireland cannot rule this man," he at once replied, "Then he shall rule all Ireland." And accordingly Kildare was restored to his forfeited estates and honours, and again appointed lord deputy, though, at the same time, the monarch retained his eldest son, Gerald, as a hostage. And well, both by his fidelity and his talents as a statesman and a soldier, did the great earl repay the king's confidence. Perkin Warbeck, on his landing at Cork in 1497, was successfully opposed by the Earls of Kildare and Desmond, and narrowly escaped being taken prisoner. For this good service, King Henry conferred on Kildare several manors in the counties of Warwick and Gloucester. With a strong hand, too, the earl controlled the unruly native chieftains, and if he could not entirely extinguish the spirit of revolt, yet he so well managed his affairs, that rebellion never dared to show its head, but it was instantly put down, and forced to save itself by submission. So pleasing were his efforts to Henry, that he was received by him with the highest favour upon his again visiting England to give an account of his government, and returned *magno cum honore et novis instructionibus,* taking with him his son Gerald, who shortly afterwards was made high treasurer of Ireland.

That unquiet spirit, to which we have just alluded, again broke out, and showed itself in a formidable array against the king's authority, amongst many of the most powerful native chiefs under the Lord of Clanricarde, who had married Kildare's daughter, but had so neglected her as to excite much ill blood between the lady's husband and her father. Never had Gerald's pre-eminent skill and courage been more severely tasked. When he came in sight of the rebels they were drawn up in full force upon *Knock Tuagh,* or the *hill of axes,* now called Knockdoe, about seven miles from Galway. Many of the lords of the pale began to be alarmed for the result, on seeing the overwhelming strength of the enemy, who had collected the largest army ever seen in the country since the invasion of 1169. They would have persuaded the earl to offer terms of peace, but the stout old soldier refused to listen for a moment to such timid counsels. Having drawn up his men in battle array, he bluntly told them that their own safety, as well as the king's honour, rested on their unflinching valour in that day's service.

The onset was made by the rebels, and in a gallant style; but they were received with such a volley of arrows from the Leinster men that they fell back in confusion. The earl then commanded his vanguard to advance, when his son Gerald, in the impatience of youthful courage, charged without orders at the head of his men in such a brave and resolute manner as no one could do better. "Far away from the troops," says the Irish chronicler, "were heard the violent onset of the martial chiefs, the vehement efforts of the champions, the charge of the royal heroes, the noise of the swords, the clamour of the troops when endangered, the shouts and exultations of the youths, the sound made by the falling of brave men, and the triumph of nobles over plebeians."

It was a fierce battle, such as had not been known in later times. Of Clanricarde's nine divisions which were in solid array, there survived only one broken battalion. The rebels were completely routed, their slain being computed at nearly nine thousand men; and, though this may be exaggeration, there can be no doubt that the battle of Knock Tuagh broke the strength of the western and southern septs. For this good service Kildare was created by Henry a Knight of the Garter.

The days of this great man were now drawing fast to a conclusion. In 1513, he marched against Lemyvannon, or O'Carroll's Castle, now called "Leap Castle," in the King's County: but as he was watering his horse in the river Greese, at Kilkeen, he was shot by one of the O'Mores, of Leix, and after lingering for a few days, he died of his wound, and was buried in his own chapel, at Christ Church, before the high altar. Holinshed describes him as a "mightie man of stature, full of honoure and courage, who had bin lord deputie and lord justice of Ireland three and thirtie yeares. Kildare was in government milde, to his enemies sterne. He was open and playne, hardly able to rule himself when he was moved; in anger not so sharp as short, being easily displeased and soon appeased."

GEROIT OGE, *i. e.* GERALD the younger, the NINTH EARL OF KILDARE, entered upon his office of lord deputy under less favourable auspices than his predecessor had done; for Henry VIII., if not more suspicious than his father, was much inferior to him in his knowledge of men, and in the way of ruling them by the show of a magnanimous confidence. Still, it must be allowed, that Gerald, as governor of Ireland, seemed to consider himself as representing the King's interests only in the pale, which, at that time, included the counties of Dublin, Louth, Meath, and Kildare; ruling the rest of his possessions as independently as any native chief, and these were tolerably extensive, for he and his kinsmen occupied the counties of Kildare and Carlow as far as the bridge of Leighlin, exacting coin and livery within those bounds. In fact, while he was English to the Irish, he was, to a certain degree, Irish to the English who were placed in this unfortunate dilemma; they must of necessity support the lord deputy from his influence over the pale, which was their instrument for curbing the rest of Ireland, then divided amongst about thirty great Anglo-Irish lords, and sixty Irish chieftains. On the other hand, there was always a danger of the lord deputy's growing over-powerful, and turning round upon his masters. The only thing, as it seems, that prevented such a casualty, was the rooted hatred borne by the Irish chieftains towards the pale, which they justly considered as the great obstacle to their regaining that absolute independence which was the constant object of all their struggles when not engaged in feud amongst themselves.

Thus it happened to Gerald Oge, as it had happened to his predecessors, to more than once incur the jealousy of the English government, and to be deprived of his office of lord deputy. What was yet worse, he unluckily drew down upon himself the hatred of the stern and lynx-eyed Wolsey, and nearly lost his head in consequence. The story is worth extracting, as it serves to show how the cardinal dared at times to act in independence of his master, and yet was sufficiently jealous of his royal power, and did not lightly endure any encroachments upon it. Kildare having been accused of treason by the Earl of Ossory, was ordered to England to answer for his conduct; upon his arrival he was immediately committed to the Tower, and soon afterwards appeared before the council, where, according to Holinshed, the cardinal made a furious attack upon him, and, among other things, charged him with having taken no steps to arrest the Earl of Desmond, who had fallen under the displeasure of the English government—" Yet had you," continued the haughty favourite, " lost a cow or horse of your owne, two hundred of your retayners would have come at your whistle to rescue the prey from the uttermost edge of Ulster. The Earl! nay, the King of Kildare; for when you are disposed, you reigne more like than rule the land."—While the cardinal was speaking, the earl showed signs of impatience, and at last interrupted him thus—"My lord chancellor, I beseech you pardon me, I am short-witted, and you, I believe, intend a long tale. If you proceed in this order, halfe of my purgation will be lost for lack of carriage. I have no schoole trickes, nor art of memory except you heare me, while I remember your words; your second process will hammer out the former." The lords of the council, deeming this request reasonable, besought the cardinal to allow the earl to proceed after his own fashion. He acceded, and Kildare entered on his defence; so graphic, so characteristic is the speech as reported by that trustworthy old chronicler, Holinshed, that we cannot forbear to give it:—

"It is good reason," urged the earl, "that your grace beare the mouth of this boarde. But, my lord, those mouths that put these things in your mouth, are very wyde mouths, such indeed as have gaped long for my wrack, and now, at length, for want of better stuffe, are fain to fill their mouths with smoke. What my cousin Desmond hath compassed, as I know not, so I beshrew his naked heart for holding out so long. If hee can be taken by my agents, that presently wait for him, then have my adversaryes betrayed their malice, and this heape of haynous words shall resemble a scarecrow or a man of strawe, that seemeth at a blush to carry some proportion, but when it is felt and poysed, discovereth a vanity, serving onely to fear crowes; and I verily trust your honours will see the proofe by the thinge itselfe within these few dayes. But to go too, suppose hee never bee hade, what is Kildare to blame for it, more than my good brother of Ossorie; notwithstanding his high promises, having also the King his power, is yet content to bring him in at leysure. Cannot the Earl of Desmond sheft, but I must be of counsell? Cannot hee bee hyden, except I winke? If hee bee close, am I his mate? If hee bee friended, am I a traytour? This is a doughty kind of accusation which they urge agaynst me. When was the earle within my viewe, and who stoode by when I let him slip? But I sent him worde to beware of mee. Who was the messenger? where are the letters? Of my cousin Desmond they may lie, since no man more can well contraire them. Touching myselfe, I never acted in them eyther so much wit or so fast fayth that I would have gaged upon their silence the life of a goode hounde, much lesse mine own. It grieveth me that your good grace, whom I take to be wise and sharpe, should be so far gone in crediting these corrupt informers. Little know you, my lord, how necessarie it is not onely for the governour, but also for every nobleman in Ireland, to hamper his uncivil neighbours at discretion, wherein if they waited for process of lawe, and had not those lyves and landes within their reach, they might happe to lose their own lyves and landes without lawe. Touching my kingdome, I know not what your lordship should meane thereby. If your grace imagin that a kingdom consisteth in serving God, in obeying the prince, in governing with love the commonwealth, in shouldering subjects, in suppressing rebelles, in executing justice, in brideling blind affections, I would be willing to be invested with so virtuous and royall a name. But if, therefore, you terme me a king, in that you are persuaded that I repine at the government of my soveraigne, or winke at malefactors, or oppress civil livers, I utterly disclayme in that odious tearme, marveyling greatly that one of your Grace his profound wisdome should seeme to appropriate so sacred a name to so wicked a thing. But, however it be, my lorde, I would you and I had changed kingdoms but for one monthe, I woulde trust to gather up more crummes in that space than twice the revenues of my poore earledom. But you are well and warme, and so holde you and upbrayde not me with such an odious terme. I slumber in a hard cabyn, when you sleepe in a softe bed of downe. I serve under the king his cope of heaven, when you are served under a canopie. I drinke water out of my skull, when you drinke wine out of golden cuppes. My courser is trayned to the field, when your genet is taught to amble. When you are begraced and beloved, and crouched and kneeled unto, then find I small grace with our Irish borderers, except I cut them off by the knees."

Holinshed continues—

"The cardinal perceiving that Kildare was no babe, rose in a fume from the counsayle-table, and commyted the earle, and deferred the matter till more direct probations came out of Irelande. There he was heartily beloved of the lieutenant, pittied in all the court; and standing in so harde a case, altered little his accustomed hue, comforted other noblemen, prisoners with him, dissembling his owne sorrow. One night, when the lieutenant and he, for their disport, were playing at slide-grote or shuffle board, sodainely commeth from the cardinall a mandatum to execute Kyldare on the morrow. The earle, marking the lieutenant's deep sigh, 'By St. Bride, lieutenant,' quoth he, 'there is some madde game in that scrole; but, fall how it will, this throw is for a huddle.' When the worst was tolde him, 'Nowe, I pray thee,' quoth he, 'doe no more, but learne assuredly from the King his own mouth, whether his highness be witting thereto or not.' Sore doubted the lieutenant to displease the cardinall, yet of verrie pure love to his friend, he posteth to the king at midnight, and delivered his errand (for at all houres of the night the lieutenant had access to the prince upon occasions). The king, controlling the sauciness of the priest (for those were his termes), delivered to the lieutenant his signet in token of countermande; which, when the cardinall had seen, he beganne to breake into unseasoned language, which the lieutenant was loath to hear. Thus broke up the storm for that time."

Thus did the stout earl weather the storm which had so well-nigh foundered him, and even again attained to his former dignity; but it was only to relapse into suspicion and disgrace. He was once more called over to England, and recommitted to the Tower.

"He was," says the old chronicler, "a wise and prudent man, valiant without rashness, and politic without treachery; such an oppressor of rebels that they dared not beare armour to the annoyance of any subject; whereby he heaped no small revenues to the crowne; guarded in safety the pale; continued the honour of his house, and purchased envy to his person. His great hospitalitie is to this day rather of each man commended than of any followed. He was so religiously addicted to the service of God as what tyme soever he traveyled to any part of the countrey, such as wear of his chapell should be seur to accompanie him."

Before his departure from Ireland, he constituted his son Thomas, Lord Offaly, vice-deputy; and strictly enjoined him to be "wise and prudent," and to submit in all things to "the sounde and sage advice of the council." Nevertheless, "the hot and active temper" of the young lord could not be restrained. The murder of Archbishop Alen, perpetrated by his followers, led to the severe sentence of excommunication pronounced against him; which being shown to the old earl in the Tower, had such an effect on him, that he died shortly after, of a broken heart. His remains received sepulture within the Tower walls, in St. Peter's Church—a sorry recompense for all his services.

The excess of jealous suspicion which made the English government so uncertain in their treatment of the Fitz-Geralds—one day creating them lord deputies, and the next imprisoning them in the Tower—provoked the very evils they were so anxious to avoid. Some time before the ninth earl died, a report reached Ireland that he was to be beheaded. A strange story is told by Holinshed, how this report was further confirmed in secret letters, written by certain servants of Sir William Skeffington. "One of these letters fell into the hands of a priest, who threw it among other papers, meaning to read it at leisure.

That nighte a gentleman, a retainer of Lord Thomas,
lodged with the priest, and sought in the morning when
he rose for some paper to darn on his strayte stockings;
and, as the divell would, he hit upon the letter, and bore
it away in the heele of his stocke." At night he found
the paper, and seeing that it announced the earl's death,
he carried it to his son, LORD THOMAS, who immediately
resolved to throw off his allegiance to the English crown.
From this moment the adventures of THOMAS, 10TH EARL
of KILDARE,* (known from the fringes on the helmets of

* The Lady Elizabeth Fitz-Gerald,—the "Fair Geraldine" of
Surrey's poetry—was half sister of Silken Thomas, and daughter
of Gerald, ninth Earl of Kildare, by the Lady Elizabeth Grey,
his second countess, whose grandmother, Elizabeth Woodville,
became Queen of Edward IV. The Fair Geraldine was educated
at Hunsdon, and, in 1543, married Sir Anthony Browne, K.G.,
then sixty years of age:—

> "From Tuscane came my lady's worthy race,
>   Fair Florence was some time her ancient seat;
> The western isle, whose pleasant shore doth face
>   Wild Camber's cliffs, did give her lively heat.
> Fostered she was with milk of Irish breast;
>   Her sire an earl, her dame of princes' blood.
> From tender years in Britain doth she rest
>   With king's child, where she tasteth costly food.
> Hunsdon did first present her to mine eyne.
>   Bright is her hue, and Geraldine she hight;
> Hampton me taught to wish her first for mine,
>   And Windsor, alas! doth chase me from her sight.
> Her beauty of kind, her virtues from above,
>   Happy is he that can attain her love."
>   *The Earl of Surrey to the Fair Geraldine.*

It is said that Lord Surrey, at a tournament at Florence, defied his retainers) as "Silken Thomas," would form no uninteresting chapter of a romance; and, after all, his determination was not so hopeless of success as many at the time imagined it to be, so extensive was the influence of the Geraldines. In disclaiming the English rule, the young Earl proceeded with all the chivalric honour of a knight of old. He called a meeting of the council at St. Mary's Abbey, and when he had seated himself at the head of the table, a party of his followers rushed in, to the sore amazement of those who had not been previously warned of his intentions. The words in which he then addressed them were worthy of his great ancestors, and show of what metal the Geraldines were made:

"Howsoever," he began, "howsoever injuriously we may be handled, and forced to defend ourselves in arms, when neither our service nor our good meaning towards our prince's crown availeth, yet say not hereafter but that in this open hostility which we here profess and proclaim, we have showed ourselves no villains nor churls, but warriours and gentlemen. This sword of estate is yours, and not mine. I received it with an oath, and used it to your benefit. I should destain mine honour if I turned the same to your annoyance. Now have I need of mine own sword, which I dare trust. As for the common sword, it

all the world to produce such beauty as hers, and was victorious. He is also said to have visited, at that time, Cornelius Agrippa, the celebrated alchymist, who revealed to him, in a magic mirror, the form of the fair Geraldine, lying on a couch, reading one of his sonnets by the light of a taper. This incident has been happily introduced by Sir Walter Scott, in his "Lay of the Last Minstrel."

flattereth me with a painted scabbard, but hath indeed a pestilent edge, already bathed in the Geraldine blood, and now is newly whetted in hope of a further destruction. Therefore save yourselves from us as from open enemies. I am none of Henry's deputie: I am his foe. I have more mind to conquer than to govern; to meet him in the field than to serve him in office. If all the hearts of England and Ireland, that have cause thereto, would join in this quarrel (as I hope they will), then should he soon aby (as I trust shall) for his tyranny, for which the age to come may lawfully scourge him up among the ancient tyrants of most abominable and hateful memory."

He then tendered his sword of state to the chancellor (Cromer). The gentle prelate, who was a well-wisher of the Geraldines, besought him, with tears in his eyes, to abandon his purpose; and might, perhaps, have succeeded, but that Nelan, an Irish bard, then present, burst out on the sudden into a heroic strain, in his native tongue, eulogistic of "Silken Thomas," and concluded by warning him, that he had "lingered there over long." The earl was roused by the fervour of this appeal. Addressing the chancellor somewhat abruptly, he renounced all allegiance to the English monarch, saying, that he chose rather "to die with valiantness and liberty."

Never was there a finer scene for poet and painter than this at St. Mary's Abbey; and never has ancient history left us a happier theme for either of them than "Silken Thomas." His subsequent career fully corresponded with this commencement. For a length of time he resisted, successfully, the famous lord deputy, Skeffington, with all the support that England could afford him, or that he derived from such of the native Irish septs as had been previously hostile to the earl, or were bought over by the hope of present advantage. When, finally, deserted by the last of his allies, Kildare found himself obliged to surrender, it was upon a promise, sealed upon the holy sacrament, that he should receive a full pardon on his arrival in England. But this pledge was shamefully violated by Henry VIII. For sixteen months the earl was incarcerated in the Tower of London, and then, together with his five uncles, two of whom had always been stanch adherents of the king, was hanged, drawn, and quartered at Tyburn, on the 8th of February, 1537, being then but twenty-four years of age.

The rebellion of "silken Thomas" is well and ably told by Lord Kildare; and perhaps the whole range of history produces no more affecting story.

"This unfortunate earl was," says Holinshed, "a man on whom nature poured beauty and fortune, and withal somewhat ruddy, delicately in each lymme featured; of nature flexible and kinde; a young man not devode of wit."

It is melancholy to contrast the early condition of the gay, glittering noble, "the Silken Lord," Vice Deputy of Ireland, and head of one of the most illustrious families in the world, with that bitter suffering which he described in a letter to an adherent, while a prisoner in the Tower:—"I never had eny money syns I cam unto prison but a nobull, nor I have had nethyr hosyn, dublet, nor shoys, nor shyrt, but on. . . . . . I have gone barefote dyverse tymes (when ytt hath not been very warme), and so I should have don styll, and now, but that pore prysoners, of their gentyles, hath sometyme gevyn me old hosyn and shoys and old shyrtes. This I wryte unto you, not as complayning on my fryndes, but for to shew you the trewth of my great nede." The generous, self-sacrificing spirit of the youth still shines through all his sufferings; and the reader will scarcely fail to be struck with the marked resemblance between "Silken Thomas" and another equally ill-fated Geraldine, of a much later period —the amiable and high-minded Lord Edward Fitzgerald. Both were led away by the enthusiasm of their nature; both were chivalrously honourable; both displayed, throughout the contest, an unflinching spirit; and each, in the bloom of manhood, paid the penalty of his error in a violent death.

Though attainder followed, the house of Kildare was not destined to perish. Thomas's half brother, GERALD, the eleventh Earl of Kildare, then a minor, only twelve years old, became the male representative of the Geraldines. So great was the sympathy in his favour, from one end of Ireland to the other, that the English government became anxious, beyond measure, to get him into their power; but all their efforts were in vain to corrupt the fidelity of those to whose charge he had been entrusted. By them he was safely conveyed to the Continent, where he found a welcome reception; and, though the English monarch was successful in having him dismissed from one place of refuge after the other, yet he could not persuade any one of his friendly allies to give the boy up. At length, the young Earl obtained a safe retreat in Rome, with his kinsman, Cardinal Pole, who caused him to be educated, and subsequently sent him, at his own desire, upon his travels. He afterwards entered the service of Cosmo de Medici, Duke of Florence, who appointed him Master of his Horse. Returning to England, after the death of King Henry, in company with some foreign ambassadors, he was present at a masque given by Edward VI., where he met, wooed, and won his future wife, Mabel, daughter of Sir Anthony Browne, K.G. Through Sir Anthony's influence, the young king gave Gerald back his Irish estates and conferred on him knighthood; and at a later period, Queen Mary restored to him his hereditary honours. After a brilliant career, Earl Gerald died in London, in 1585, but his body was taken back to Ireland, and buried in Kildare.

There is less of romance, but scarcely less of historical interest, in the lives of the succeeding Earls of Kildare; but the details are suited rather to the genealogical than the general reader. In this brief sketch our purpose has been to shadow forth the career of as noble a race as ever graced the page of history; but, to be felt and comprehended in its full extent, the tale should be read in the delightful pages of Lord Kildare's own book.

There is abundant evidence of research in his lordship's labours. It is, however, to be regretted that the manuscript sources, locked up and unknown in the public offices of Dublin, and loudly calling for a new Record

Commission, to give their treasures to the world, could not be more thoroughly ransacked. Mention is made of a "chest or secure place in the Castle of Mainothe," for the custody of family papers, to which three locks were, for their better safety, to be affixed during the minority of George, sixteenth earl. We trust the "secure place" was not robbed of its deposit at the ruin of the castle by Preston and the confederate Catholics, who plundered "the library of great value" in 1642, and dismantled the building in 1646, since which time it has remained uninhabited.

Though there thus seems, unfortunately, but too good grounds for apprehension that the muniment room of Carton is less rich than that of the great rival race of Ormonde, in Kilkenny Castle; still report states that many valuable manuscripts are preserved at the former mansion, as, for instance, the "Book of Kildare" (perhaps the manuscript mentioned at page 113, as "the Earl of Kildare's Red Book,") and the "Book of *Obits* of diverse gentlemen of the Geraldys," which would, if given in an appendix, have been a valuable document in illustration of the collateral branches of the family. The history of those offshoots, in many instances deduced by Lodge, does not enter into the plan of the present work. This we regret, as the Duke of Leinster, however times have changed, is still a great chief, the head of a widely-spread and powerful clan, who look up to him with all the respect given to the ancient leader, though he no longer calls on them to follow his feudal banner to the field.

In conclusion we will only add that few will rise from

the perusal of Lord Kildare's memorials of the great race from which he springs, without cordially coinciding in the remark that the family of the Geraldines is " so ancient, that it seems to have no beginning, and so illustrious that it ought to have no end."

www.ingramcontent.com/pod-product-compliance
Lightning Source LLC
Chambersburg PA
CBHW022145300426
44115CB00006B/355